Table of contents

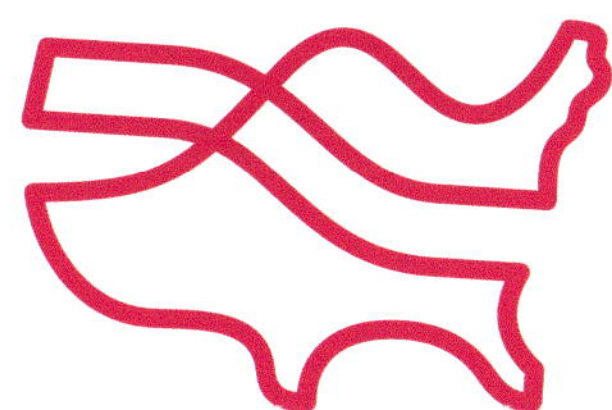

USAFacts is founded and funded by Steve Ballmer, Ballmer Group co-founder, Chairman of the LA Clippers, and former CEO of Microsoft.

USAFacts Institute
PO Box 1558, Bellevue, WA 98009-1558

ISBN-13: 979-8-9904493-6-7

Required notices:

About USAFacts

About USAFacts

Our mission: Empower Americans with facts.

USAFacts provides a data-driven portrait of the American population, governments' finances, and governments' impact on society. We are a nonpartisan, not-for-profit civic initiative without a political agenda.

Our principles:

UNBIASED

We rely only on numbers from government agencies and present them without bias. You can use the data to judge the country's direction for yourself. We don't answer to a board or political group. We have no agenda other than improving debates — and, by extension, American democracy — with government facts that every American deserves to know.

UNDERSTANDABLE

We gather metrics from government sources and standardize them so they're easy to grasp. That means detailed reports and clear, vibrant visualizations illustrating the data.

COMPREHENSIVE

We offer a complete view of government finances and impact, from the federal level to the community where you live. We're always collecting and adding metrics from the nation's more than 90,000 governments.

CONTEXTUAL

We use government data from many different sources, allowing you to see the big picture in one place. Our reports include historical context and our visualizations are simple to navigate so that you can measure changes over time.

TRANSPARENT

We are open about our data sources and methods. We cite our sources and note if we have made any changes, such as adjusting for inflation or population.

Our approach to the data:

All Americans are stakeholders in this democracy. To find solutions to issues affecting the United States, everyone, from regular citizens to top policymakers, needs data to understand how the government serves the people. At USAFacts, we believe a vibrant democracy requires informed debate grounded in facts. We exclusively use publicly available government data to provide this grounding.

About this report:

In this report, *America in Facts 2025: A Data-Driven Report for Congress*, we leverage nonpartisan government data to inform critical policy debates of particular interest to the 119th Congress, including taxes, federal finances, and immigration and border security, among others. While excellent nonpartisan, unbiased government data is available to illuminate some of these debates, in other instances, there is only limited or deficient data.

We envision this report serving as a catalyst for informed policy discussions among members of Congress and their teams.

For more information about USAFacts' data, reports, and recommendations, email us at congress@usafacts.org.

CHAPTER 01

Federal finances

Federal finances facts

Questions about how the federal government raises and spends money are front and center in 2025. With debates intensifying over the future of major programs like Social Security, Medicare, Medicaid, and interest payments consuming a growing share of the budget, this chapter offers a factual baseline to understand how the federal government raises and allocates money. It highlights recent trends in taxes, spending, deficits, and debt and provides essential context for evaluating fiscal policy choices.

Revenue

- In FY 2024, the federal government collected $4.9 trillion in revenue. Nearly half (49%) came from individual income taxes, 35% from payroll taxes, and 11% from corporate income taxes.
- Federal revenue increased 2.4 times since FY 1980, after adjusting for inflation, while the population grew 1.5 times.

Spending

- Total federal spending in FY 2024 was $6.8 trillion, including transfers to state and local governments. Social Security, transfers to state and local governments, and defense and support for veterans made up more than half of all spending.
- Federal spending rose by 7% in FY 2024 after two years of decline and remained 24% above FY 2019 levels.
- Spending has increased 2.9 times since FY 1980 when adjusted for inflation, outpacing population growth.

Spending by category

- Mandatory spending accounted for 60% of the budget in FY 2024, up from 45% in FY 1980.
- Of the $4.1 trillion in mandatory spending, Social Security was the largest program at $1.5 trillion (35%), followed by Medicare (21%) and Medicaid/CHIP (16%).
- Discretionary spending was $1.8 trillion, with national defense making up 47%, followed by aid to individuals (9%) and support for veterans (7%).
- Social Security, Medicare, and Medicaid made up 44% of all federal spending in FY 2024. While Social Security and Medicare costs rose, spending on Medicaid and CHIP declined compared to the previous fiscal year.
- Debt interest payments totaled $879.9 billion — 13% of all federal spending and the highest share since FY 1999.

Debt and deficit

- The federal government ran a deficit of $1.8 trillion in FY 2024, spending more than it collected.
- The deficit rose in FY 2024 compared to FY 2023, though it remained below the $3 trillion highs of FY 2020 and 2021.
- The total federal debt reached $36.2 trillion by the end of 2024 with 80% held by the public, including individuals, businesses, banks, and foreign investors. Debt held by the public was 97% of GDP.

How did federal government revenue and spending compare in 2024?

In FY 2024, the federal government spent 37% more than it collected, resulting in a $1.8 trillion deficit.

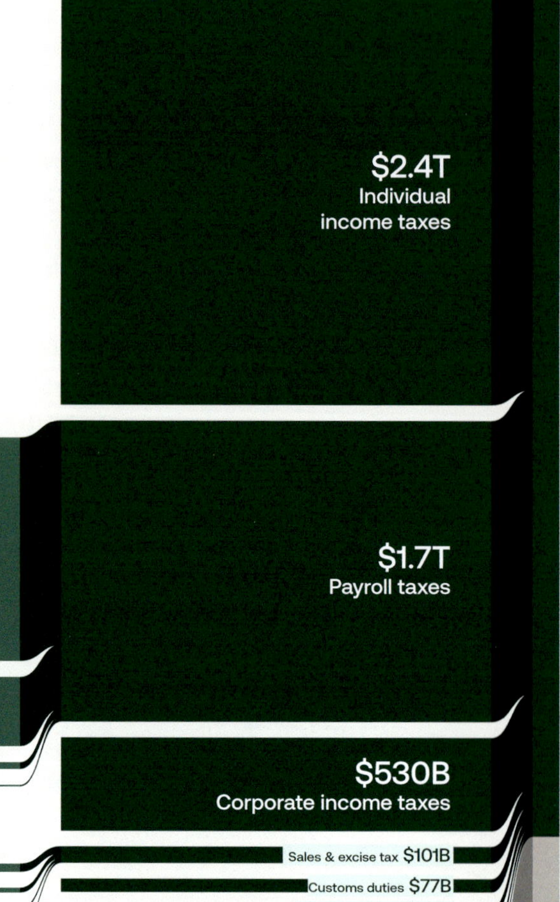

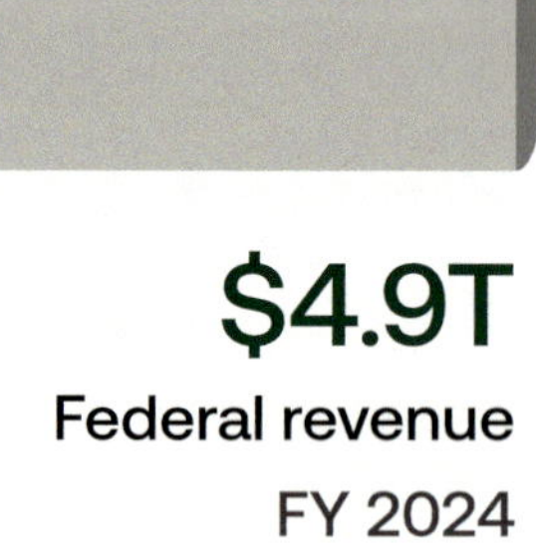

$4.9T
Federal revenue
FY 2024

Denotes negative spending/deficit

Federal government finances (FY 2024)

Source: USAFacts aggregation of data from Office of Management and Budget, Census Bureau, and Bureau of Economic Analysis
Note: Adjusted for inflation (FY 2024 dollars). Charts are shown to scale for comparison. Numbers may not add due to rounding.

$3.3T
Wealth & savings
$1.2T
National defense & support for veterans
$454B
Standard of living & aid to individuals
$151B Economy & infrastructure
$133B Education
$91B Sustainability & self-sufficiency
$88B Crime & disaster
$87B Health
$72B Foreign affairs
$25B Immigration & border security
$25B General government
$11B Consumer & employee safety
$1.1T
Transfers to states & local governments
$1.5T
Social Security
$976B
Obligations
$874B
Medicare
$23B General retirement programs
-$33B Housing support
$874B
National defense
$323B Support for veterans
$264B Non-cash programs
$150B Cash programs
$34B Unemployment Insurance
$3B Employment & training
$2B Child & social services
$41B Transportation
$37B Banking & finance
$24B Space
$18B Technology infrastructure
$17B General science & basic research
$5B Community & regional development
$4B General commerce
$4B Postal service
$129B Education inside the classroom
$4B Education outside the classroom
$44B Environment & natural resources
$34B Agriculture
$13B Energy
$36B Disaster relief
$32B Law enforcement & corrections
$20B Justice system
$85B Public health
$2B Other health, hospitals, & medical assistance
$638B
Medicaid & CHIP
$126B Other aid to individuals
$100B Elementary & secondary education
$95B Transportation
$55B Other
$49B Housing assistance
$38B Child & social services
$33B Disaster relief
$12B Community & regional development
$1.3T
Retirement (FOASI)
$156B Disability (FDI)
$54B Other Social Security
$880B
Net interest on debt
$96B Net employee retirement & disability benefits
$161B Veterans pension & disability benefits
$120B Veterans medical care
$42B Veteran readjustment benefits, housing, & other services
$112B Other medical assistance to poor
$96B SNAP & other nutrition programs
$35B Pell grants
$21B Housing assistance
$40M Other non-cash programs
$12M Child care assistance
$60B Earned Income Tax Credit
$59B Supplemental Security Income
$26B Child Tax Credit
$5B Refugee assistance, TANF, & other
$24B Air transportation
$13B Water transportation
$4B Other transportation (incl. highway, railroad, & unallocable)
$126B Higher education
$4B Elementary & secondary education
$24M Vocational education
$23B Law enforcement
$9B Corrections
$6.8T
Federal spending
FY 2024

How has federal government revenue changed over time?

Federal government revenue increased 2.4 times between FY 1980 and FY 2024, while the population increased 1.5 times.

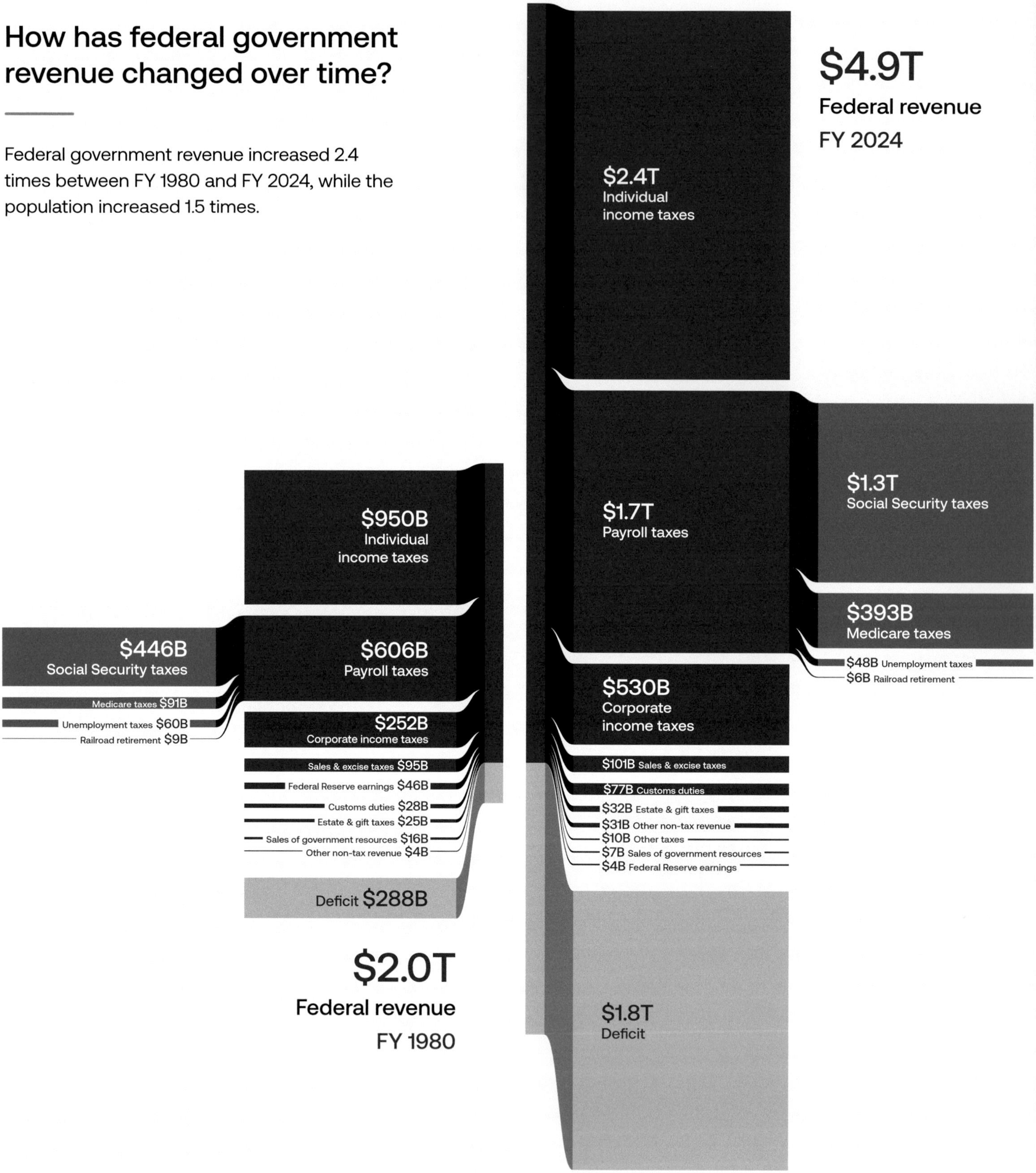

Federal government revenue (FY 1980 vs. FY 2024)

Source: USAFacts aggregation of data from Office of Management and Budget, Census Bureau, and Bureau of Economic Analysis
Note: Adjusted for inflation (FY 2024 dollars). Charts are shown to scale for comparison. Numbers may not add due to rounding.

What are the federal government's primary revenue sources?

In FY 2024, the federal government collected $4.9 trillion in revenue. Nearly half (49%) came from individual income taxes, while 35% came from payroll taxes that fund Social Security and Medicare. Other revenue sources include corporate income taxes, sales and excise taxes, customs duties, and estate and gift taxes.

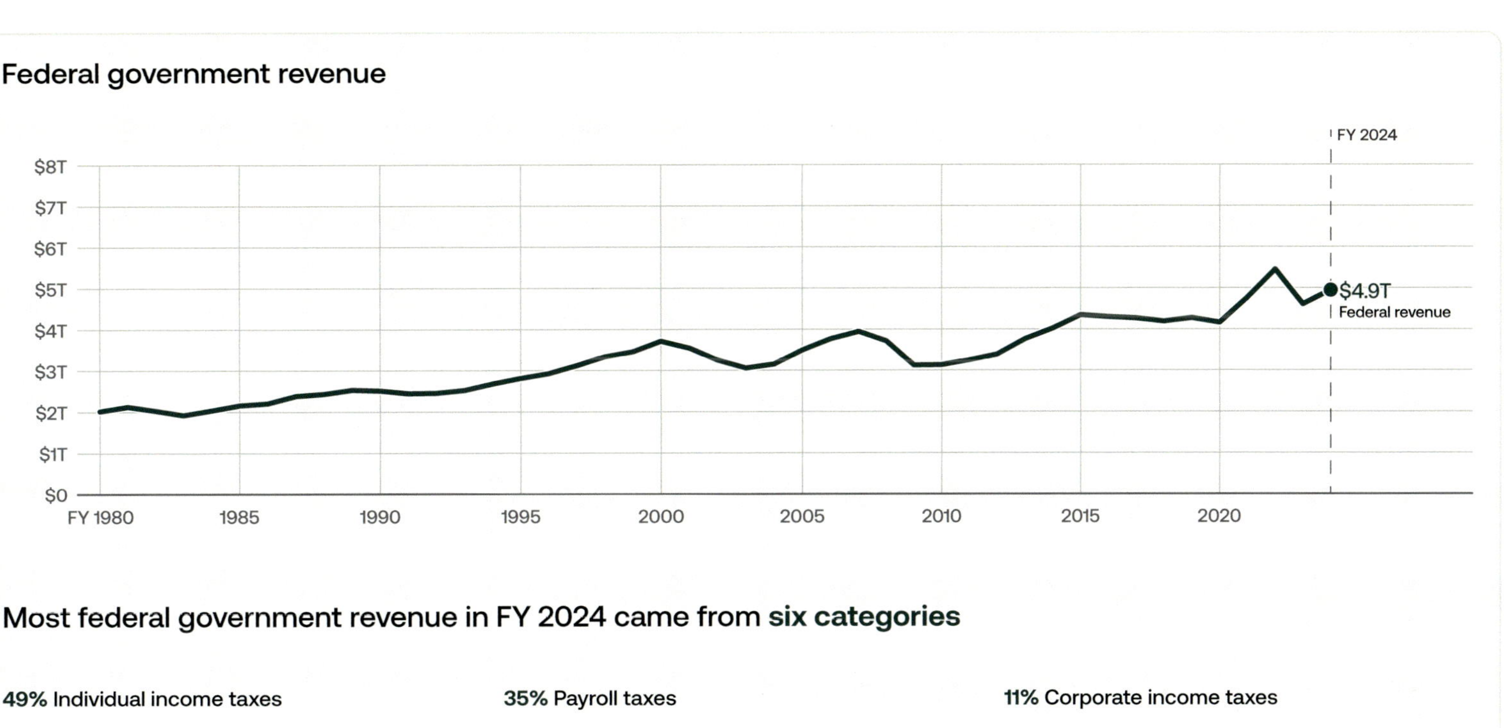

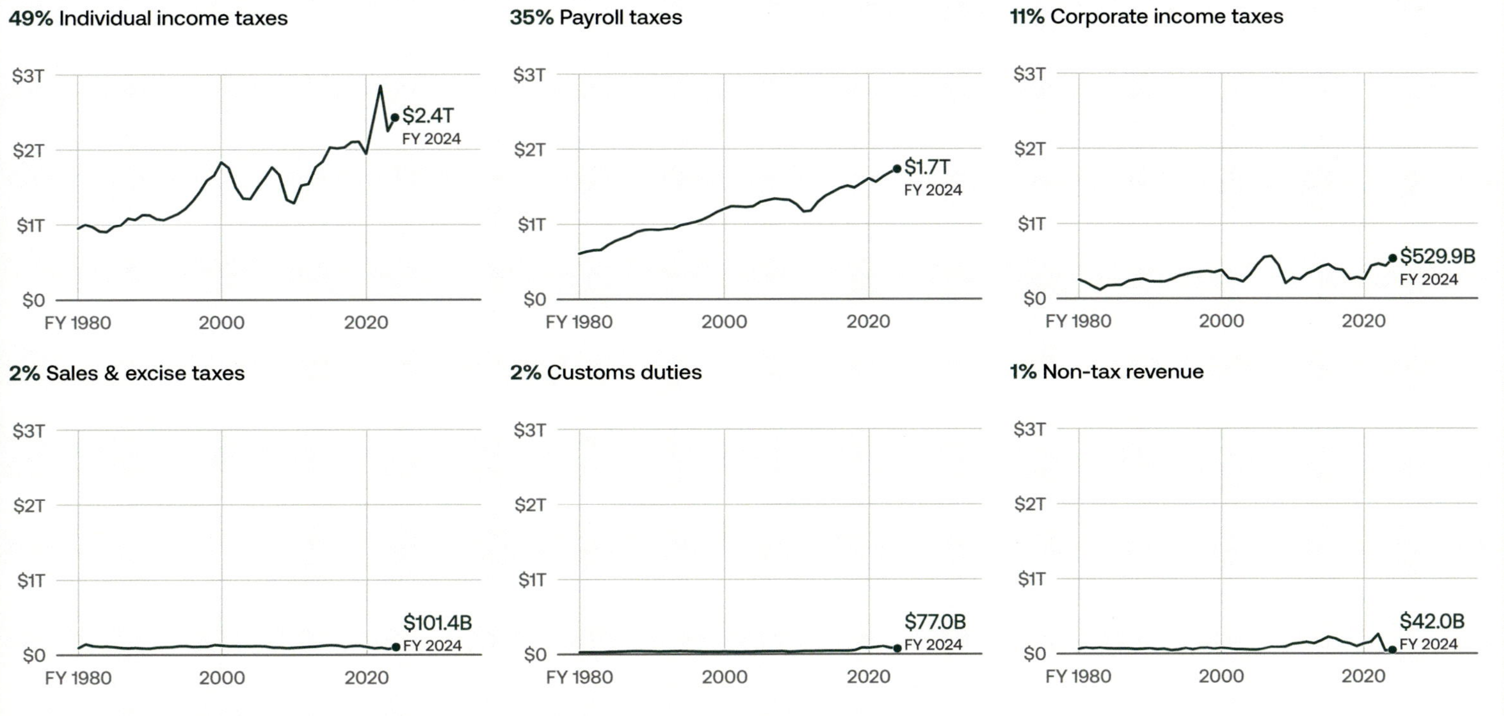

Source: USAFacts aggregation of data from Office of Management and Budget, Census Bureau, and Bureau of Economic Analysis
Note: Adjusted for inflation (FY 2024). Numbers may not add due to rounding.

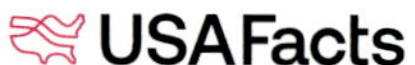

How has federal spending changed over time?

Federal government spending increased 2.9 times between FY 1980 and FY 2024, when adjusted for inflation, while the population increased 1.5 times.

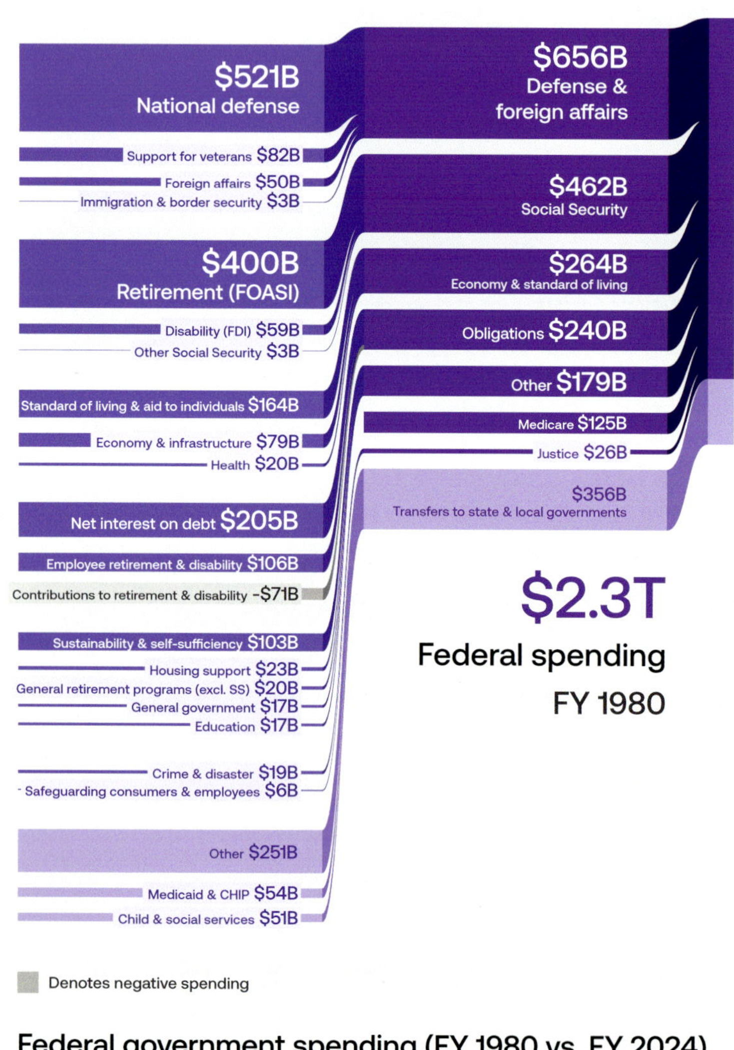

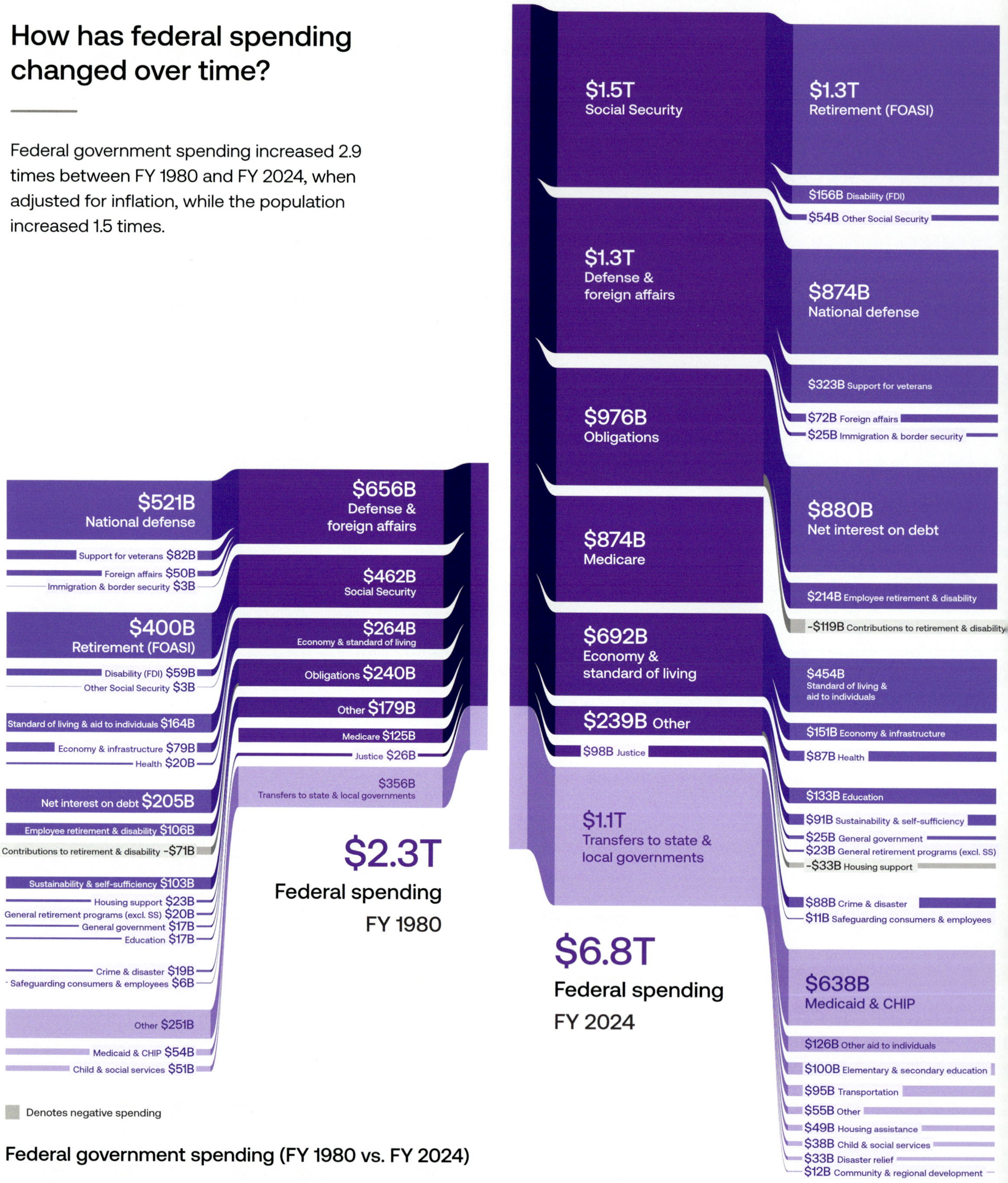

$521B National defense
Support for veterans $82B
Foreign affairs $50B
Immigration & border security $3B
$400B Retirement (FOASI)
Disability (FDI) $59B
Other Social Security $3B
Standard of living & aid to individuals $164B
Economy & infrastructure $79B
Health $20B
Net interest on debt $205B
Employee retirement & disability $106B
Contributions to retirement & disability -$71B
Sustainability & self-sufficiency $103B
Housing support $23B
General retirement programs (excl. SS) $20B
General government $17B
Education $17B
Crime & disaster $19B
Safeguarding consumers & employees $6B
Other $251B
Medicaid & CHIP $54B
Child & social services $51B
$656B Defense & foreign affairs
$462B Social Security
$264B Economy & standard of living
Obligations $240B
Other $179B
Medicare $125B
Justice $26B
$356B Transfers to state & local governments
$2.3T
Federal spending
FY 1980
$1.5T Social Security
$1.3T Defense & foreign affairs
$976B Obligations
$874B Medicare
$692B Economy & standard of living
$239B Other
$98B Justice
$1.1T Transfers to state & local governments
$6.8T
Federal spending
FY 2024
$1.3T Retirement (FOASI)
$156B Disability (FDI)
$54B Other Social Security
$874B National defense
$323B Support for veterans
$72B Foreign affairs
$25B Immigration & border security
$880B Net interest on debt
$214B Employee retirement & disability
-$119B Contributions to retirement & disability
$454B Standard of living & aid to individuals
$151B Economy & infrastructure
$87B Health
$133B Education
$91B Sustainability & self-sufficiency
$25B General government
$23B General retirement programs (excl. SS)
-$33B Housing support
$88B Crime & disaster
$11B Safeguarding consumers & employees
$638B Medicaid & CHIP
$126B Other aid to individuals
$100B Elementary & secondary education
$95B Transportation
$55B Other
$49B Housing assistance
$38B Child & social services
$33B Disaster relief
$12B Community & regional development
Denotes negative spending

Federal government spending (FY 1980 vs. FY 2024)

Source: USAFacts aggregation of data from Office of Management and Budget, Census Bureau, and Bureau of Economic Analysis
Note: Adjusted for inflation (FY 2024 dollars). Charts are shown to scale for comparison. Numbers may not add due to rounding.

What does the federal government spend the most money on?

The federal government spent $6.8 trillion in FY 2024, including transfers to states. Social Security (22%), defense and veterans (18%), and transfers to state and local governments (17%) accounted for more than half of spending. Federal spending increased by 7% in FY 2024, following two years of decreased spending. Federal spending remained 24% above that of FY 2019.

Federal government spending

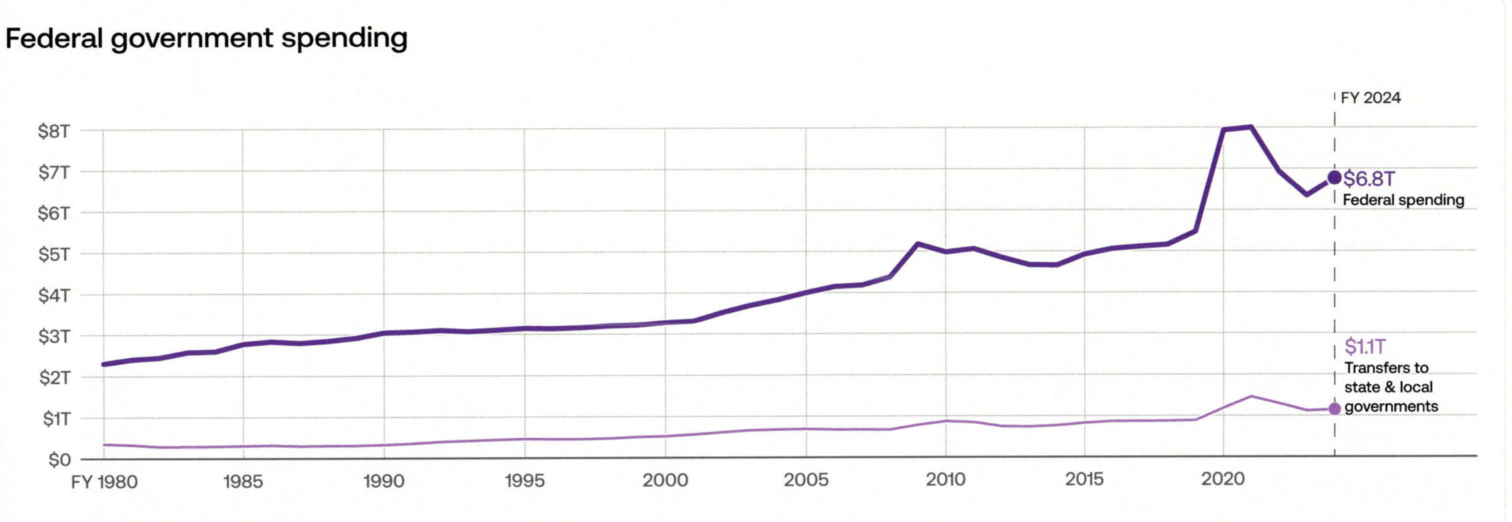

90% of federal government spending in FY 2024 went to six categories

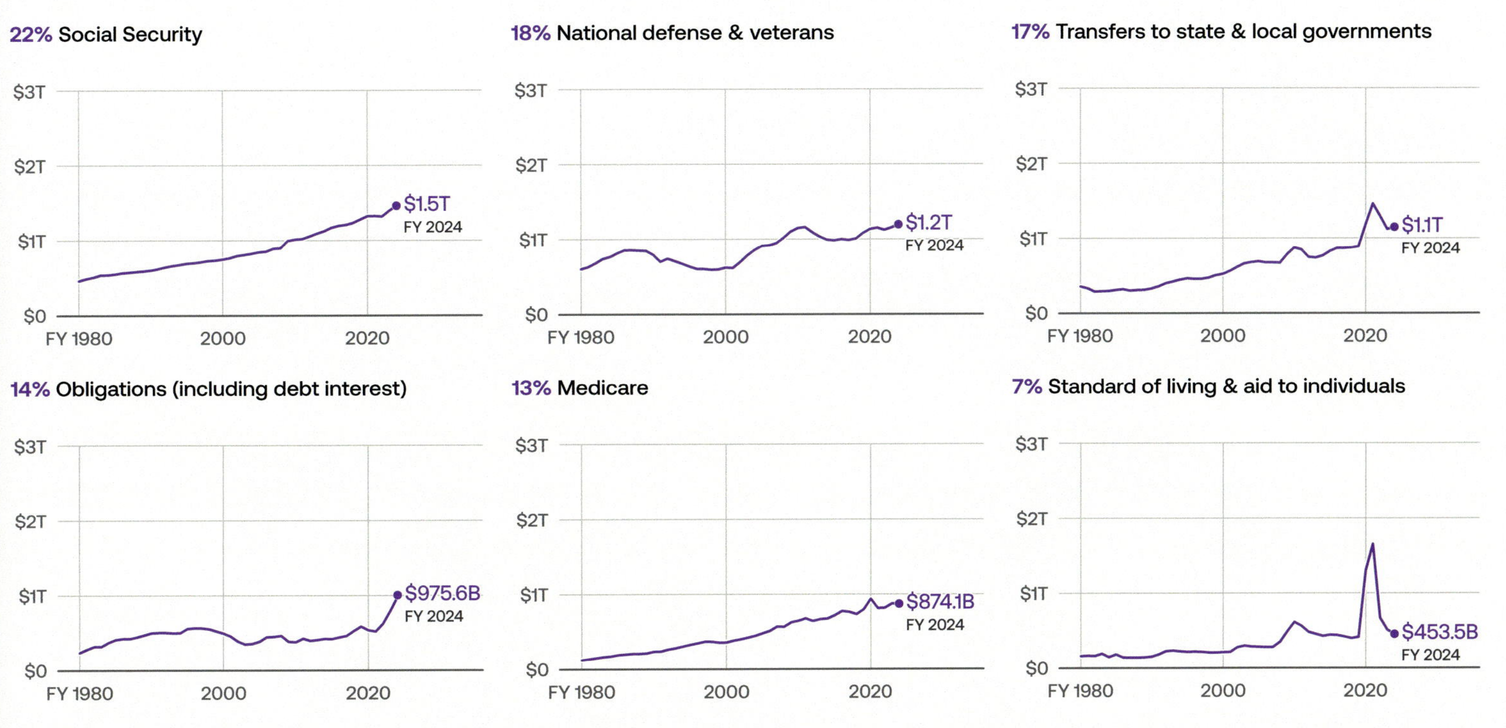

Source: USAFacts aggregation of data from Office of Management and Budget, Census Bureau, and Bureau of Economic Analysis
Note: Adjusted for inflation (FY 2024). Numbers may not add due to rounding.

What are the components of federal government spending?

There are three types of federal government spending: mandatory, discretionary, and interest. Mandatory spending must be funded as the law requires, unless Congress changes the rules or laws regarding the programs themselves. This type of spending made up 60% of the budget in FY 2024, up from 45% in FY 1980. Discretionary spending is determined each year through the appropriations process and can change depending on national priorities. In FY 2024, it made up 27% of the budget. The government also pays interest on the national debt, which is the cost of borrowing from previous years. These payments aren't tied to any specific program and must be paid regardless of what Congress decides each year.

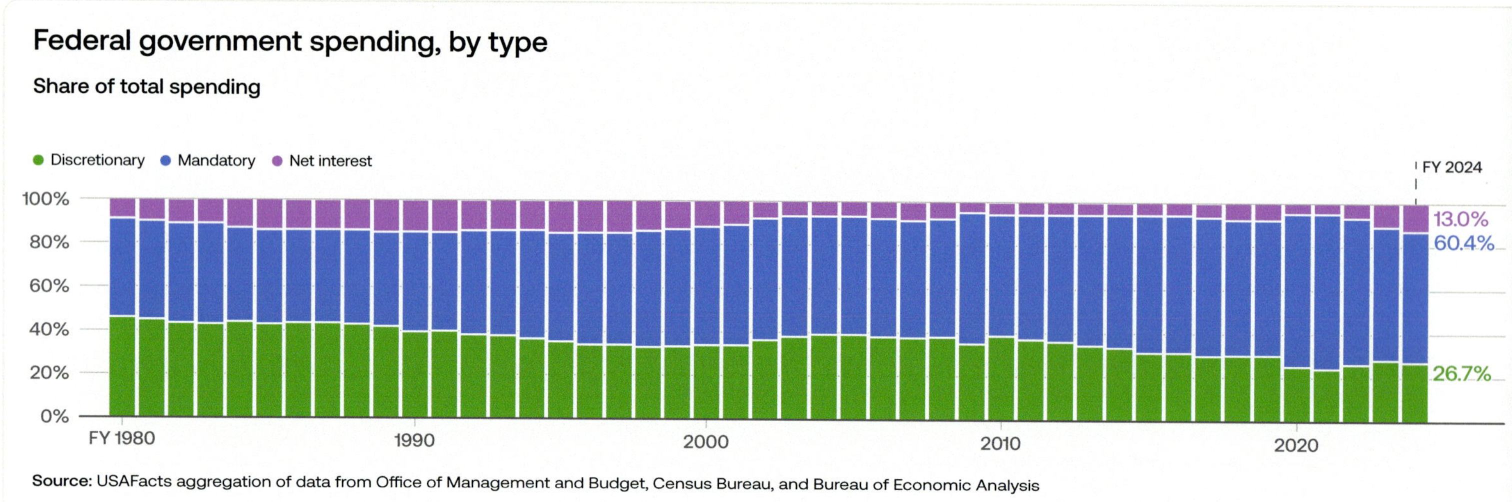

What programs make up mandatory and discretionary spending?

Of the $4.1 trillion in mandatory spending spent in FY 2024, the largest program was Social Security at $1.5 trillion, making up 35% of the total. It was followed by Medicare (21%) and Medicaid and CHIP (16%). Of the $1.8 trillion in discretionary spending in FY 2024, the largest category was national defense at $850.7 billion, making up 47% of the total.

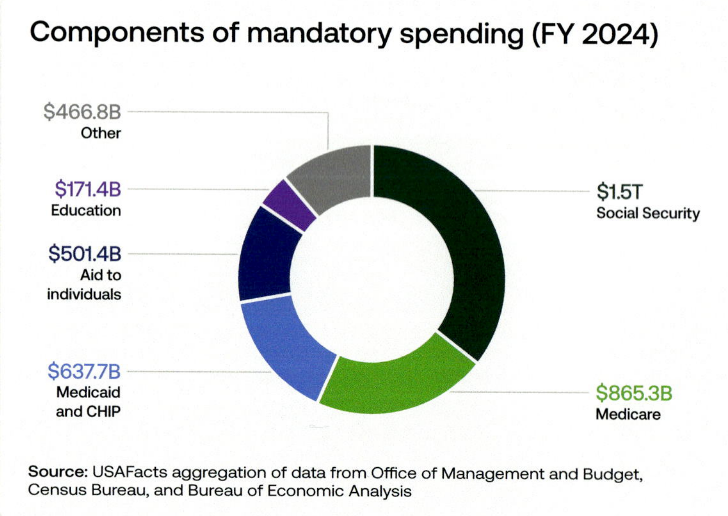

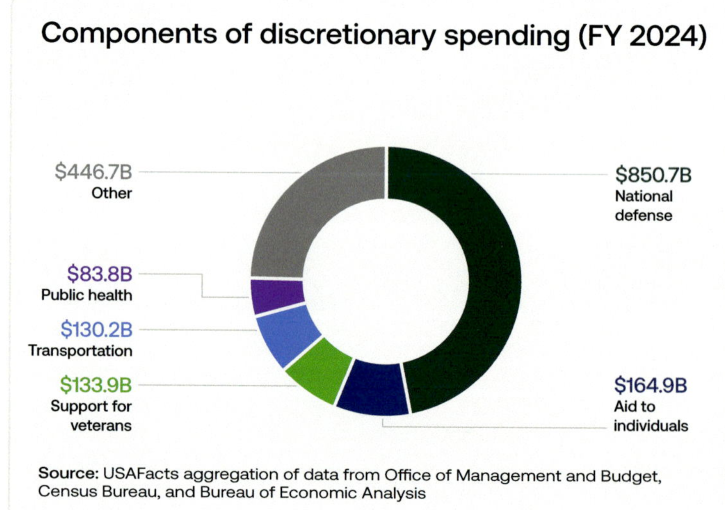

How much is spent on Social Security?

Social Security is a federal program that provides income to retired workers, eligible family members of deceased workers (survivors), and people with qualifying disabilities. The law requires the government to pay benefits to all who qualify; most Social Security-related spending is mandatory. In FY 2024, Social Security spending totaled $1.5 trillion, or 22% of federal spending, making it the largest government program. Spending rose 5% from the previous year, higher than the FY 1980–2023 average growth rate of 3%.

Social Security spending

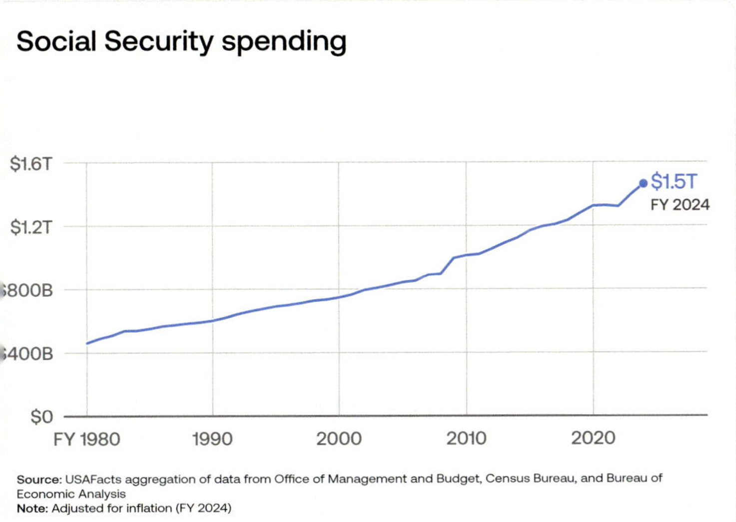

Source: USAFacts aggregation of data from Office of Management and Budget, Census Bureau, and Bureau of Economic Analysis
Note: Adjusted for inflation (FY 2024)

Social Security spending

Share of federal spending

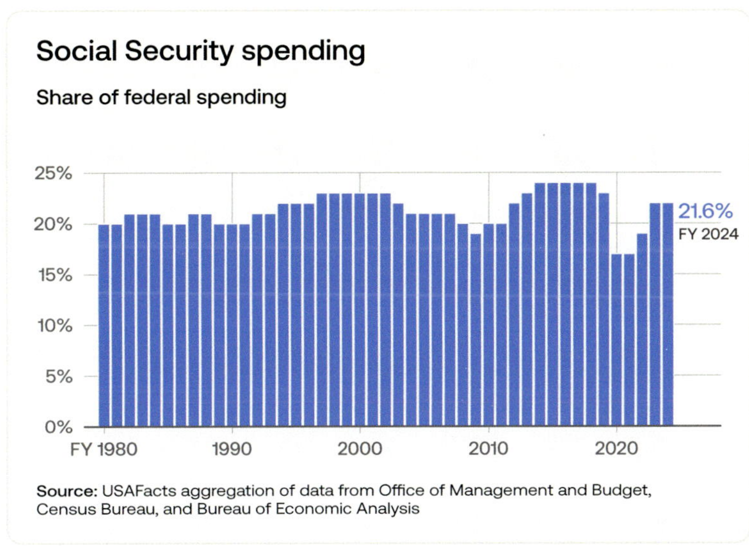

Source: USAFacts aggregation of data from Office of Management and Budget, Census Bureau, and Bureau of Economic Analysis

How many people collect Social Security benefits? How much do they receive?

In September 2024, there were 68.2 million Social Security recipients. Most of these, 54.0 million, received retirement benefits; 8.4 million received disability benefits and 5.8 million received survivor benefits. The number of retirement recipients increased by 3% from a year prior, while the number of disability and survivor recipients decreased. Retirement recipients received an average monthly benefit of $1,864, disability recipients received $1,395, and survivors received $1,501.

Social Security recipients

By type

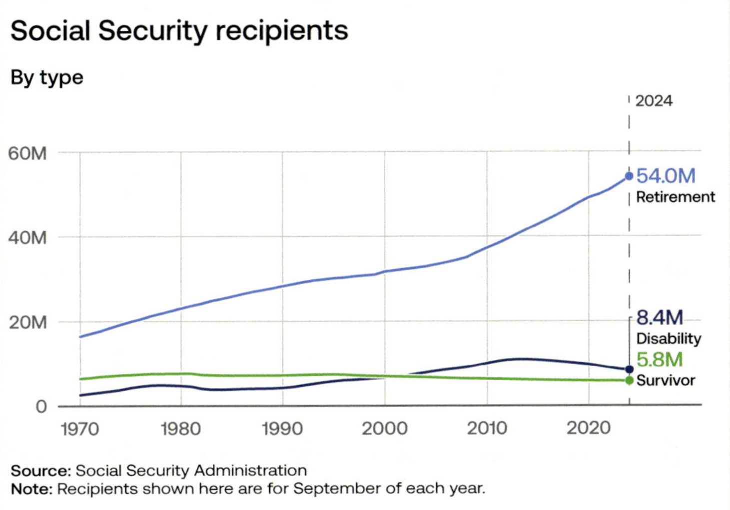

Source: Social Security Administration
Note: Recipients shown here are for September of each year.

Social Security average monthly benefit

By type

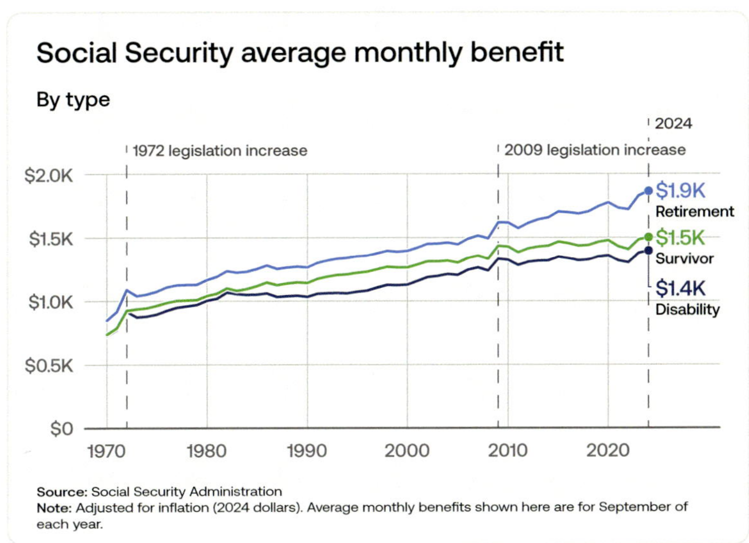

Source: Social Security Administration
Note: Adjusted for inflation (2024 dollars). Average monthly benefits shown here are for September of each year.

What is Medicare? How much does the government spend on it?

Medicare is a federal program that provides health insurance to people age 65 and older and certain younger individuals with disabilities or serious health conditions. Its funding comes from payroll taxes and premiums, and a majority of its spending is mandatory. In FY 2024, Medicare spending totaled $874.1 billion, or 13% of federal spending. Spending increased by less than 1% from the previous year, below the FY 1980–2023 average rate of 5% growth. Its share of the total budget declined from FY 2023.

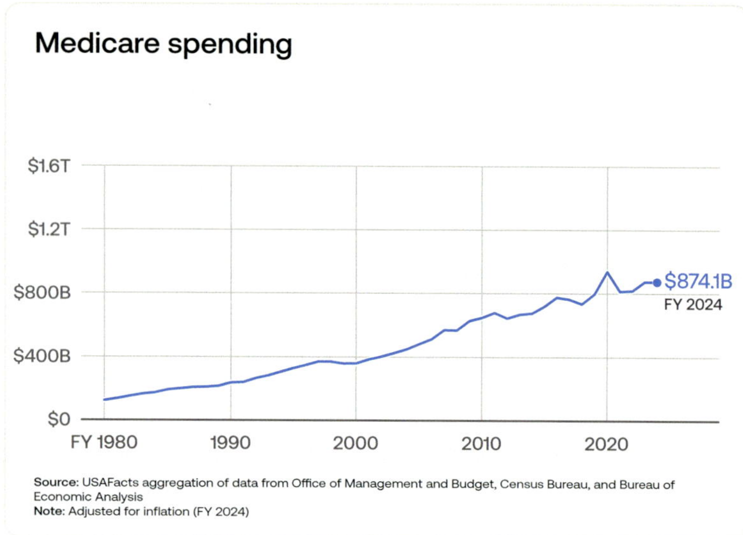

Source: USAFacts aggregation of data from Office of Management and Budget, Census Bureau, and Bureau of Economic Analysis
Note: Adjusted for inflation (FY 2024)

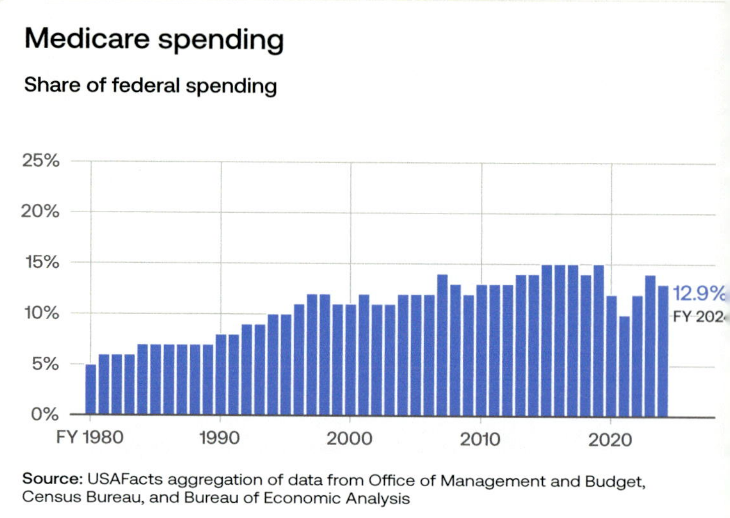

Source: USAFacts aggregation of data from Office of Management and Budget, Census Bureau, and Bureau of Economic Analysis

How many people are enrolled in Medicare? How much does it cost per person?

67.6 million people were enrolled in Medicare in 2024, 1.5% more than in 2023. The average cost of Medicare per beneficiary was $17,786, a new high (after adjusting for inflation). Nearly half of this cost was for Part B, which supports medical and preventative care.

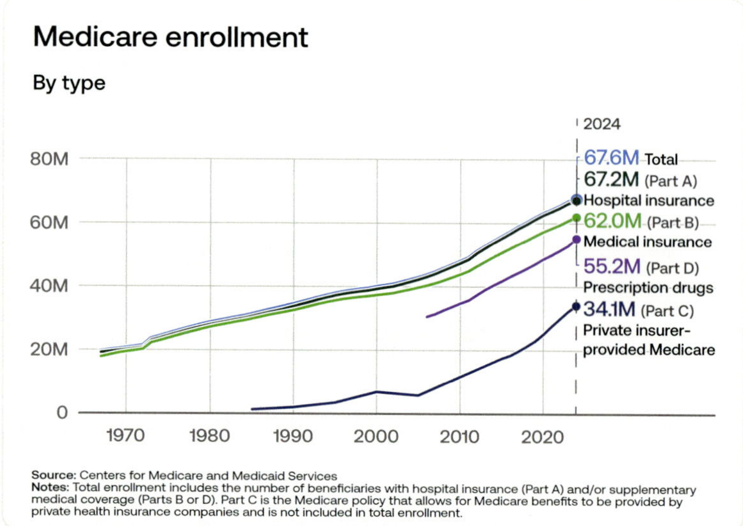

Source: Centers for Medicare and Medicaid Services
Notes: Total enrollment includes the number of beneficiaries with hospital insurance (Part A) and/or supplementary medical coverage (Parts B or D). Part C is the Medicare policy that allows for Medicare benefits to be provided by private health insurance companies and is not included in total enrollment.

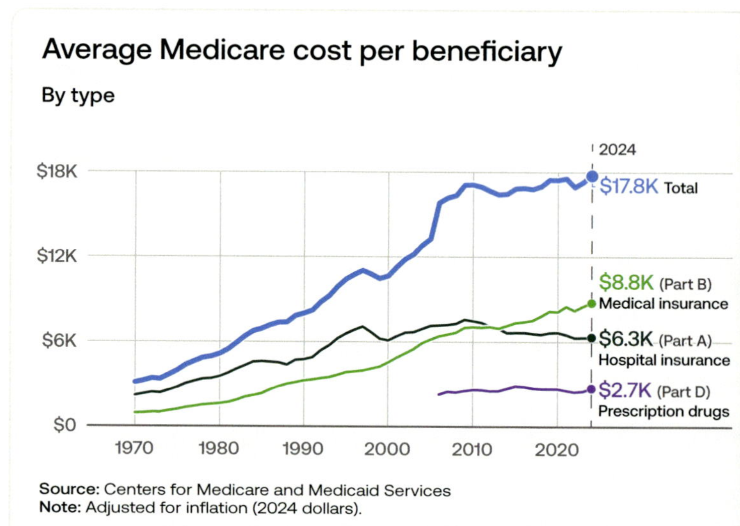

Source: Centers for Medicare and Medicaid Services
Note: Adjusted for inflation (2024 dollars).

What are Medicaid and CHIP? How much does the federal government contribute to them?

Medicaid and the Children's Health Insurance Program (CHIP) are joint federal and state programs that provide health coverage to low-income individuals and families, including children, pregnant women, people with disabilities, and some older adults. The federal government covers at least 50% of each state's Medicaid costs, making these programs a large part of federal mandatory spending. In FY 2024, federal Medicaid and CHIP spending totaled $637.7 billion, or 9% of federal spending. Spending decreased 2% from the previous year, below the FY 1980–2023 average rate of 6% growth. Its share of the total budget also declined from FY 2023 by about 1 percentage point.

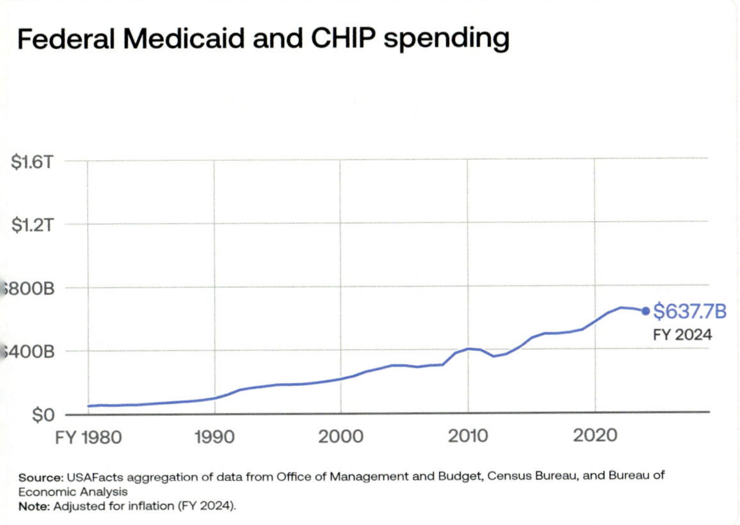

Source: USAFacts aggregation of data from Office of Management and Budget, Census Bureau, and Bureau of Economic Analysis
Note: Adjusted for inflation (FY 2024).

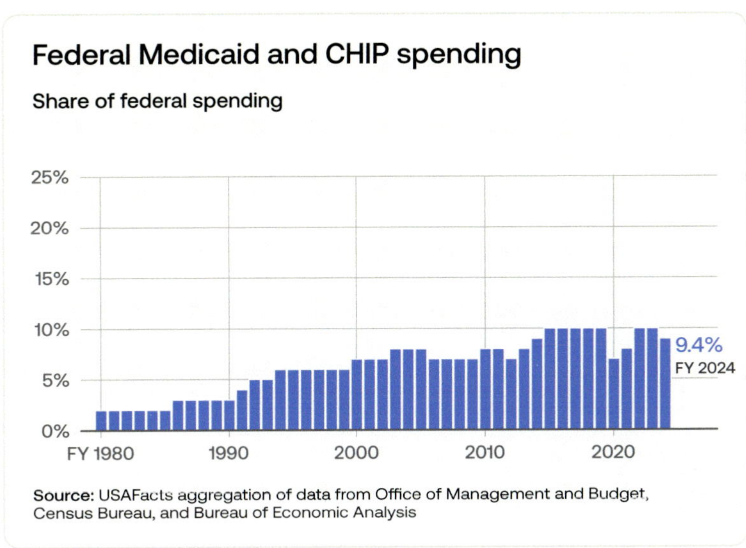

Source: USAFacts aggregation of data from Office of Management and Budget, Census Bureau, and Bureau of Economic Analysis

How many people are enrolled in Medicaid and CHIP? How much does the program cost per person?

There were 91.7 million Medicaid enrollees in 2023, costing an average of $9,782 per person. The number of recipients increased nearly 1% and average per-enrollee costs increased by 3% from 2022, after adjusting for inflation. Total CHIP enrollees increased 1% to 7.3 million in 2023, and the average per-enrollee cost was $3,469, down 2% from the previous year.

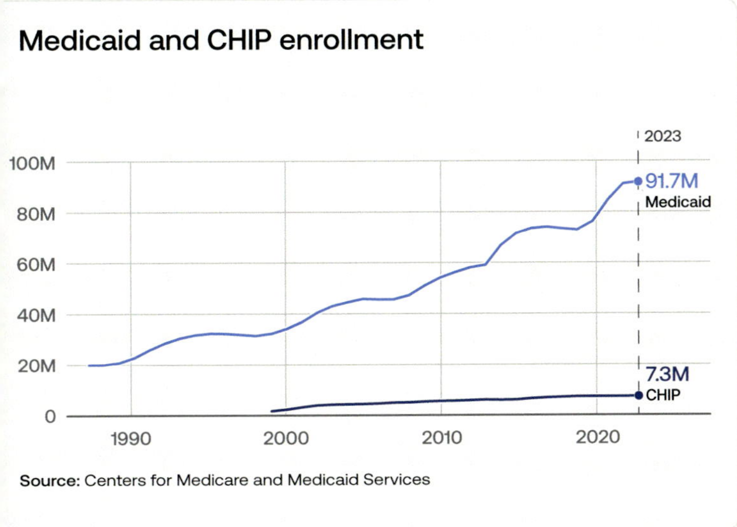

Source: Centers for Medicare and Medicaid Services

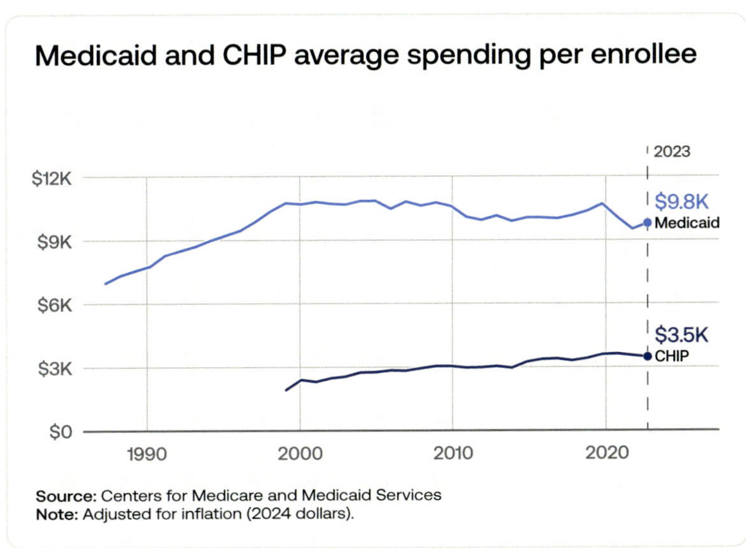

Source: Centers for Medicare and Medicaid Services
Note: Adjusted for inflation (2024 dollars).

How much does the US pay in interest on its debt?

The government pays interest on its debts the same way individuals pay interest on credit card bills, mortgages, and car payments. Interest payments aren't fixed and change based on the size of the debt and interest rates. In FY 2024, the US spent $879.9 billion in debt interest. It was equivalent to 13% of total government spending, the highest share since 1999.

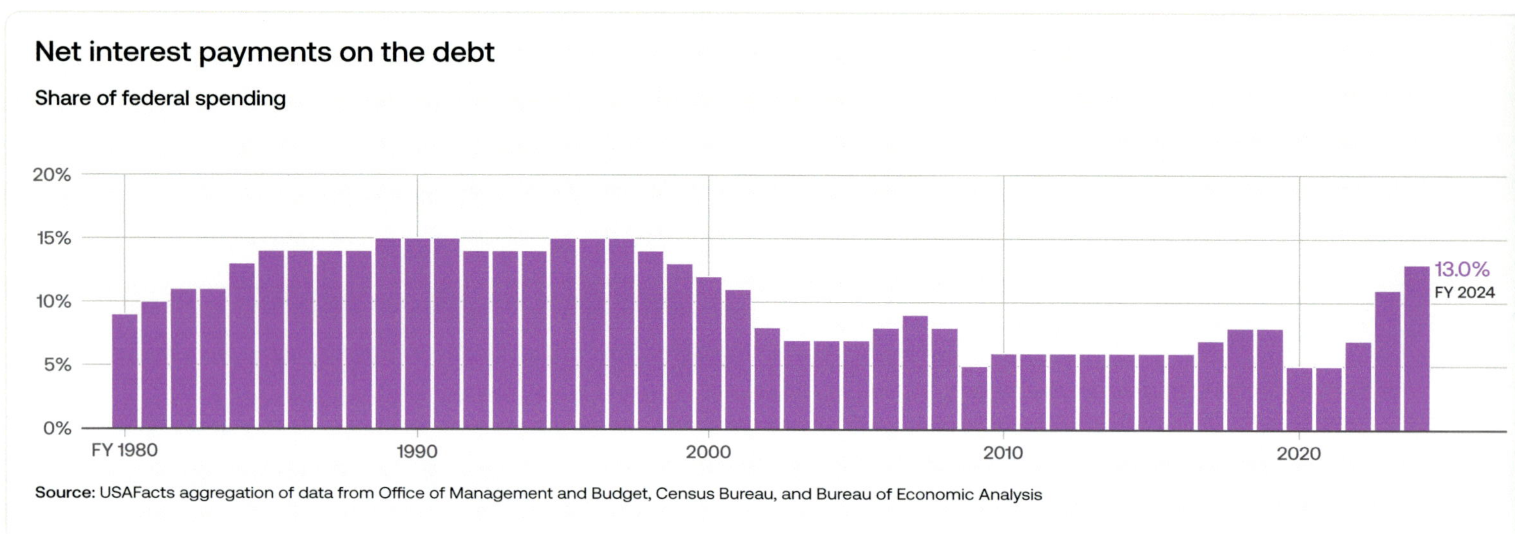

How much debt does the federal government have?

The total debt owed by the federal government reached $36.2 trillion by the end of 2024. About 80% of the debt was owned by the public (individuals, businesses, banks, the Federal Reserve, and foreign entities). Debt held by the public was equivalent to $84,852 per person in the US, or 97% of GDP. Public debt as a percentage of GDP reached a peak in 2020, when it was 98% of GDP.

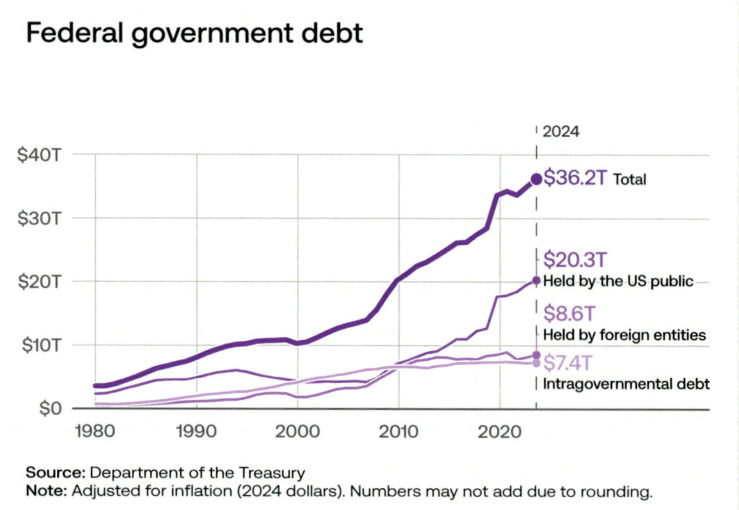

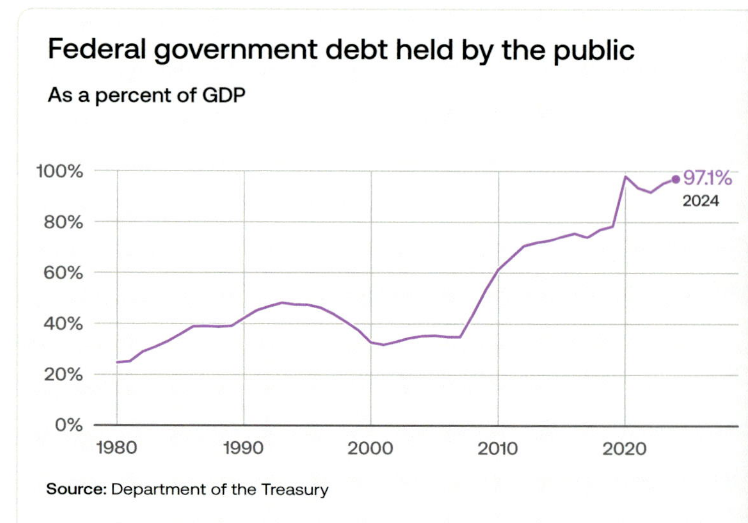

How has the federal government deficit changed over time?

Spending in FY 2024 increased by $427.8 billion (adjusted for inflation) compared to FY 2023, while revenue increased by $342.6 billion. As a result, the budget deficit increased to $1.8 trillion from $1.75 trillion in FY 2023. The deficit was lower than FY 2020 and FY 2021 highs (both exceeding $3.0 trillion).

Federal government finances

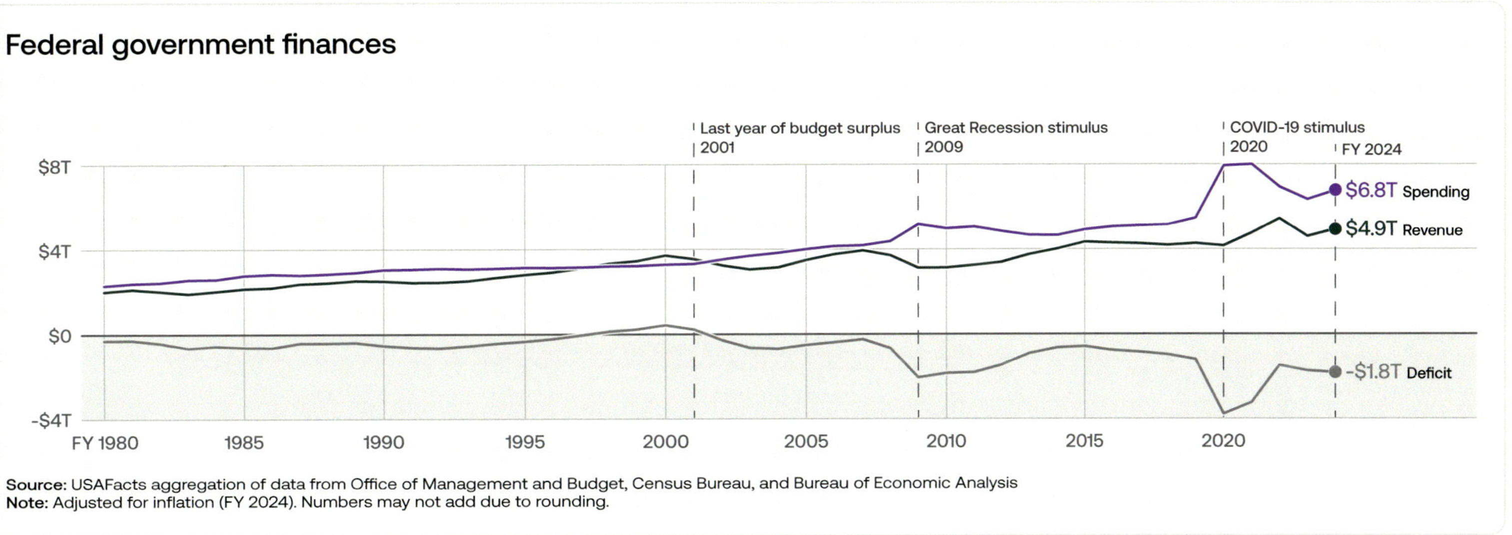

Source: USAFacts aggregation of data from Office of Management and Budget, Census Bureau, and Bureau of Economic Analysis
Note: Adjusted for inflation (FY 2024). Numbers may not add due to rounding.

Chapter sources and data timeliness

Publishing agency	Program	Publication name	Release date	Most recent period in the data
Office of Management and Budget	Public Budget Database	Budget of the United States Government	As of August 2025, the public budget database for FY 2024 has not been published	FY 2023
Centers for Medicare and Medicaid Services	Data & Research	National health expenditure data	Dec. 2024	2023
		2025 Annual Report of the Boards of Trustees of the Federal Hospital Insurance and Federal Supplementary Medical Insurance Trust Funds	June 2025	2024
Social Security Administration	Office of the Chief Actuary	Benefits paid by type of beneficiary	Monthly releases	July 2025
Department of the Treasury	Treasury Bulletin	Distribution of federal securities by class of investors and type of issues	Quarterly releases	June 2025

See sources and notes section at the end of this report for detailed citation information.

USAFacts adjusts government finance data for inflation so comparisons can be made over time. To learn more about the financial analysis methodology, visit usafacts.org/methodology.

- The data in this section is in fiscal years. The federal fiscal year is from October to September. For example, the 2024 fiscal year covers the period of October 2023 through September 2024.
- The Office of Management and Budget's annual budget tables are often released months after the start of the fiscal year. This lag can make it difficult to analyze the most recent federal revenue and spending trends. This year, the delay was particularly pronounced with tables released in late June 2025, months later than is typical.
- USAFacts relies upon the Public Budget Database to provide detailed analysis of the US federal budget. This data is typically released early spring each year. As of mid-August 2025, the FY 2024 database is not published.

Federal income taxes

Federal individual income taxes facts

The Tax Cuts and Jobs Act (TCJA) was passed in 2017 and was first effective during the 2018 tax season. It made sweeping changes to the individual provisions of the federal tax code, particularly the standard deduction and itemized deductions. The One Big Beautiful Bill Act (OBBBA) of 2025 made some of those changes permanent, tweaked others, and introduced new tax code provisions.

It's not just policy changes that affect federal income tax collection; the number of filers and their incomes play a role. This chapter, which describes taxpayers and their behavior over the last decade, serves as a benchmark to evaluate the effects of the TCJA and the OBBBA.

Federal income tax collection trends

- The IRS collected $2.1 trillion in individual income taxes in 2022, 33.3% more than in 2017 (not inflation adjusted).
- From 2017 to 2022, the number of tax returns increased 5.5%, and average adjusted gross income rose 27.7%.
- In 2022, the average effective income tax rate was 14.1%, up from 13.0% in 2018 and down from 14.4% in 2017.
- Returns with income over $100,000 paid 86.8% of all federal individual income taxes in 2022, up from 81.1% in 2017.

Earned Income Tax Credit (EITC)

- The EITC provided $60.1 billion in credits across 24.1 million tax returns in 2022.
- Over 95% of EITC dollars went to filers with children.

Child Tax Credit (CTC)

- The TCJA doubled the maximum CTC, raised the refundable portion of the credit, and made it available to higher-income families. The OBBBA increased the maximum CTC again and indexed it for inflation.
- The number of returns claiming the non-refundable portion increased 78% the first year the TCJA was effective.
- In 2022, families with AGI over $100,000 received, as a group, $42.0 billion in CTC credits. That was over eight times more than in 2017.

Standard deduction vs. itemized deductions

- Both the TCJA and OBBBA increased the standard deduction and limited some popular deductions.
- The share of returns that itemized fell to 9.5% in 2022, down from 30.6% in 2017.

Itemized deductions

- From 2017 to 2022, the average state and local tax (SALT) deduction fell from $13,457 to $8,303. The average deduction fell 96% among the highest-income tax returns.
- The share of returns claiming the charitable deduction dropped from 24.8% in 2017 to 7.5% in 2022, mirroring the reduction in itemized returns.
- The average charitable contributions deduction rose as the pool of taxpayers claiming it became more concentrated among higher-income filers.
- In 2022, 11.6 million returns claimed the mortgage interest deduction for a total of $147.0 billion.
- High-income households claim the largest mortgage interest deductions, though their average deduction decreased from 2017 to 2022.
- In 2022, 25.7 million returns claimed the qualified business income (QBI) deduction, totaling $216.1 billion. The QBI deduction was established by the TCJA.
- Nearly three-quarters of returns with income over $1 million claimed the QBI deduction, averaging nearly $160,000 per return.

How much does the IRS collect from individual income taxes?

The IRS collected $2.1 trillion in individual income taxes in 2022. This was down from $2.2 trillion the year before. Compared to 2017, the year before the implementation of the Tax Cuts and Jobs Act (TCJA), total individual income taxes collected increased 33.3%.

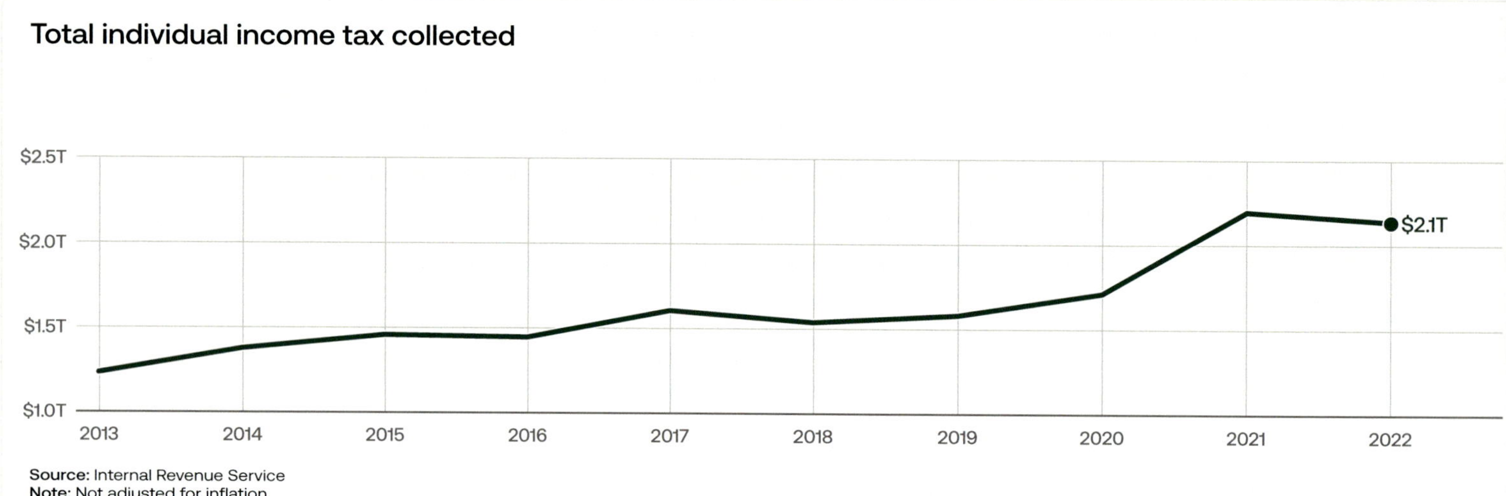

Adjusted gross income (AGI) is a tax filer's total income from all sources — wages, tips, interest, dividends, capital gains, business income, and retirement income — minus certain adjustments. These adjustments include contributions to a retirement account or a health savings account. In other words, AGI is income before deductions or credits, but after subtracting a few specific expenses the IRS allows.

How has the pool of federal taxpayers changed over time?

What the federal government collects from individual income taxes depends on the number of tax filers and their incomes. Increases in either may raise income tax revenue while declines may have the opposite effect. The number of tax returns filed increased from 160.8 million in 2021 to 161.3 million in 2022. Average adjusted gross income (AGI) declined 0.1%. Compared to 2017, the number of tax returns filed in 2022 increased 5.5%, and average AGI increased 27.7%.

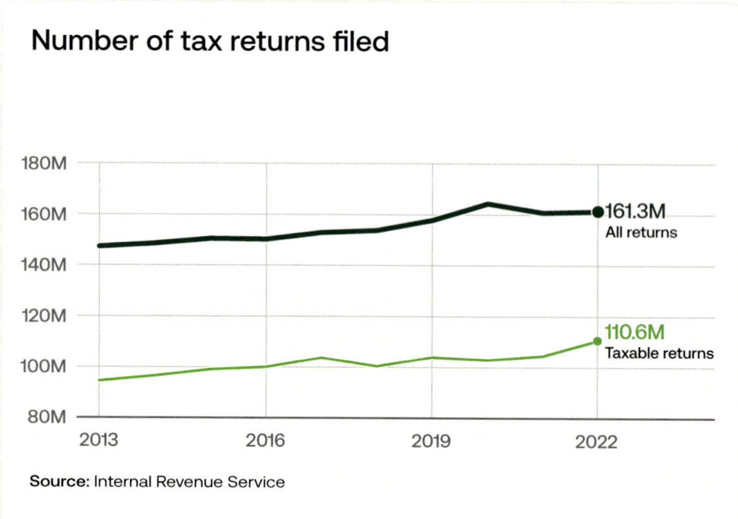

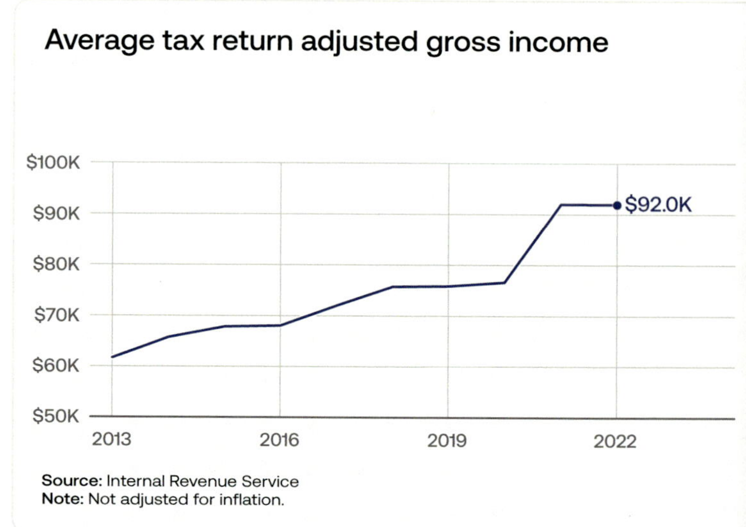

What are federal income tax rates?

The United States has a progressive federal income tax system, meaning tax rates increase as income rises. The TCJA reduced tax rates for most income levels and adjusted the income ranges subject to each tax rate. For example, it changed the highest federal marginal income tax rate — the rate applied to the last dollar of income for the highest earners — from 39.6% on income over $418,400 for single filers to 37% on income over $500,000. (This increased to $539,900 by 2022 due to inflation adjustments applied by the IRS.) These changes were set to expire at the end of 2025, but were made permanent by the OBBBA.

Realized capital gains, which are the profits from selling assets such as stocks, bonds, or real estate, are also taxed. Profits from selling assets held less than one year are taxed at the same rate as regular income. If they're held longer than one year, though, they are taxed at lower rates than other income. While the TCJA did not change the capital gains tax rate, the income brackets to which each rate is applied shifted to align with the regular tax rate schedule.

Regular and capital gains tax rates, 2017 and 2018, by select filing statuses

Pre-TCJA (2017)				TCJA (2018)			
Select filing statuses		Tax rates		Select filing statuses		Tax rates	
Single	Married filing jointly	Regular tax rate	Capital gains tax rate	Single	Married filing jointly	Regular tax rate	Capital gains tax rate
$0–$9,325	$0–$18,650	10%	0%	$0–$9,525	$0–$19,050	10%	0%
$9,326–$37,950	$18,651–$75,900	15%		$9,526–$38,700	$19,051–$77,400	12%	
$37,951–$91,900	$75,901–$153,100	25%	15%	$38,701–$82,500	$77,401–$165,000	22%	15%
$91,901–$191,650	$153,101–$233,350	28%		$82,501–$157,500	$165,001–$315,000	24%	
$191,651–$416,700	$233,351–$416,700	33%		$157,501–$200,000	$315,001–$400,000	32%	
$416,701–$418,400	$416,701–$470,700	35%		$200,001–$500,000	$400,001–$600,000	35%	
Over $418,400	Over $470,700	39.6%	20%	Over $500,000	Over $600,000	37%	20%

Source: Internal Revenue Service
Note: The OBBBA made the TCJA changes to tax brackets and tax rates permanent.

What share of taxpayer income is taxed at capital gains rates?

In 2022, 9.1% of tax filers' adjusted gross income (AGI) was taxed at the long-term capital gains rates. Over the last decade, this percentage averaged 7.8%, reaching as low as 5.3% and as high as 13.0%. A larger share of high-income tax filers' AGI comes from realized long-term capital gains: 32.7% in 2022 for people with an AGI over $1 million. Filers with AGI under $25,000 may include retirees who rely on investment income and have little wage or salary income, or high-wealth individuals who had low income due to business losses or other factors, but still realized capital gains.

Long-term capital gains as a share of AGI

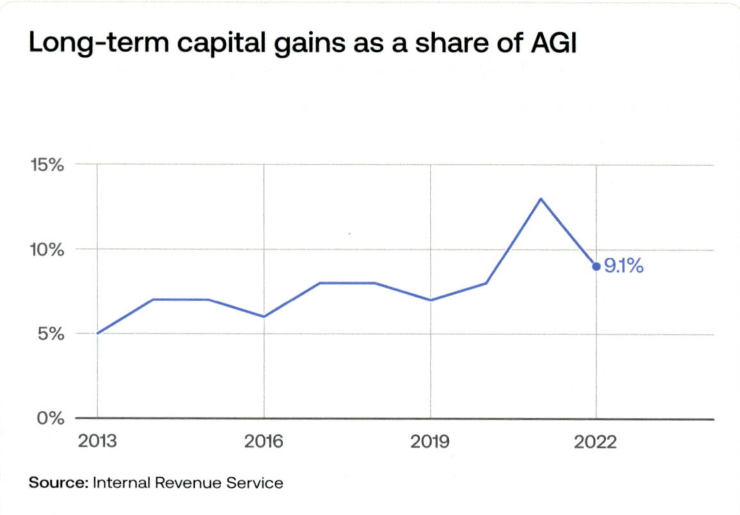

Source: Internal Revenue Service

Share of AGI from long-term capital gains (2022)

By AGI group

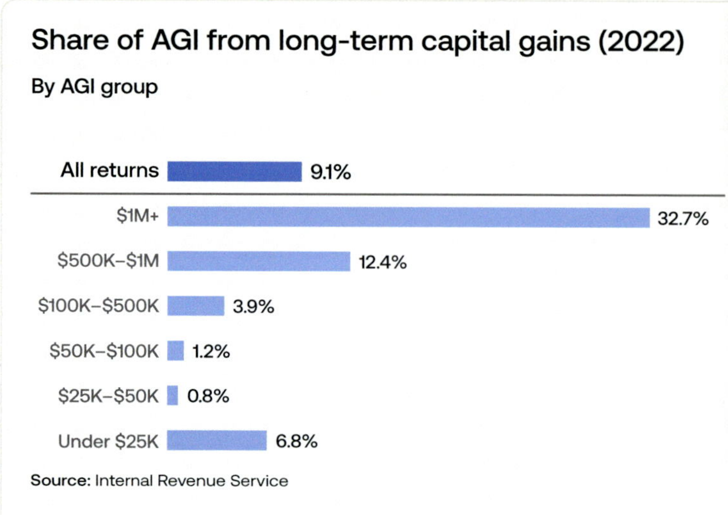

Source: Internal Revenue Service

How much do people pay in federal individual income taxes?

A filer's effective tax rate, or the percentage of their income paid in taxes, is typically lower than their tax bracket. That's for two reasons: 1) because marginal tax rates apply to the last dollars earned rather than all income, and 2) because lower tax rates are applied to some income, such as capital gains and dividends. In 2022, the average effective federal income tax rate was 14.1%, up from 13.0% in 2018, but below the 2017 pre-TCJA level of 14.4%. Effective tax rates ranged from 1.6% for filers earning under $25,000 to 25.4% for people earning over $1 million.

Average effective federal income tax rate

By AGI group

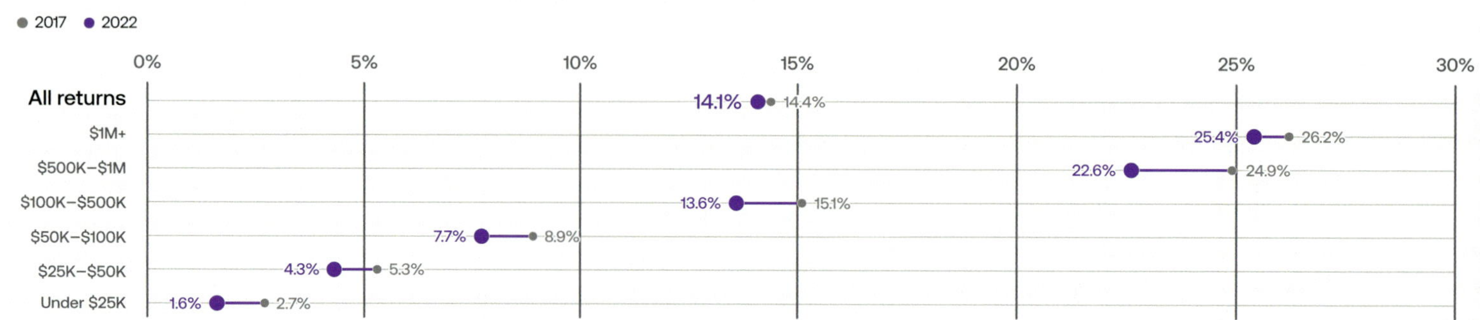

Source: Internal Revenue Service
Note: Effective rates are calculated based on income tax paid after tax credits.

How do effective federal income tax rates vary by state?

Taxpayers had the highest effective federal income tax rate in higher-income states like Connecticut (17.0%), New York (16.7%), and Massachusetts (16.6%). The lowest effective tax rates were in lower-income states like West Virginia (10.8%) and Mississippi (10.9%). Since 2017, the effective tax rate has increased in 18 states and fallen in 31.

Average effective federal income tax rate, by state

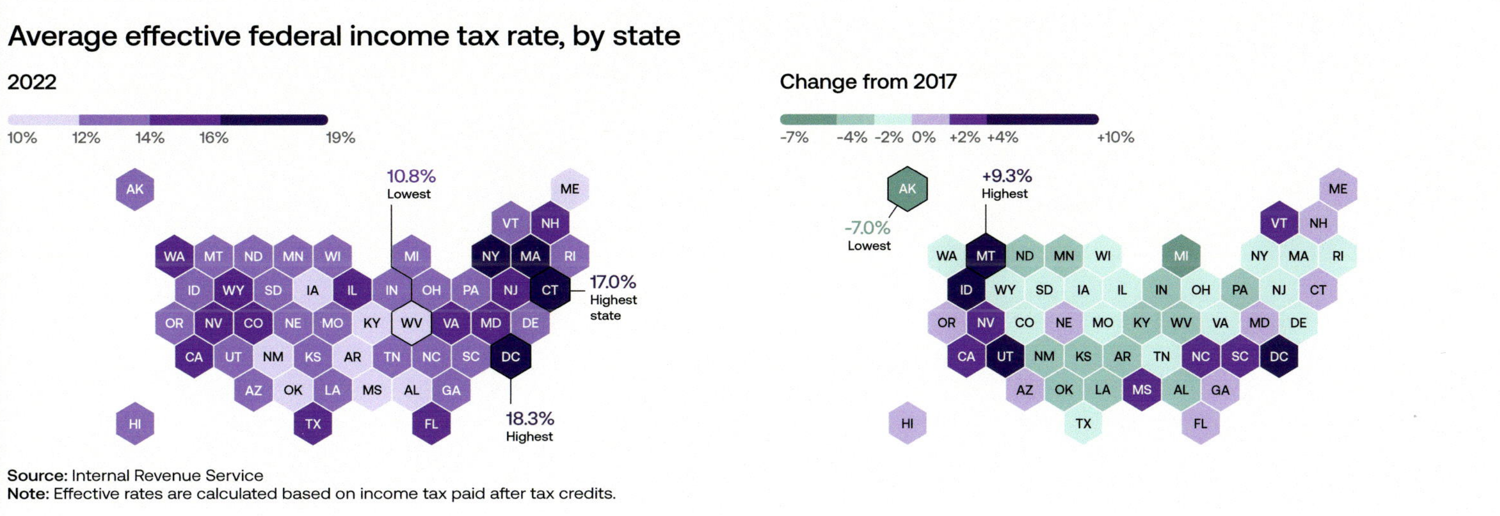

Source: Internal Revenue Service
Note: Effective rates are calculated based on income tax paid after tax credits.

What is the distribution of taxes paid by income level?

The portion of total income taxes paid by higher-income tax filers has grown since 2017, mirroring rising incomes. Between 2017 and 2022, the share of tax returns with AGIs over $100,000 increased by 5.7 percentage points, up from 18.1% to 23.8%. The share of income taxes paid by the group also increased 5.7 percentage points from 81.1% to 86.8%.

Share of federal income taxes collected

By AGI group

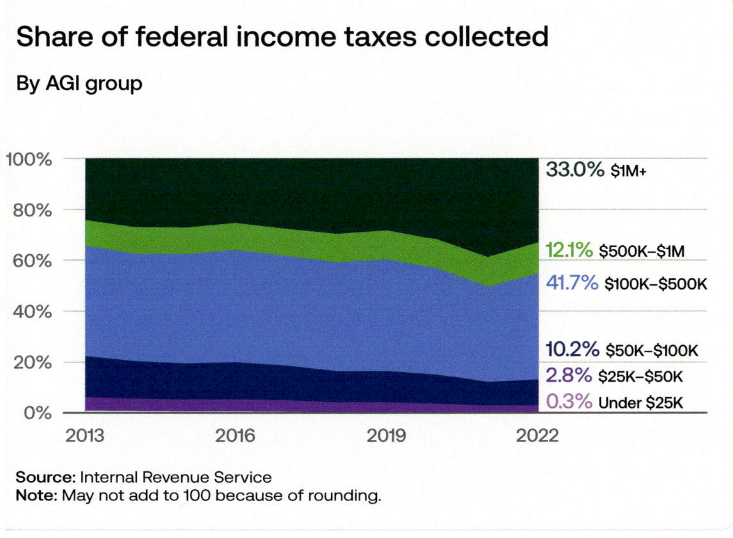

Source: Internal Revenue Service
Note: May not add to 100 because of rounding.

Share of tax returns filed

By AGI group

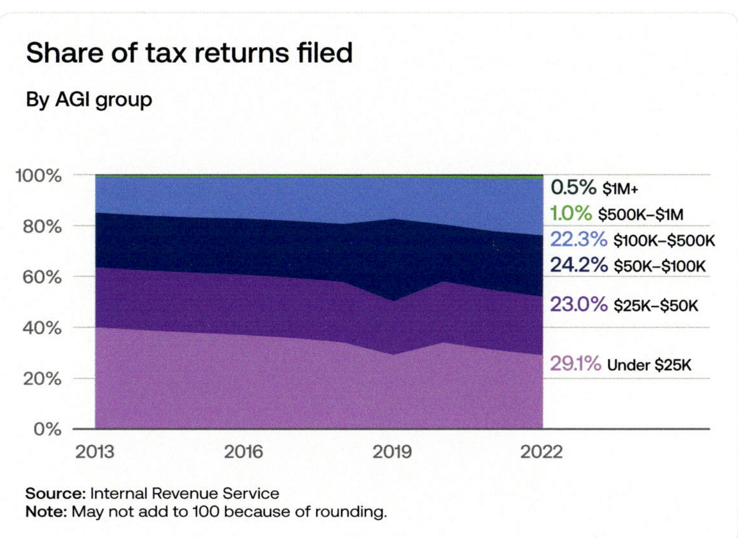

Source: Internal Revenue Service
Note: May not add to 100 because of rounding.

What is the standard tax deduction?

The standard deduction reduces a taxpayer's taxable income by a fixed amount. When taxpayers file their federal individual income tax return, they choose between the standard deduction or a series of itemized deductions. The TCJA nearly doubled the standard deduction to $12,000 for individuals and to $24,000 for joint filers. The OBBBA further increased the standard deduction and made those new levels permanent.

Standard deduction, by filing status

Filing status	Pre-TCJA (2017)	TCJA (2018)	OBBBA (2025)
Individual	$6,350	$12,000	$15,750
Joint	$12,700	$24,000	$31,500
Head of household	$9,350	$18,000	$23,625

Source: Internal Revenue Service
Note: Without OBBBA, the standard deduction would have been $15,000 for individuals, $30,000 for joint filers, and $22,500 for heads of household in 2025.

How many people itemize their taxes?

Itemizing means listing specific deductible expenses incurred throughout the year to reduce taxable income. Typically, tax filers choose to itemize only when their itemized deductions exceed the standard deduction. It is most common among high-income taxpayers. Following the implementation of the TCJA, the portion of itemized returns fell from 30.6% in 2017 to 11.4% in 2018. Itemizing declined by nearly 50 percentage points among returns with an AGI of $100,000 to $500,000. While itemizing fell among the highest-income taxpayers as well, more than 50% of returns with an AGI over $500,000 continued doing so in 2022.

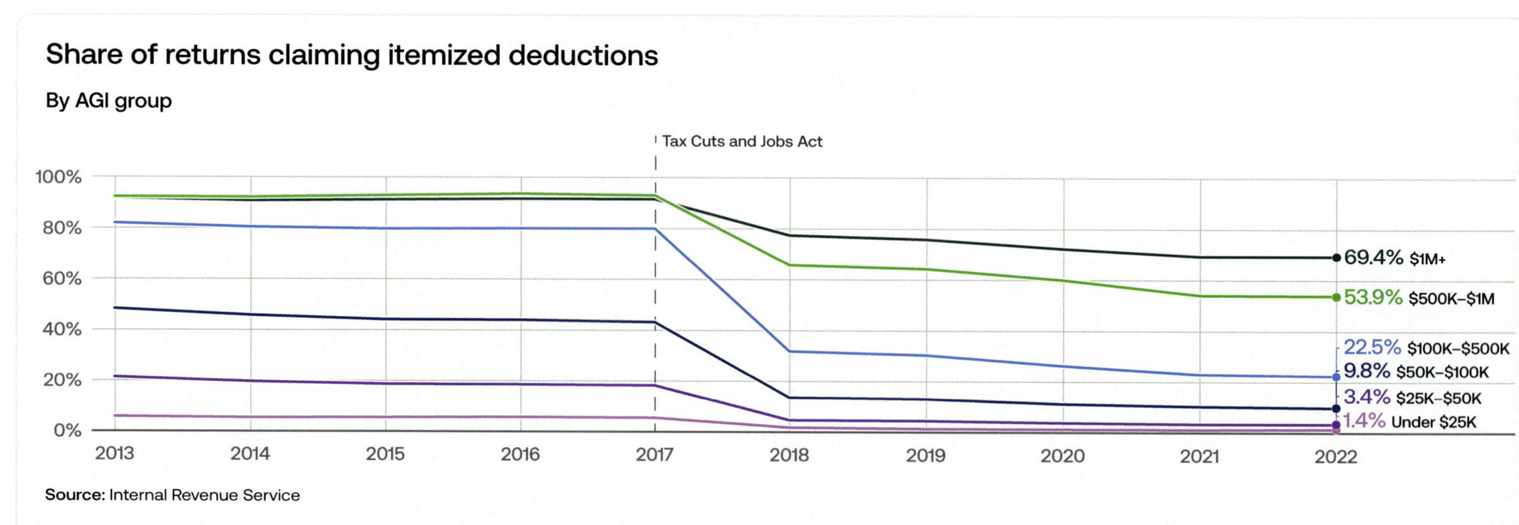

What are the most common income tax deductions?

The state and local tax (SALT), home mortgage interest, and charitable contribution deductions are the three most frequently claimed by taxpayers who itemize. SALT was claimed on the most returns (15.1 million), while the charitable contributions deduction had the highest dollar value ($222.4 billion) in 2022.

Number of returns and amount claimed, by itemized deduction (2022)

Type of itemized deduction	Total returns	Total amount claimed
SALT	15.1 million	$125.2 billion
Mortgage interest	11.6 million	$147.0 billion
Charitable contributions	12.2 million	$222.4 billion

Source: Internal Revenue Service

Are more or fewer filers claiming popular deductions since TCJA?

Mirroring the decline in itemization, the share of tax returns claiming SALT, mortgage interest, and charitable contributions deductions has declined since 2017. In 2022, 9.3% of returns claimed SALT, 7.5% claimed the charitable contribution deduction, and 7.2% claimed the mortgage interest deduction. More than 20% of returns claimed these deductions before the TCJA.

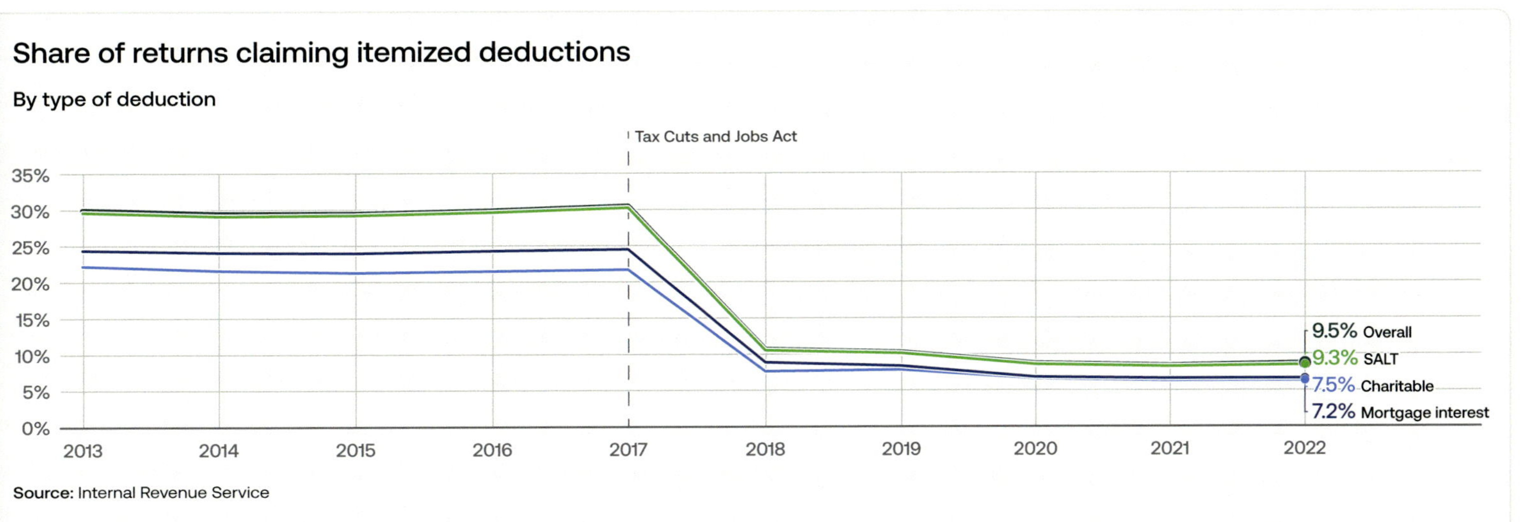

How has the use of the SALT deduction changed since the TCJA?

During the 2018–2025 tax seasons, the SALT deduction allowed taxpayers who itemize to deduct up to $10,000 in state and local property taxes and either income or sales taxes paid. The OBBBA increased this cap to $40,000 until 2030, at which point it will revert to $10,000 unless further legislative action is taken. Prior to the TCJA, there was no cap on how much could be deducted. The cap doesn't apply to state and local taxes associated with a trade or business (there is no upper limit). In 2022, 15.1 million returns claimed SALT deductions — nearly all the returns that itemized. The average SALT deduction fell from $13,457 in 2017 to $8,303 in 2022. High-income filers with AGI over $1 million were most affected by the change with their average deduction per return falling 96.0% from $282,402 to $11,233.

Share of returns claiming SALT deduction

By AGI group

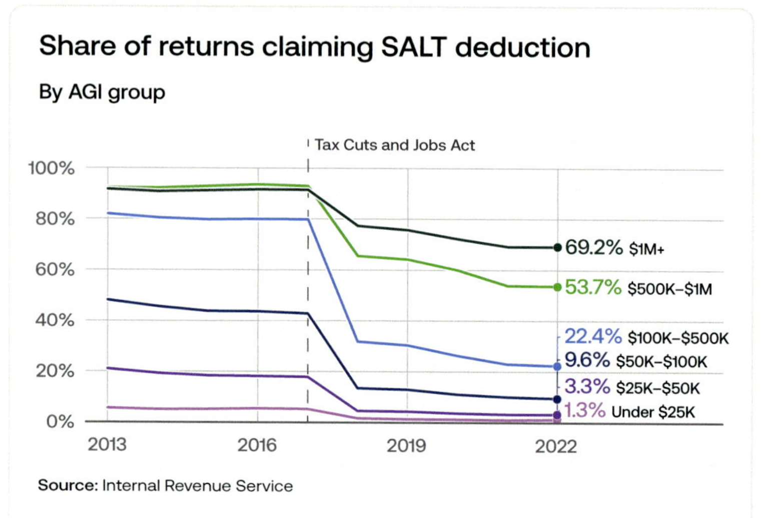

Source: Internal Revenue Service

Average SALT deduction

By AGI group

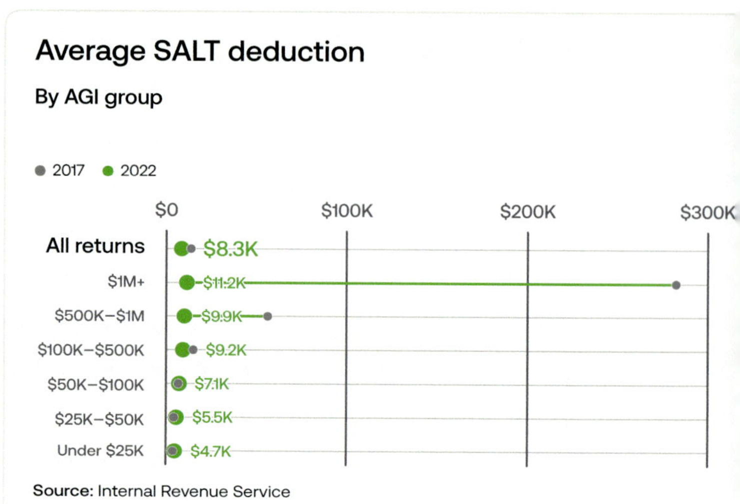

Source: Internal Revenue Service

How have SALT deductions changed by state?

From 2017 to 2022, the share of taxpayers claiming the SALT deduction declined in every state. In Wisconsin, West Virginia, and Ohio, the share of returns claiming SALT fell by more than 80%. It declined least, but by still more than 50%, in California, Maryland, and Hawaii.

Share of returns claiming SALT deduction, by state

2017

17.4% Lowest

46.5% Highest

3%
12%
21%
30%
39%
47%

2022

3.4% Lowest

19.9% Highest state

20.4% Highest

Source: Internal Revenue Service

Has use of the charitable contributions deduction changed since the TCJA?

The charitable contributions deduction allows itemizers to deduct qualified donations to nonprofit organizations from their taxable income. In 2022, 12.2 million returns claimed the deduction, totaling $222.4 billion — the largest itemized deduction by dollar amount. While the share of returns claiming the charitable contributions deduction fell from 24.8% in 2017 to 7.5% in 2022, the average deduction increased across all income groups. High-income taxpayers are more likely to claim this deduction due partly to their greater likelihood of itemizing. The drop in claims after TCJA follows the broader decline in itemizing.

Share of tax returns claiming charitable contributions deduction

By AGI group

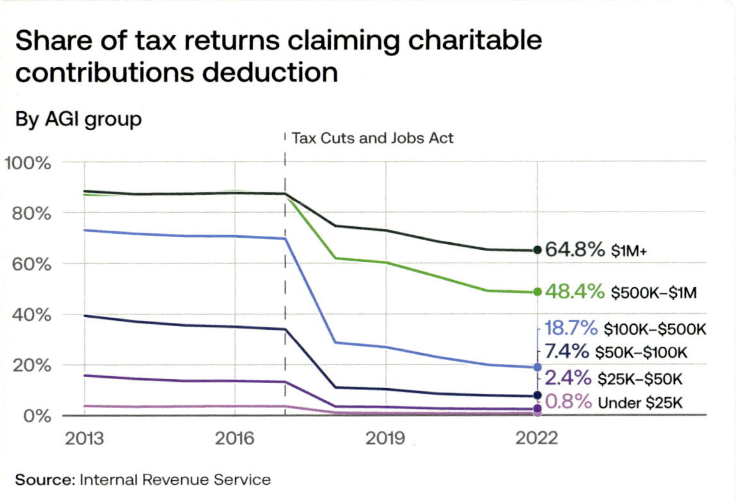

Source: Internal Revenue Service

Average charitable deduction

By AGI group

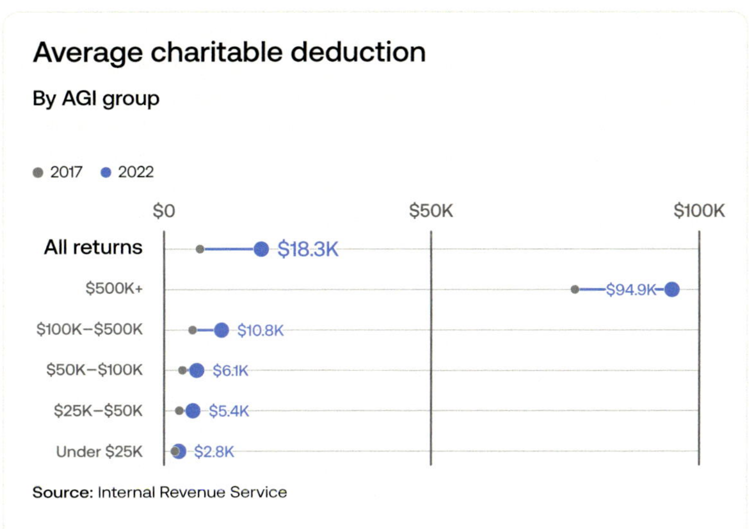

Source: Internal Revenue Service

How have charitable deductions changed at the state level?

From 2017 to 2022, the share of taxpayers claiming the charitable contributions deduction fell in every state. In some states, including Connecticut, New Jersey, and Minnesota, the share of returns claiming the deduction fell by more than 22 percentage points.

Share of returns claiming charitable contributions deduction, by state

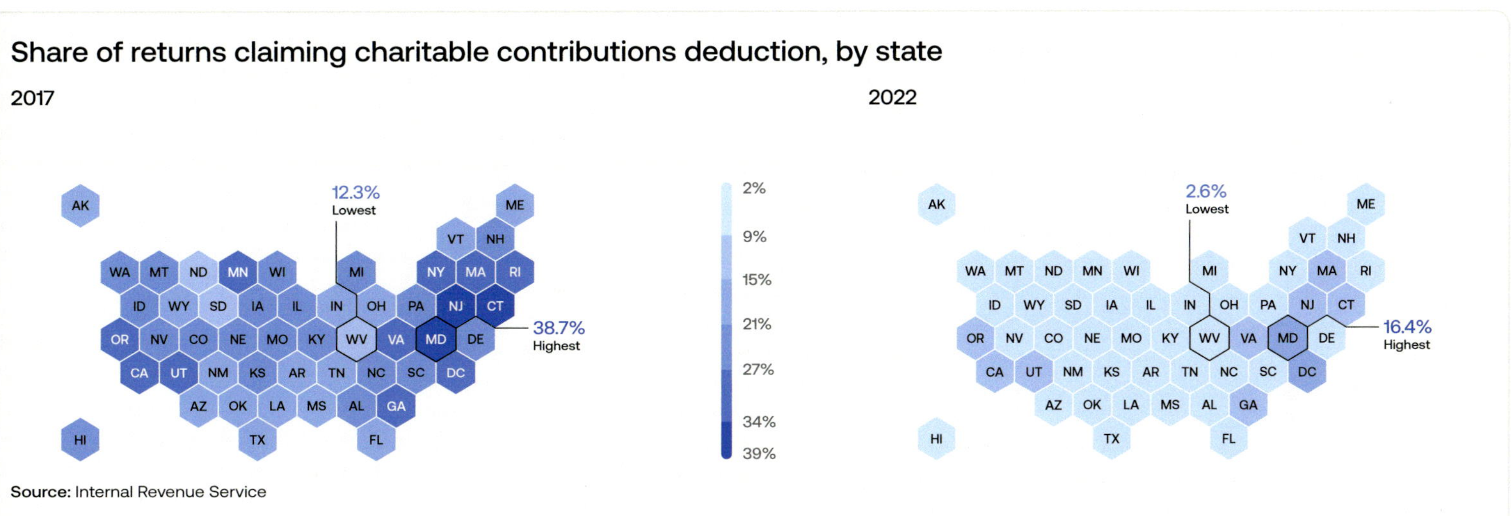

Source: Internal Revenue Service

How has the use of the mortgage interest deduction changed since the TCJA?

The mortgage interest deduction lets itemizers deduct a limited amount of interest paid on home loans from their taxable income. The TCJA reduced the amount of mortgage debt eligible for the deduction for new loans from $1 million to $750,000 and the OBBBA made this change permanent. In 2022, 11.6 million returns claimed the deduction, totaling $147.0 billion.

As with other itemized deductions, the share of returns claiming this fell after the TCJA. Higher-income households still take the largest deductions, although the average deduction taken decreased from 2017 to 2022 for filers with an AGI of $1 million or more.

Share of tax returns claiming home mortgage interest deduction

By AGI group

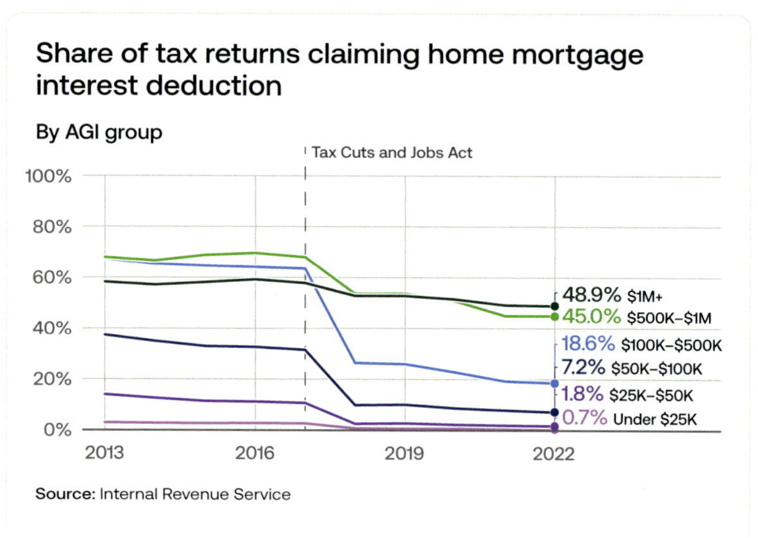

Source: Internal Revenue Service

Average mortgage interest deduction

By AGI group

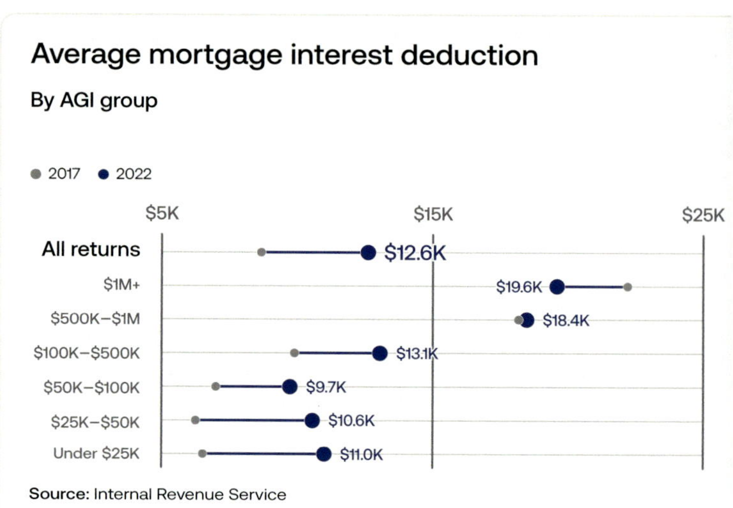

Source: Internal Revenue Service

How has use of the mortgage interest deduction changed across states?

The share of returns claiming the mortgage interest deduction fell by more than 80% between 2017 and 2022 in Wisconsin, Iowa, Ohio, West Virginia, Kentucky, Nebraska, and Vermont.

Share of returns claiming home mortgage interest deduction, by state

2017

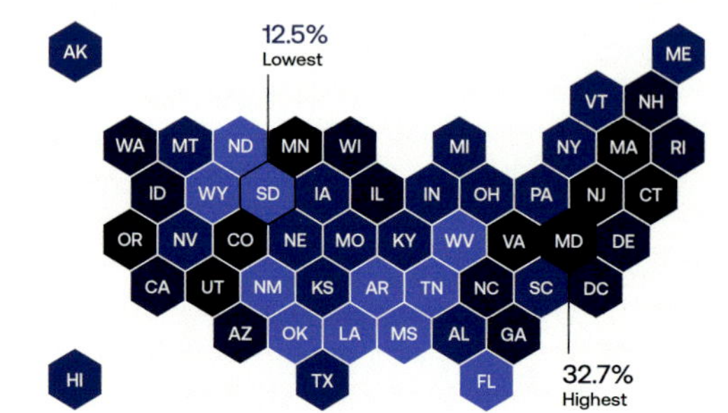

2022

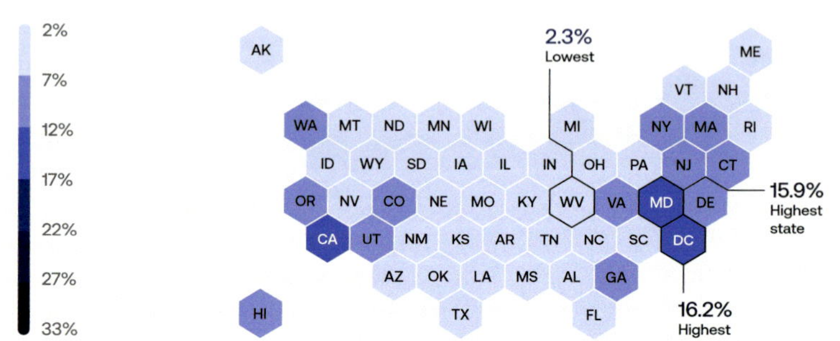

Source: Internal Revenue Service

What is the Qualified Business Income (QBI) deduction?

The TCJA established the QBI deduction. This deduction lets owners of pass-through businesses, such as sole proprietorships and LLCs, deduct up to 20% of their qualified business income (with some limitations and restrictions). It is not an itemized deduction and can be used by filers claiming the standard deduction.

In 2022, 25.7 million returns claimed QBI deductions totaling $216.1 billion. The average deduction was $8,423. High-income filers were most likely to claim it: 73.8% of returns with earnings over $1 million used it, reducing their taxable income by an average of $159,978 per return. By contrast, filers with AGIs under $50,000 claimed an average deduction of less than $1,500 per return. The deduction provision was scheduled to expire at the end of 2025, but was made permanent by the OBBBA.

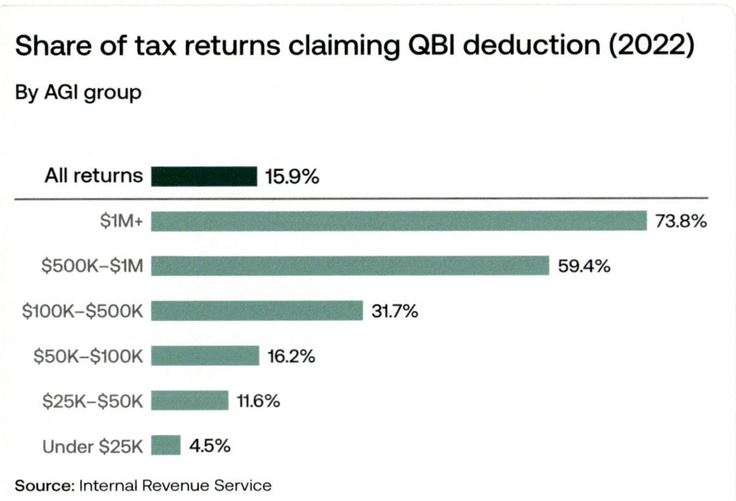

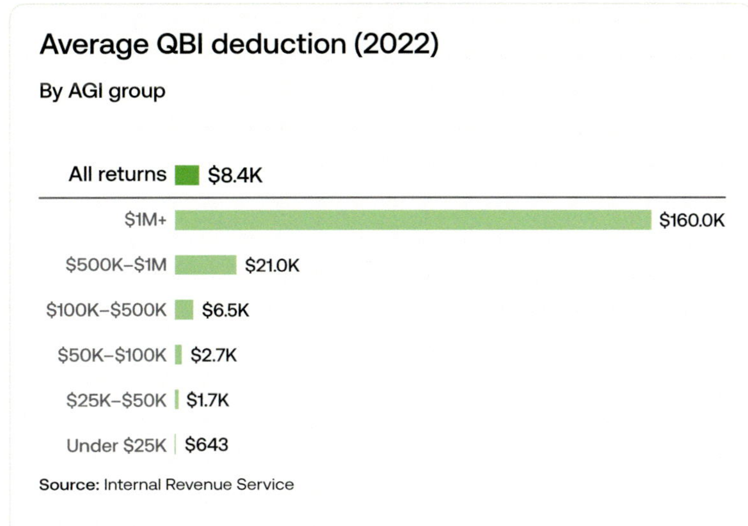

How do QBI claims vary by state?

In 2022, the share of returns claiming the QBI deduction ranged from about 10% in West Virginia to more than 20% in Colorado, South Dakota, and Washington, DC. The highest average deduction was taken in Nevada at nearly $13,000.

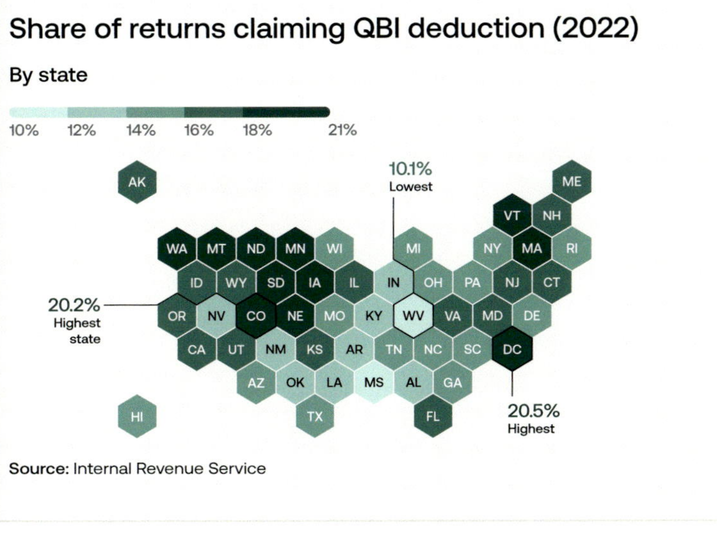

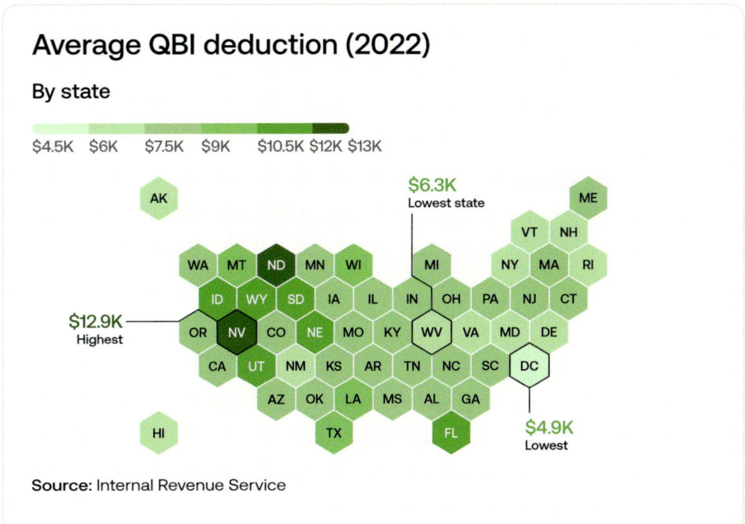

What is the Earned Income Tax Credit (EITC)?

The EITC is a fully refundable tax credit for low- and moderate-income workers, particularly those with children. In 2022, 24.1 million returns claimed the EITC and received $60.1 billion in benefits. The average credit was about $2,500. Sixty-five percent of total benefits went to tax filers with an AGI under $25,000, and provided a benefit equal to more than 20% of their pre-tax incomes.

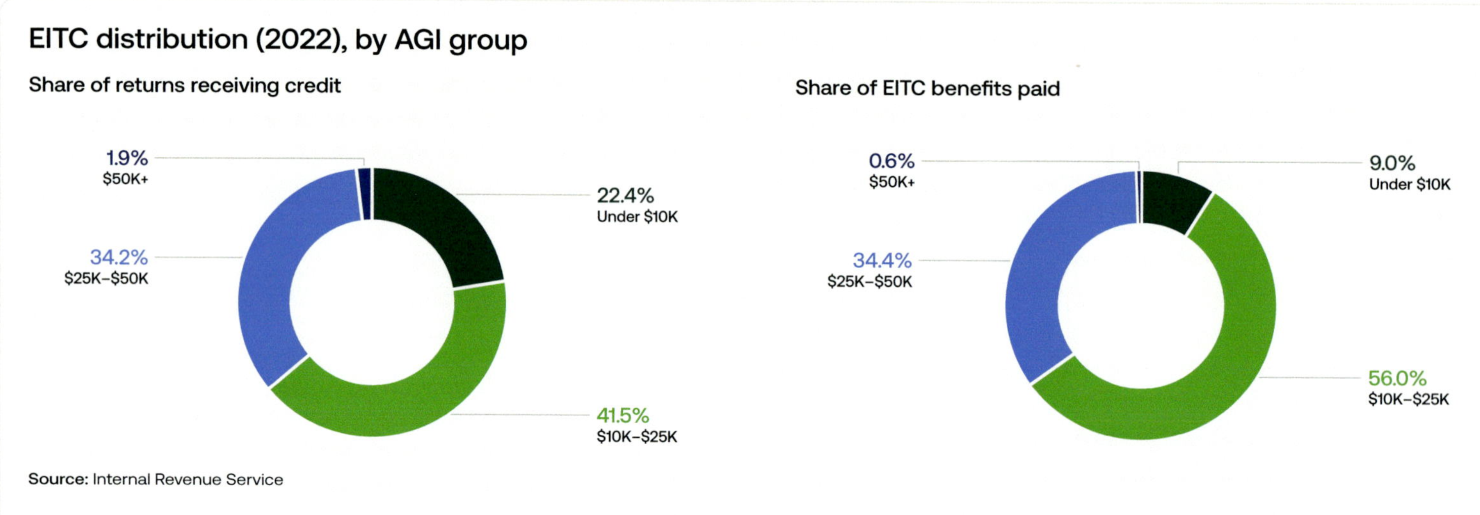

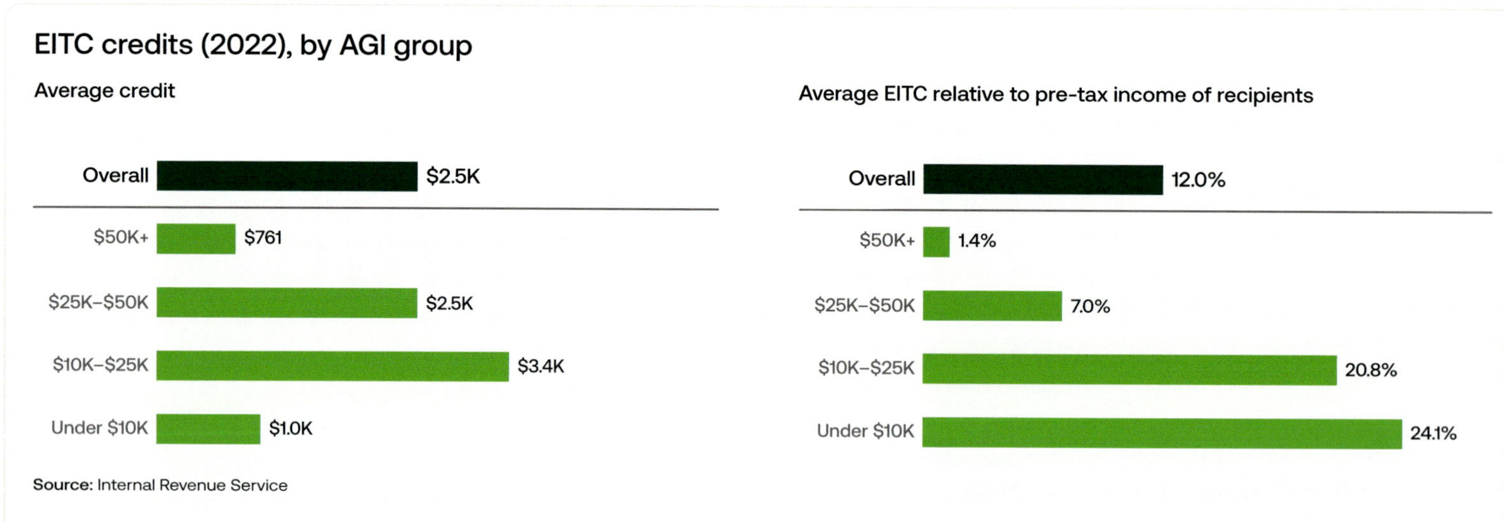

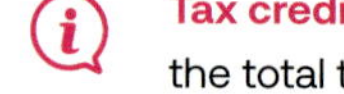

Tax credits are taken off the taxes filers owe. Some tax credits are **refundable**. This means that even if a tax filer is eligible for a credit that exceeds the total tax they owe, they can still get the full value (fully refundable) or partial value (partially refundable) of the credit as cash. The largest tax credits are the Earned Income Tax Credit, which is fully refundable, and the Child Tax Credit, which is partially refundable.

How does EITC vary by the number of children in a household?

The maximum EITC amount increases with the number of qualifying children. In 2022, over 95% of EITC dollars went to taxpayers with children. Families with one child received 35.3% of all EITC dollars, families with two children received 37.0%, and families with three or more children received 23.3%. In contrast, childless adults received 4.4% of total EITC dollars, although they accounted for 28.6% of EITC recipients.

Distribution of EITC benefits (2022), by number of qualifying children

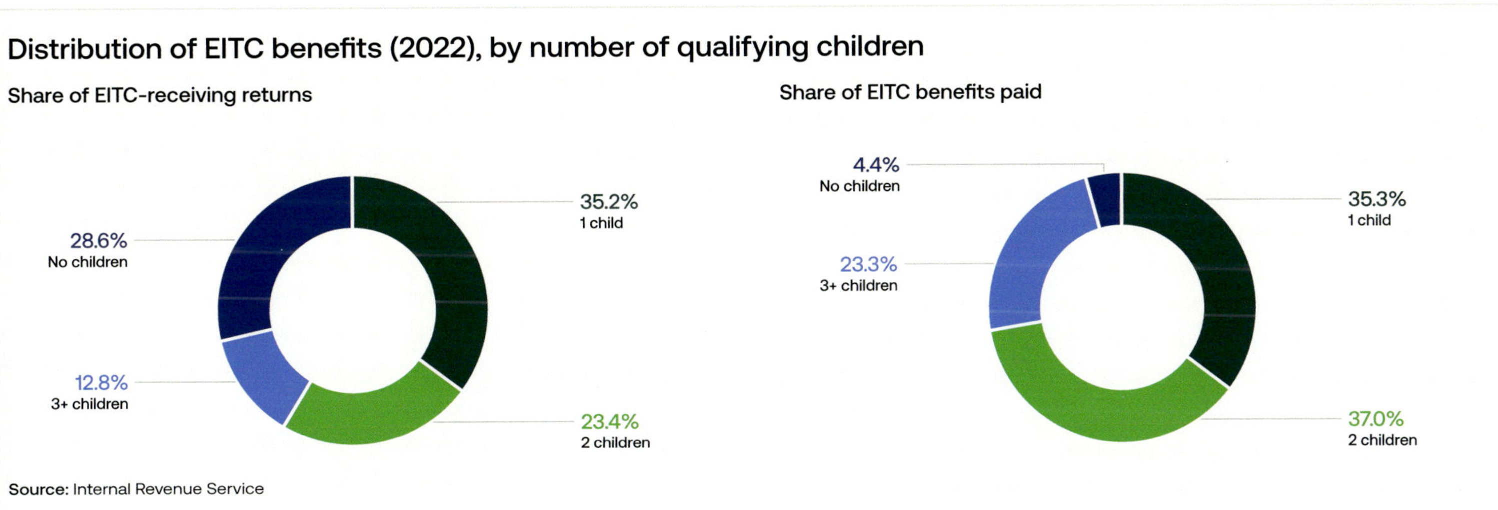

Source: Internal Revenue Service

EITC credits (2022), by number of qualifying children

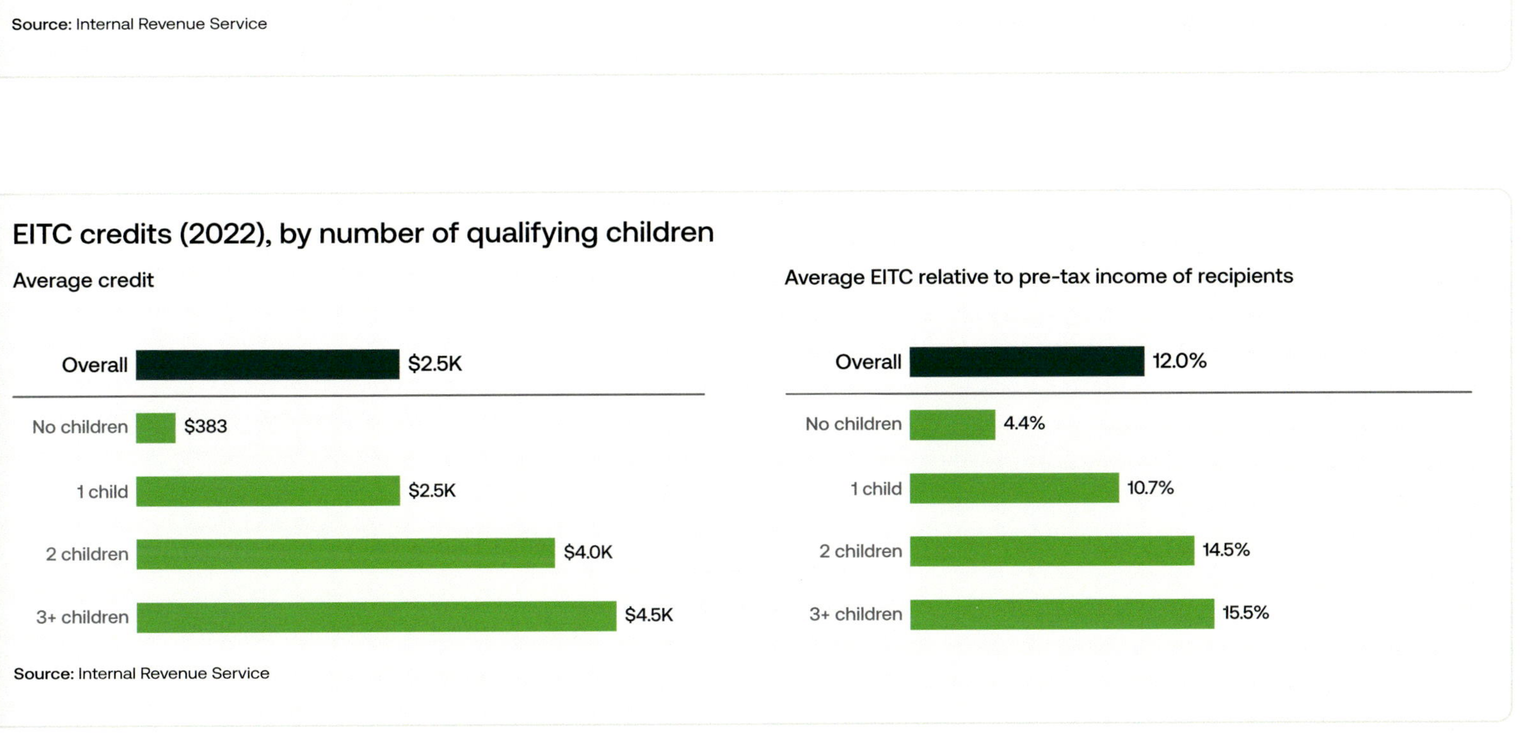

Source: Internal Revenue Service

What is the Child Tax Credit (CTC)?

The CTC is a partially refundable, per-child tax credit available to most US families. The refundable and non-refundable portions of the CTC are administered separately, and eligible families can claim both.

The TCJA doubled the maximum credit from $1,000 to $2,000 per child, lowered the minimum earnings families needed to be eligible, and expanded eligibility for higher-income families. It also increased the refundable portion of the credit, called the Additional Child Tax Credit (ACTC), from $1,000 to $1,400 (indexed to inflation). This means that if a tax filer is eligible for a credit that exceeds how much they owe in income taxes, they can receive up to the cap amount back as cash.

These changes to the CTC would have expired at the end of 2025, but were made permanent by the OBBBA. The legislation also increased the maximum non-refundable per child credit further to $2,200.

Child Tax Credit provisions

Category	Pre-TCJA (2017)	TCJA (2018)	OBBBA (2025)
Maximum credit per child (under age 17)	$1,000 per child	$2,000 per child	$2,200 per child (indexed)
Maximum Additional CTC (ACTC)	Refundable up to $1,000 per child; 15% of income over $3,000	Refundable up to $1,400 (indexed); 15% of income over $2,500	Made TCJA changes to CTC permanent
Refundability formula for ACTC	15% of earnings above $3,000, not to exceed the ACTC maximum of $1,000 per child	15% of earnings above $2,500, not to exceed the ACTC maximum of $1,400 per child	
Earned income threshold for credit to begin	$3,000	$2,500	
Income threshold for credit to begin phasing out	$75,000 (head of houshold and single) / $110,000 (married filing jointly)	$200,000 (head of household and single) / $400,000 (married filing jointly)	
Phaseout rate	Credit is reduced by $50 for every $1,000 above phaseout threshold		
Credit for other dependents (non-children)	None	$500 non-refundable credit per non-child dependent	
Refundable vs. non-refundable nature	Up to $1,000 could be refunded	Refundable up to $1,400; $600 non-refundable	
Indexing for inflation	No indexing	Refundable portion adjusted upward with inflation each year	Both refundable and non-refundable credits adjusted annually for inflation

Source: Adapted from Congressional Research Service

How many tax returns claim the CTC?

With expanded CTC eligibility, claims of the non-refundable credit jumped 78.4% between 2017 and 2018 and benefited the filers of 38.3 million returns in 2022. The number of returns claiming the refundable ACTC increased from 18.3 million in 2017 to 20.5 million in 2018. It fell to 18.1 million in 2022.

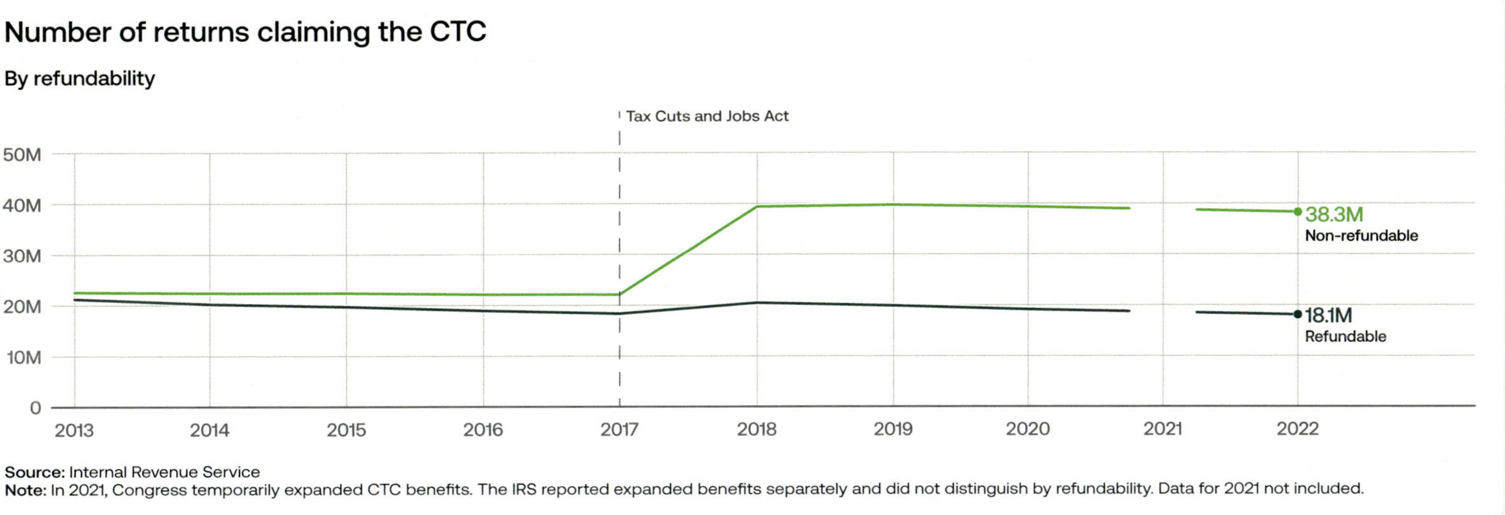

How do claims of the CTC differ by income?

In 2017, 12.0% of tax returns claimed the refundable ACTC, while 14.4% claimed the non-refundable CTC. In 2018, those shares increased to 13.3% and 25.6%, respectively.

Lower-income households are the most likely to claim the ACTC because they often owe little or no federal income tax. In 2022, 18.2% of returns with an AGI under $50,000 claimed the ACTC; 19.0% did so in 2017. Before the TCJA, the non-refundable CTC was primarily claimed by filers earning $50,000–$100,000. After the law expanded eligibility to higher income tax filers, it became most common among those with an AGI over $100,000. Between 2017 and 2018 the share of these filers claiming the non-refundable credit nearly tripled, rising from 13.7% of returns to 41.0%.

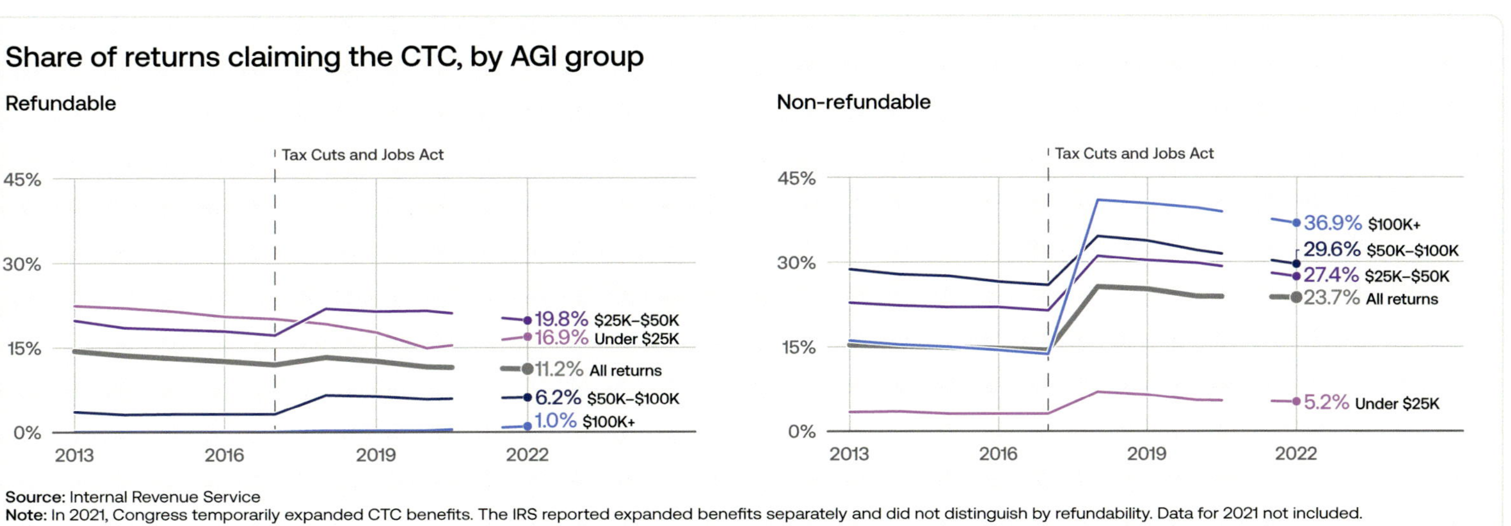

How have total CTC benefits changed since 2017?

Total CTC benefits rose from $51.4 billion in 2017 to $117.7 billion in 2018. The value of the refundable portion increased from $24.5 billion in 2017 to $36.2 billion. Non-refundable CTC benefits rose from $26.9 billion to $81.5 billion. Aside from increases in the credit in 2021 due to its temporary expansion in response to the COVID-19 pandemic, the aggregate value of the claims has remained steady since. Between 2017 and 2022, total benefits going to families with AGI over $100,000 had a more than eightfold increase, from $5.2 billion to $42.0 billion.

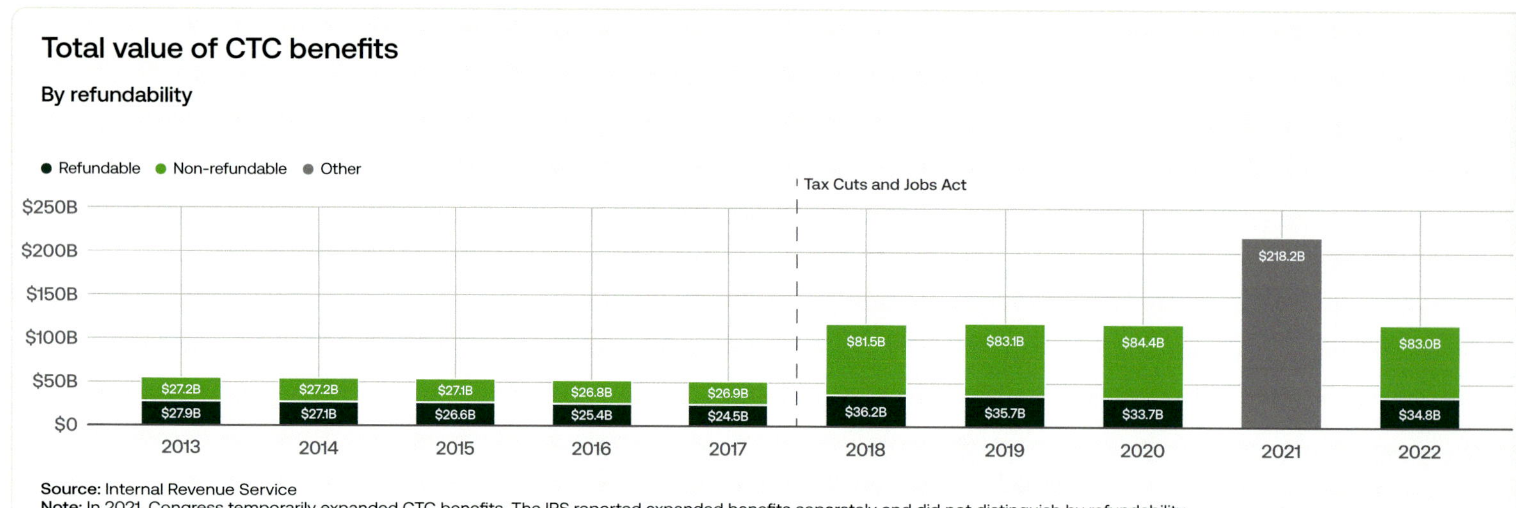

Source: Internal Revenue Service
Note: In 2021, Congress temporarily expanded CTC benefits. The IRS reported expanded benefits separately and did not distinguish by refundability.

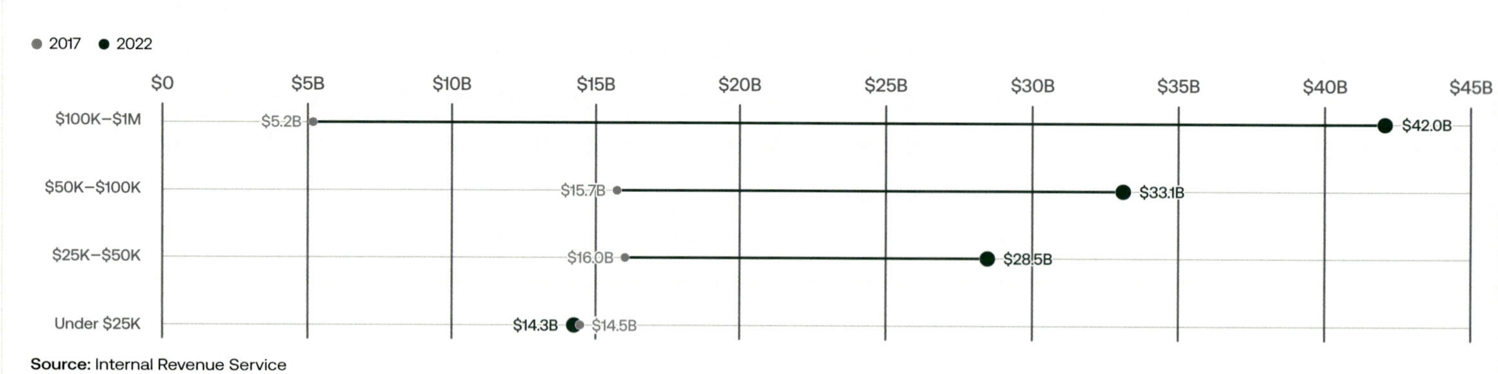

Source: Internal Revenue Service

How much do families receive from the CTC?

Average non-refundable CTC benefits grew more than refundable ones after the TCJA, since the credit doubled while the refundable portion increased 40%. Across all returns, the average non-refundable benefit rose from $1,218 in 2017 to $2,070 in 2018 to $2,168 by 2022. The average refundable portion increased from $1,336 to $1,772 in 2018 and reached $1,928 by 2022.

Refundable and non-refundable benefits increased the most for middle- and higher-income filers. For example, returns with an AGI of more than $100,000 saw their average refundable CTC rise by $434 between 2017 and 2018 and by another $507 by 2022. Meanwhile, this group's average benefit from the non-refundable CTC portion more than doubled between 2017 and 2018.

Returns with lower income had more modest increases in average benefits. Among those with AGI under $25,000, average refundable benefits increased $435 between 2017 and 2022. Non-refundable benefits were almost unchanged.

Source: Internal Revenue Service

Chapter sources and data timeliness

Publishing agency	Program	Publication name	Release date	Most recent period in the data
Internal Revenue Service	Statistics of Income	Individuals, Individual Income Tax Returns Tables and Complete Report (Publication 1304)	Oct. 2024	2022
		Historic table 2 (SOI bulletin)	Jan. 2025	2022
		SOI Tax Stats - Historical Table 23	Historic table, no longer being updated	2018
	News releases	Press release titled "IRS provides tax inflation adjustments" each year.	Annually in the fall for the following tax season	2024

See sources and notes section at the end of this report for detailed citation information.

Most of the data described in this chapter is compiled and published by the IRS's Statistics of Income (SOI) program. While these data provide valuable insight, the USAFacts team encountered some limitations in the data:

- Tabulated topline data typically lags two to three years, with the most recent individual tax data being from 2022.
- Tax data is not easily findable on the IRS's website. Users must have a strong working knowledge of existing tables and the US tax system to answer simple questions.
- Tables are only available in .csv or Excel files where there is a separate file for each table and each year. This makes the data difficult to work with.

CHAPTER 03

Standard of living

Standard of living facts

Several temporary income support provisions enacted during the COVID-19 pandemic have ended or reverted to previous levels. Congress also recently made changes to federal standard of living programs, such as the Supplemental Nutrition Assistance Program (SNAP), through the One Big Beautiful Bill Act. This chapter presents government data on key indicators of household well-being — such as poverty rates, income, and food security — to understand the current standard of living in the US and the potential effects of policy changes.

Gross domestic product (GDP) per person

- In 2024, real gross domestic product (rGDP, or GDP adjusted for inflation) per person in the US was up 1.7% from 2023.
- The change in rGDP per person from 2023 to 2024 varied by state, decreasing most in North Dakota (-1.7%) and increasing most in West Virginia (+3.6%).

Wages, income, taxes, and transfers

- In 2022, the average middle-class family (40th–60th percentile of the income distribution) made about $67,790 in market income, paid $24,487 in taxes, and received $26,918 in government assistance.
- Between 2000 and 2022, average tax payments increased (adjusted for inflation) for all families except the bottom 20% of earners; government assistance increased by more than 50% in every group, in part due to temporary COVID-19 programs.
- The nation's median annual wage, or the typical amount paid to individuals in exchange for their work or services, was $49,440 in 2024, down 0.3% from 2023 after adjusting for inflation.

Poverty

- The poverty rate was 11.1% in 2023, while the child poverty rate was 15.3%. Both remained above 2019 levels.
- In 2023, three states had poverty rates of at least 16%: Louisiana, New Mexico, and Mississippi.

Housing

- In 2023, nearly 52% of renters and about 23% of homeowners spent 30% or more of their income on housing, qualifying as housing burdened under Department of Housing and Urban Development guidelines.
- The US had 15.1 subsidized housing units per 1,000 people in 2024. This included both occupied and unoccupied units and was at the lowest level since at least 2004.
- In 2024, the average wait time for subsidized housing rose to 27 months, two months longer than in 2023.

Food insecurity

- In 2023, 13.5% of US households experienced food insecurity, meaning they were uncertain about having enough food or did not have enough food at some point in the year.
- In FY 2024, an average of 41.7 million people received SNAP benefits monthly — 17% more than in FY 2019 but below the FY 2013 peak.
- 6.7 million people received nutrition benefits through WIC, the Special Supplemental Nutrition Program for Women, Infants, and Children, in FY 2024; 21.4 million children per month received free or reduced lunch during the 2022–2023 school year.

Other government income support programs

- In 2023, 30% of US households received Social Security benefits, including retirement benefits, permanent disability insurance payments, and railroad retirement income.
- Five percent of households received Supplemental Security Income (SSI), while 2.4% received cash assistance through general welfare programs like Temporary Assistance for Needy Families (TANF).
- An average of 1.8 million people received unemployment insurance benefits each week of 2024.

The federal government also tries to boost incomes of qualifying individuals and families through some tax credits. Check out the *Federal Individual Income Taxes* section of this report to learn more.

How has gross domestic product (GDP) per person changed over time?

GDP per person is one way to measure a country's standard of living. It reflects the nation's average economic output per person by adjusting for differences in population size. This provides an idea of the amount of resources available, on average, for each person. Tracking this measure over time can indicate whether those resources are growing or dwindling.

Real gross domestic product (GDP adjusted for inflation or rGDP) per person was $69,006 in 2024, an all-time high. It increased 1.7% from 2023, higher than the 1.4% average annual change from 2000 through 2023.

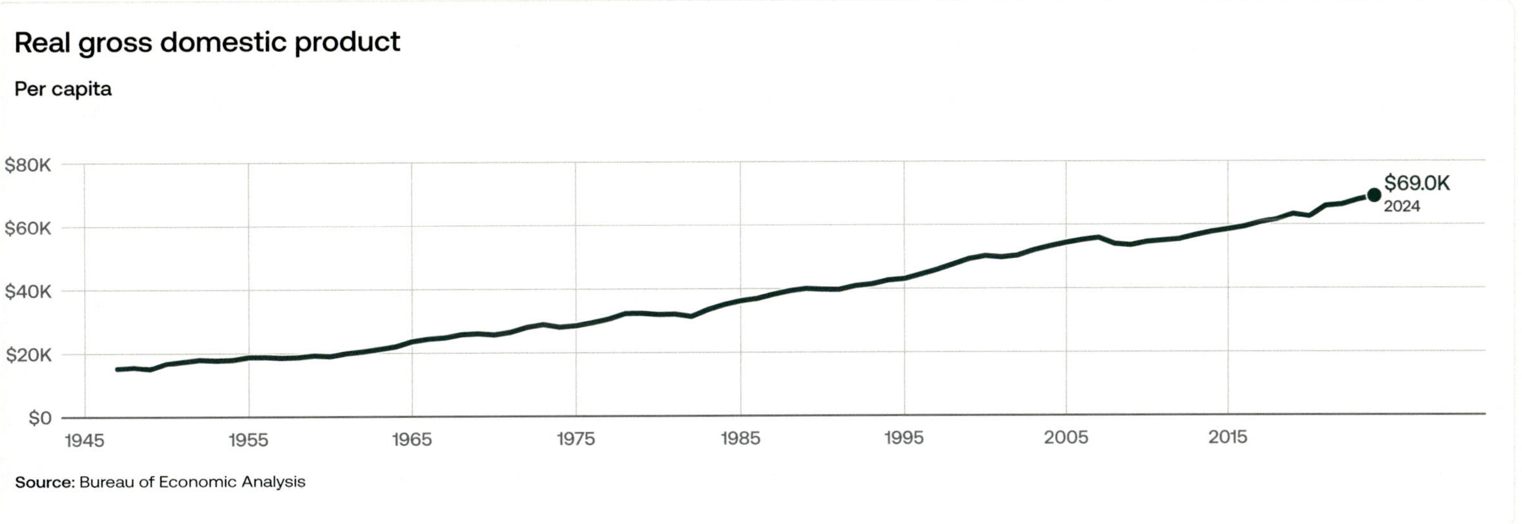

Source: Bureau of Economic Analysis

How does GDP vary by state?

In 2024, rGDP per person exceeded $85,000 in four states: New York, Massachusetts, Washington, and California. It was less than $49,000 in four states: Mississippi, West Virginia, Arkansas, and Alabama. From 2023 to 2024, the change in rGDP per person ranged from -1.7% in North Dakota to +3.6% in West Virginia.

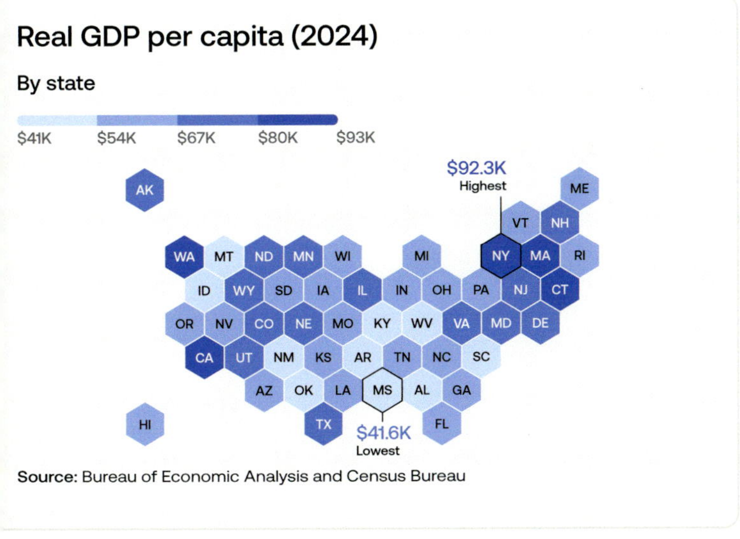

Source: Bureau of Economic Analysis and Census Bureau

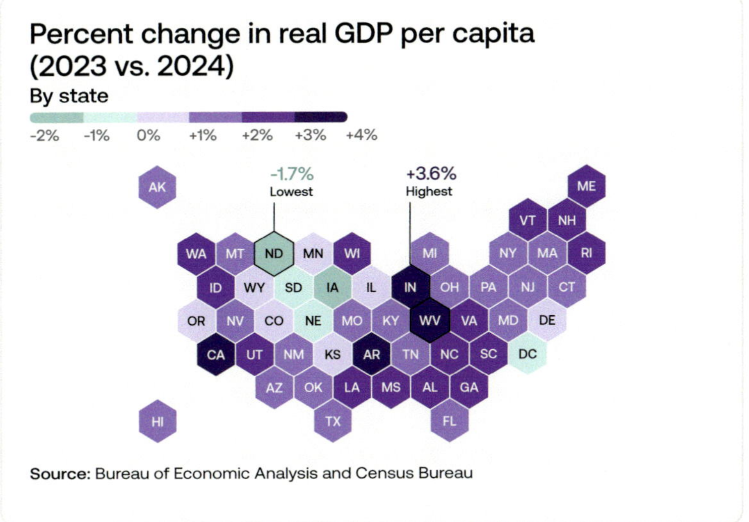

Source: Bureau of Economic Analysis and Census Bureau

How has family income changed over time?

In 2022, the average middle-class family (middle 20% of income earners) had $67,790 in market income. This is up 1.1% since 2000 (after adjusting for inflation). Meanwhile, the characteristics of these families shifted: the average age of the primary householder rose from 47 to 50, household size shrank slightly, and average weekly work hours declined from 43 to 40.

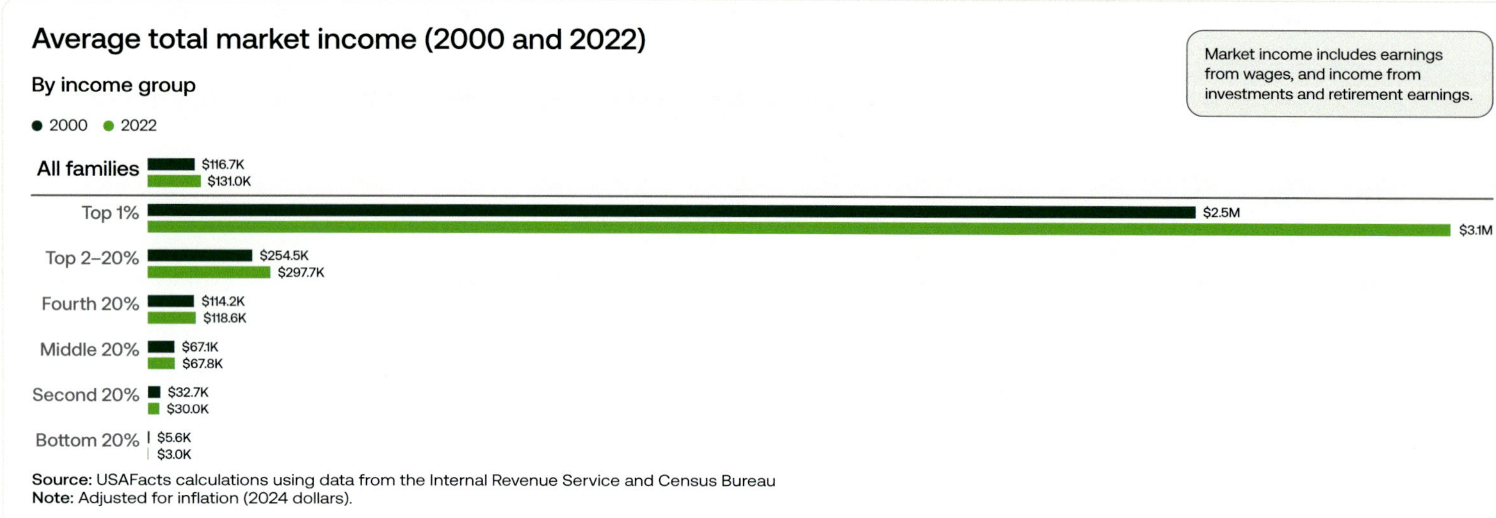

How much do families pay in taxes? How much do they receive from the government?

In 2022, the average middle-class family paid $24,487 in taxes and received $26,918 in government assistance. Taxes includes both direct (like income and sales taxes) and indirect taxes (like the employer share of the Federal Insurance Contributions Act). Transfers includes cash benefits such as Social Security, and noncash support such as Medicaid and SNAP.

Families in all but the bottom 20% paid more in taxes in 2022 than in 2000 (after adjusting for inflation), while government assistance rose over 50% across all income levels. This is partly due to COVID-19 programs that have since expired, including the expanded Child Tax Credit and emergency food aid.

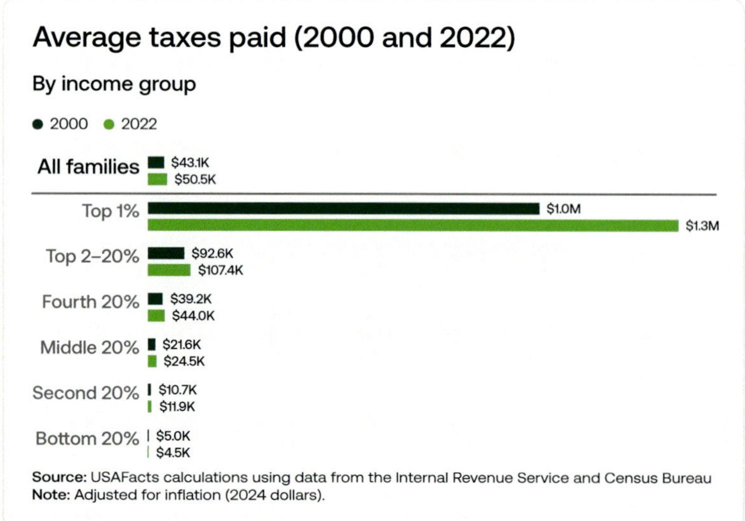

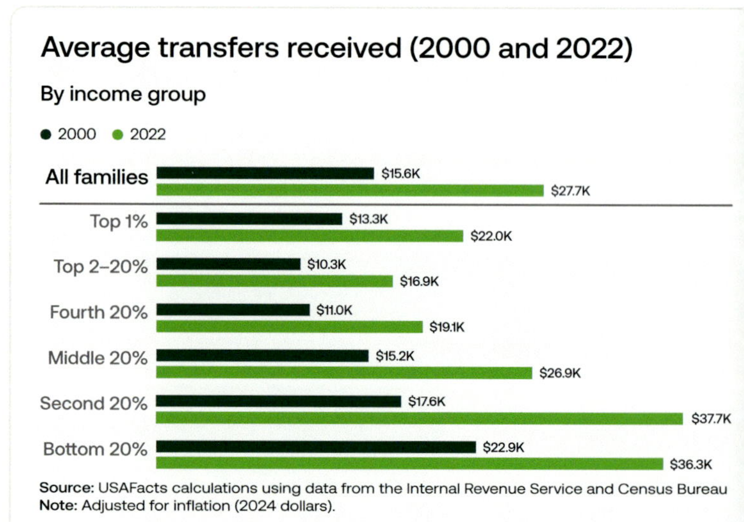

How much do US workers earn?

The nation's median annual wage was $49,440 in 2024. Median wages reflect the typical amount of money an individual receives in exchange for their work. Massachusetts, Washington, and Alaska had the highest median wages, each over $59,000. Six states had median wages under $44,000: Mississippi, Arkansas, West Virginia, Louisiana, Alabama, and Oklahoma.

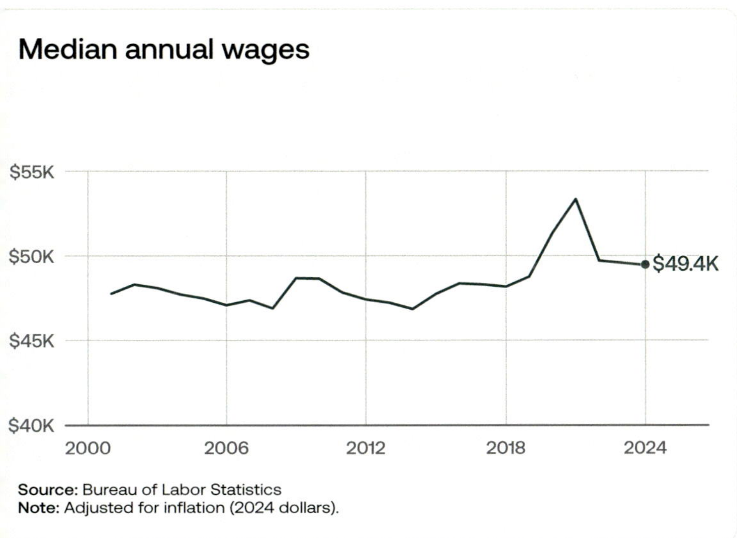

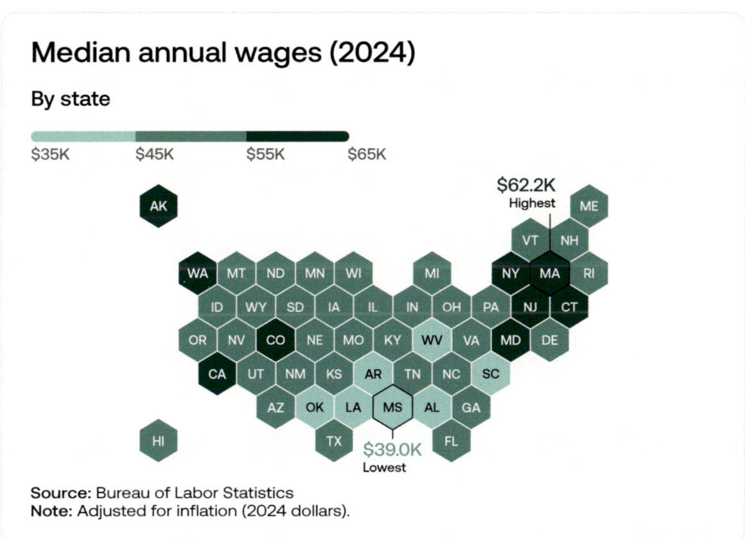

Are wages keeping up with inflation?

After adjusting for inflation, median wages decreased from 2023 to 2024 by 0.3%. Wage growth lagged behind the annual inflation rate for three consecutive years. This includes 2022, when median wages fell 6.8% compared with 2021.

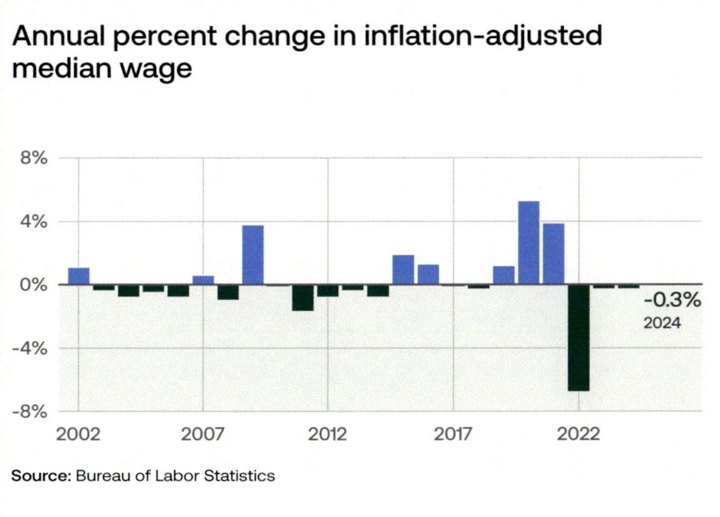

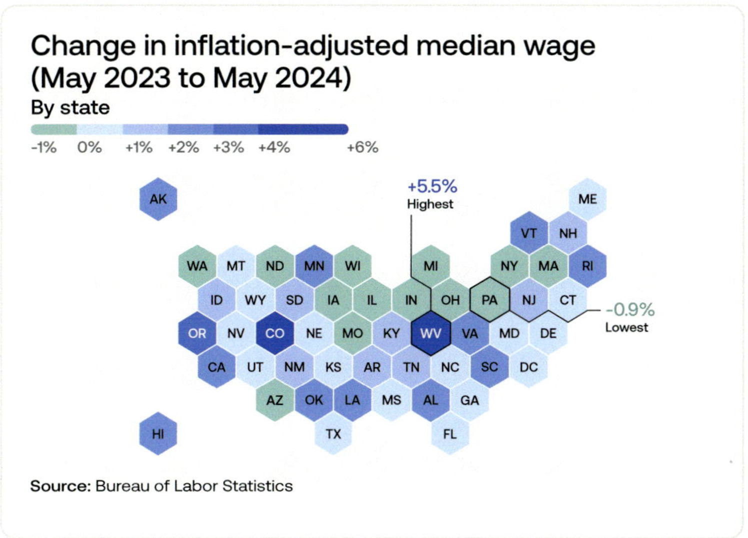

How many people receive unemployment insurance benefits?

Unemployment insurance temporarily replaces a limited amount of earnings for eligible workers who lose their jobs through no fault of their own. States run their own unemployment insurance programs with some federal oversight and funding. An average of 1.8 million people claimed unemployment insurance benefits each week of 2024 — equal to 0.7% of people ages 16 and older. The share of the population claiming these benefits has remained at or near record lows since 2022.

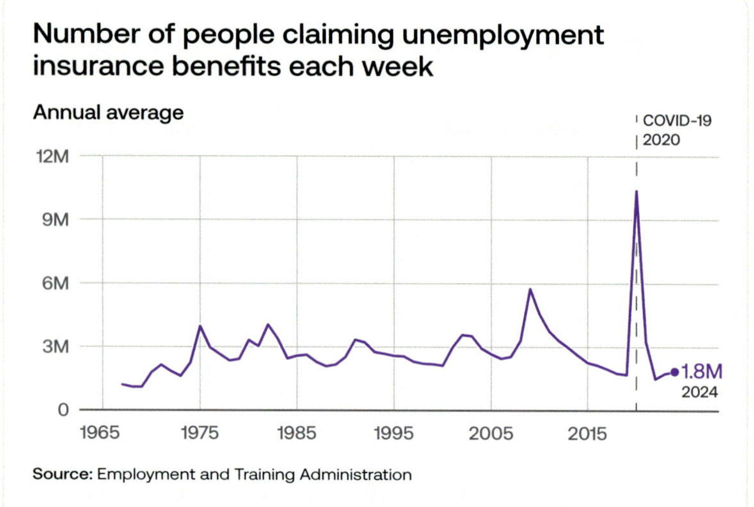

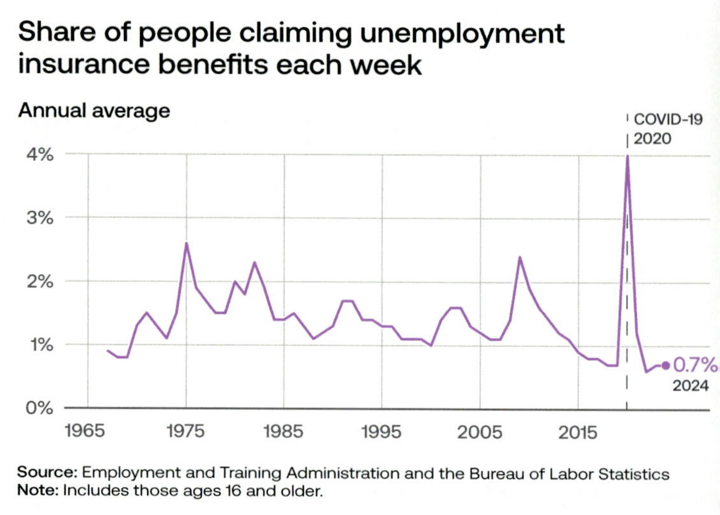

What is the US poverty rate?

The federal government's official poverty measure sets poverty thresholds, adjusted by family size; anyone whose household income falls below the threshold is counted as in poverty. The share of people in poverty (the poverty rate) was 11.1% in 2023. This was lower than any other time in the last 45 years, aside from 2019. The poverty rate among children (those under 18) was 15.3% in 2023 and has only been lower in two other years, 2019 and 2022.

In 2023, three states had overall poverty rates of at least 16%: Louisiana, New Mexico, and Mississippi. It was lowest, below 7%, in New Hampshire, Utah, and Vermont.

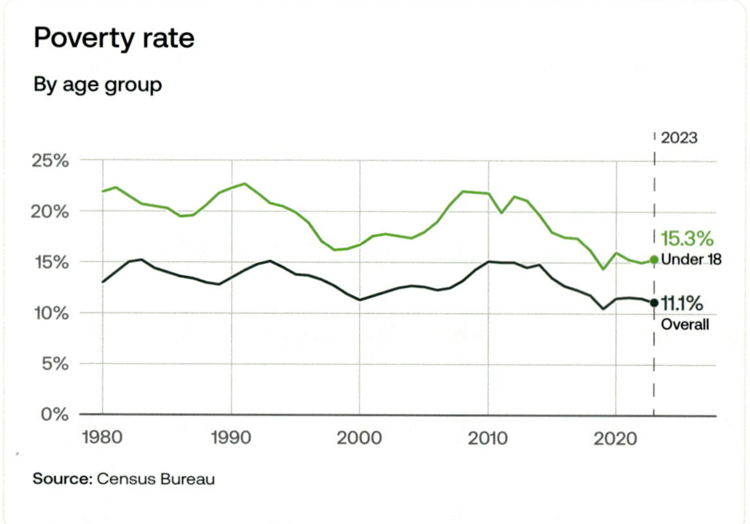

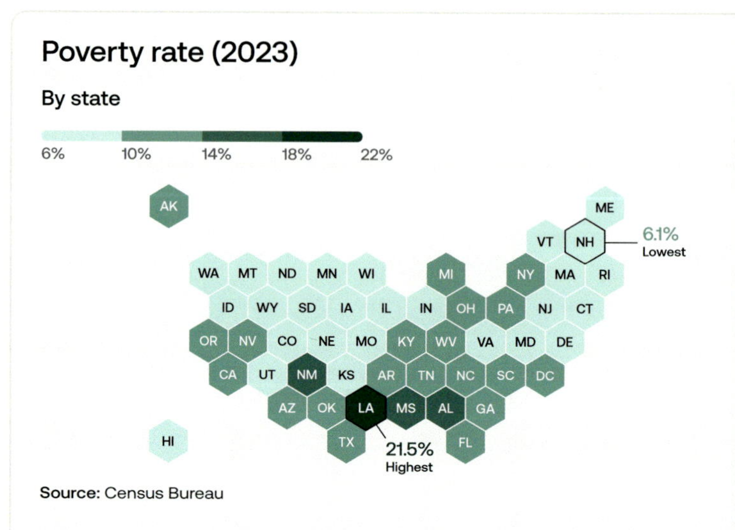

What share of households receive government public assistance income?

In 2023, 3.1 million or 2.4% of US households received cash benefits provided through Temporary Assistance for Needy Families (TANF) and general assistance programs administered by state and local governments. These programs are often called "welfare." The share of households receiving these cash benefits in 2023 ranged from 1.1% in Louisiana and South Carolina to 5.7% in Alaska.

Share of households receiving public assistance income

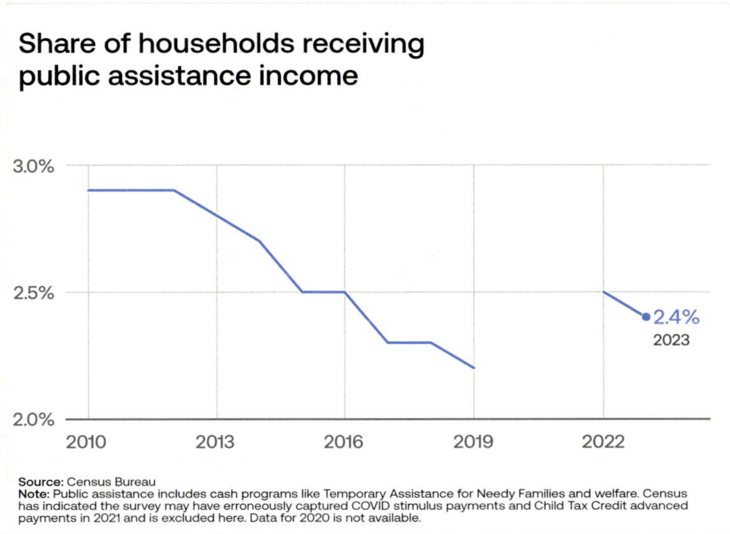

Source: Census Bureau
Note: Public assistance includes cash programs like Temporary Assistance for Needy Families and welfare. Census has indicated the survey may have erroneously captured COVID stimulus payments and Child Tax Credit advanced payments in 2021 and is excluded here. Data for 2020 is not available.

Share of households receiving public assistance income (2023)

By state

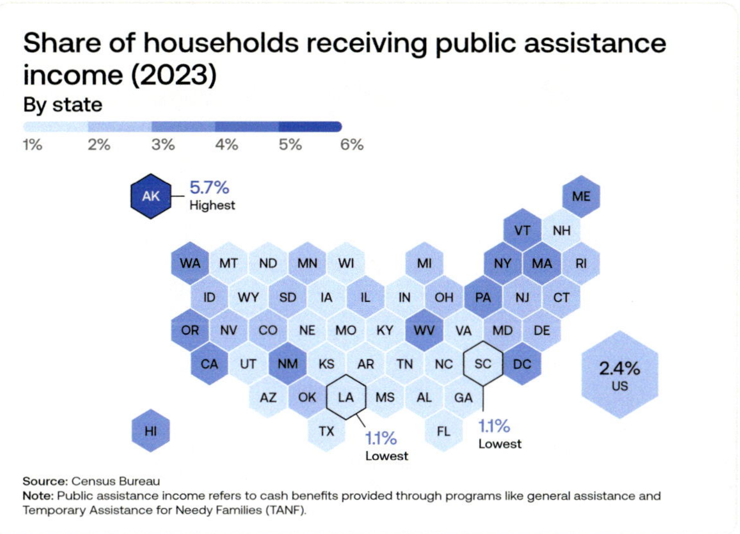

Source: Census Bureau
Note: Public assistance income refers to cash benefits provided through programs like general assistance and Temporary Assistance for Needy Families (TANF).

What share of households receive Supplemental Security Income?

The Supplemental Security Income (SSI) program provides cash assistance to people with disabilities and older adults with both low income and low wealth. One in 20 households received SSI each year from 2010 through 2023. In 2023, the share reached as high as 7.6% in Mississippi and as low as 2.9% in Colorado and North Dakota.

Share of households receiving Supplemental Security Income

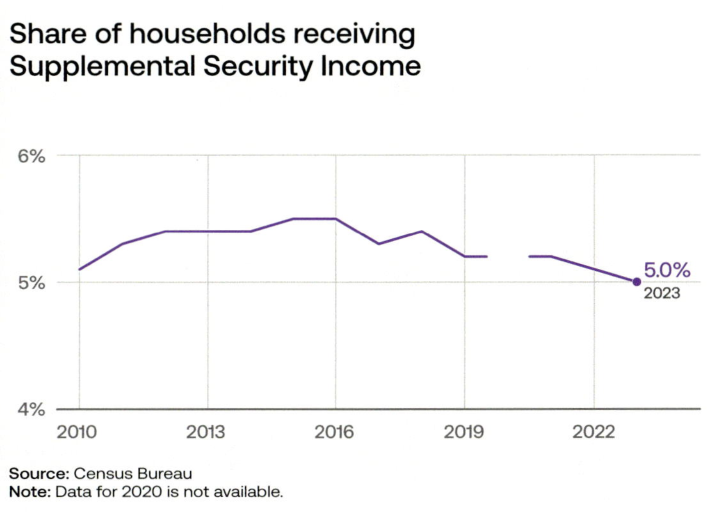

Source: Census Bureau
Note: Data for 2020 is not available.

Share of households with Supplemental Security Income (2023)

By state

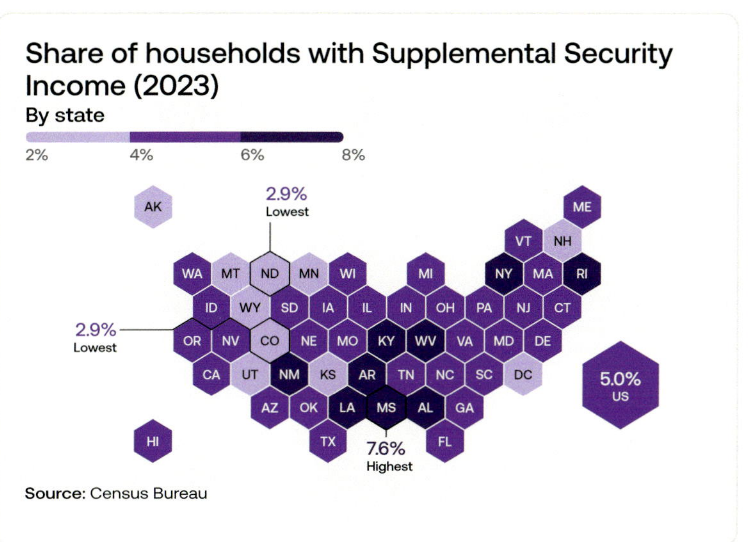

Source: Census Bureau

What share of households receive Social Security retirement or disability benefits?

Social Security is an insurance program that primarily provides monthly cash benefits to retired workers age 62 and older, or the eligible family members of deceased workers. It also has a component called Social Security Disability Insurance (SSDI), which provides benefits to people with a disability and qualifying work history.

In 2024, 12% of Social Security recipients received disability benefits, 9% received survivor benefits, and 79% received retirement benefits.[i] The share of households receiving Social Security benefits increased from 28.4% in 2010 to 31.3% in 2023. Meanwhile, the share of the population age 62 and older grew from 16.4% to 21.6%.[ii] In 2023, the proportion of households receiving Social Security benefits ranged from 23.9% in Utah to 40.4% in West Virginia.

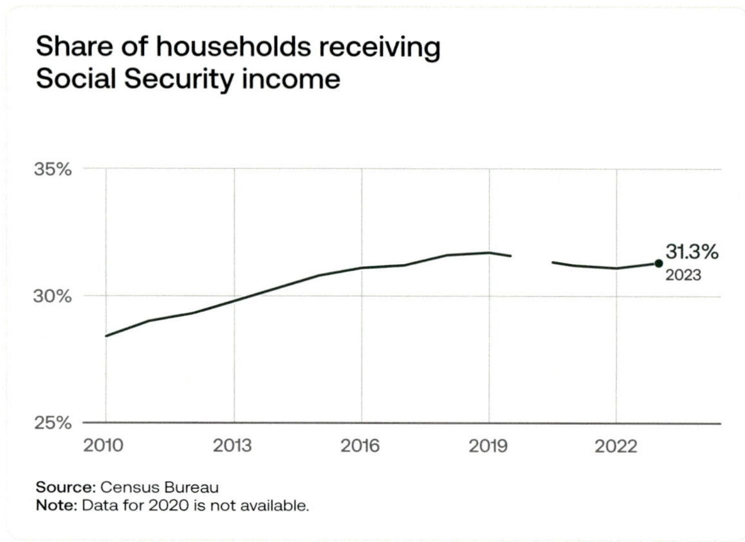

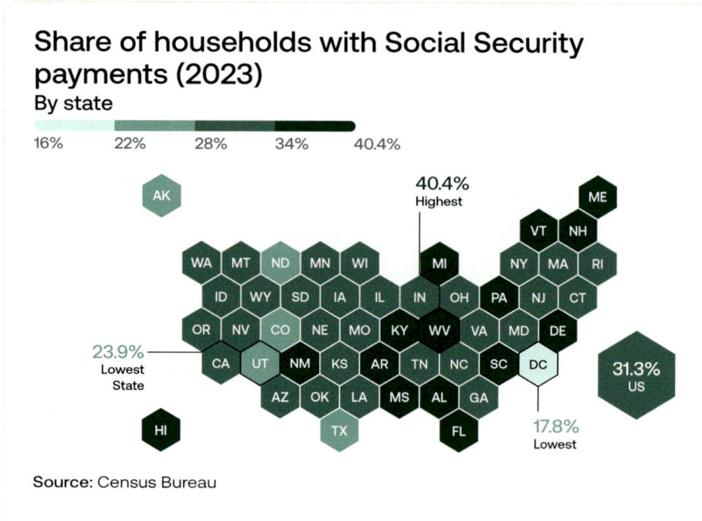

What share of people are housing burdened?

Among homeowners in 2023, median monthly income was $7,993, median housing costs were $1,320, and 23.3% were housing burdened. Among renters, median monthly household income was $4,310, median housing costs were $1,406, and 51.8% were housing burdened. This was down since 2010, but up from 48.4% in 2019. Housing burden among homeowners is down from 2010 but up two percentage points from 2019.

Share of households that are housing burdened

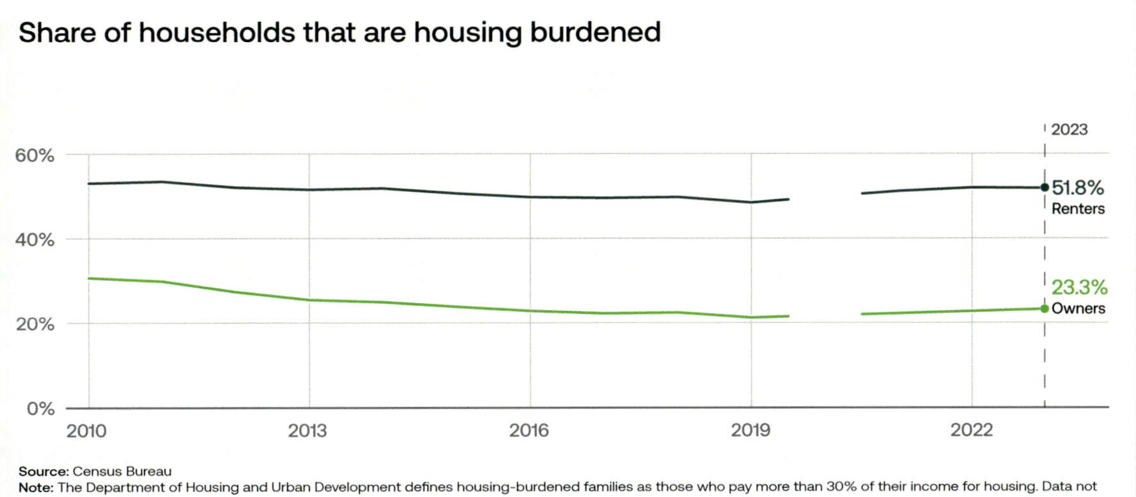

Source: Census Bureau
Note: The Department of Housing and Urban Development defines housing-burdened families as those who pay more than 30% of their income for housing. Data not available for 2020.

The Department of Housing and Urban Development (HUD) says households should spend less than 30% of their income on housing to have enough money for other needs. Households that spend more than this are considered **housing burdened.**

Where are people most and least housing burdened?

In 2023, housing-burdened households were more likely to rent than own. This was the trend in every state without exception. Florida had the highest share of renters spending more than 30% of their income on housing at 61.7%. There, median monthly household income was $4,480 and median renting costs were $1,719.

Meanwhile, the share of housing-burdened homeowners ranged from 31.9% in California ($10,231 homeowner household median monthly income; $2,137 median monthly housing costs) to 14.6% in West Virginia ($5,572 homeowner household median monthly income; $621 median monthly housing costs).

Share of households that are housing burdened, by state (2023)

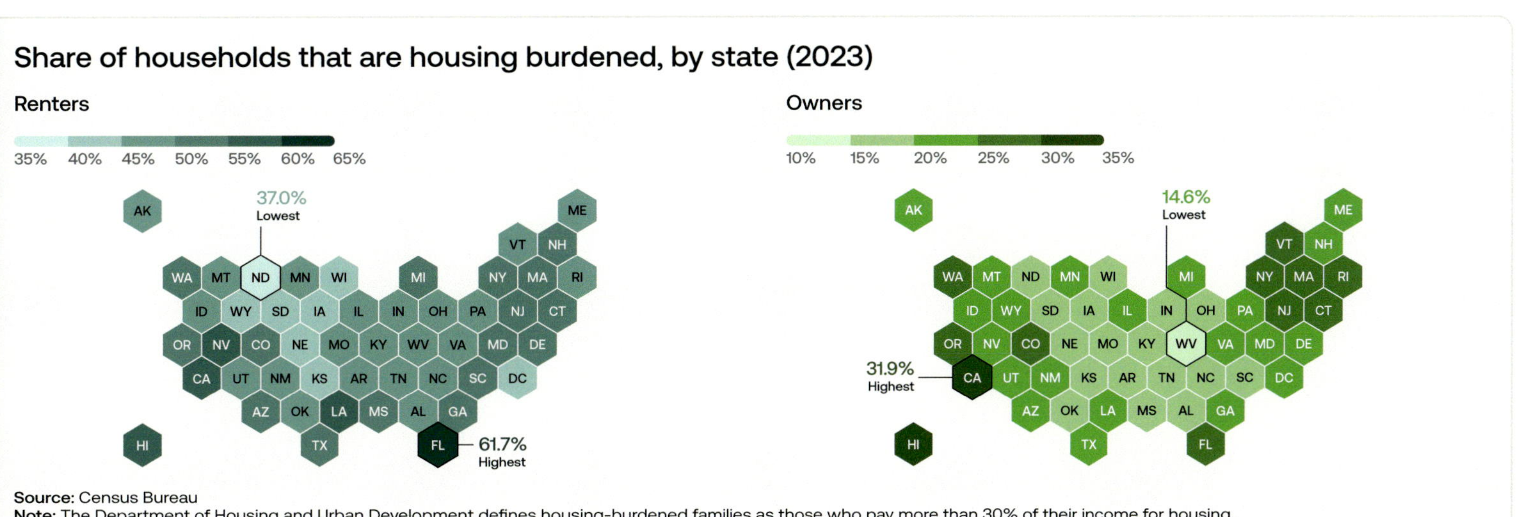

Source: Census Bureau
Note: The Department of Housing and Urban Development defines housing-burdened families as those who pay more than 30% of their income for housing.

What share of people live in subsidized housing?

In 2024, 2.7% of the US population, equal to 9 million people, lived in subsidized housing. The percentage has roughly been the same since 2022. The highest share in recent history was 3.2% in 2013, or 10.1 million people.

The share varies by state. In Utah, 0.9% of residents lived in subsidized housing in 2024 compared to a high of 5.3% in Rhode Island.

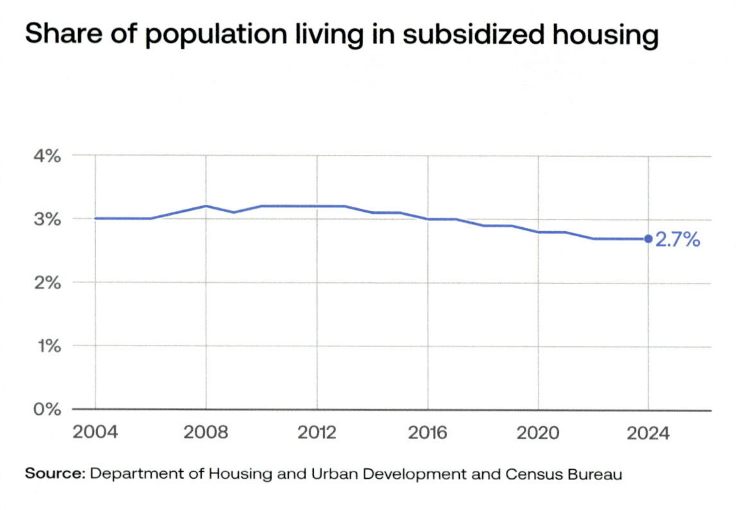

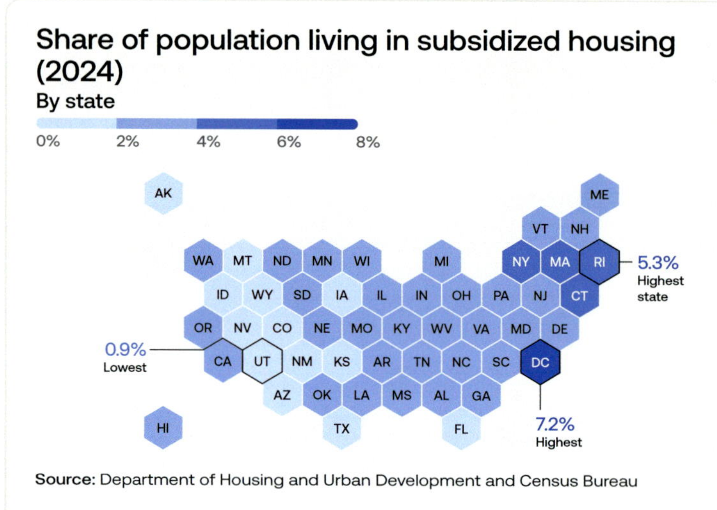

Subsidized housing is housing provided below market rates to low-income families and individuals. This assistance can include reduced rents in publicly owned buildings or programs that provide vouchers to help cover rent in privately owned housing.

How many subsidized housing units are available?

There were 15.1 subsidized housing units available per 1,000 people in 2024, the fewest since at least 2004. While there were nearly 82,000 (or 1.6%) more subsidized units in 2024 than 2004, this increase lagged behind the 16.2% population growth in the US. On average, people who received subsidized housing in 2024 had waited 27 months. Average wait times were two months longer than in 2023.

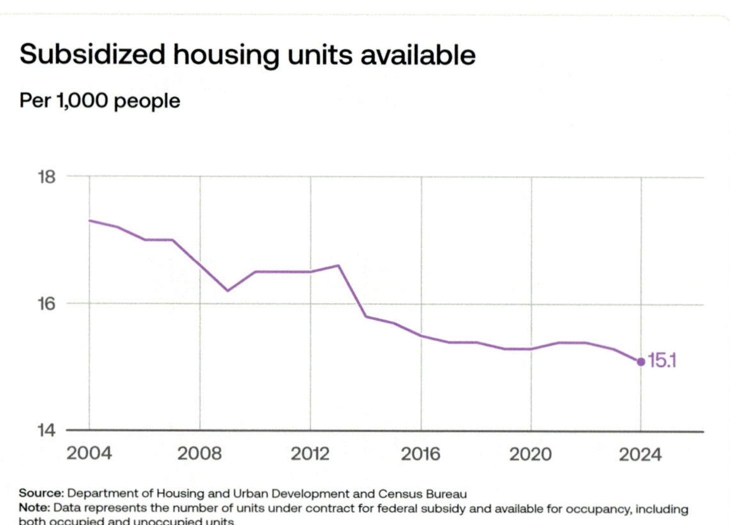

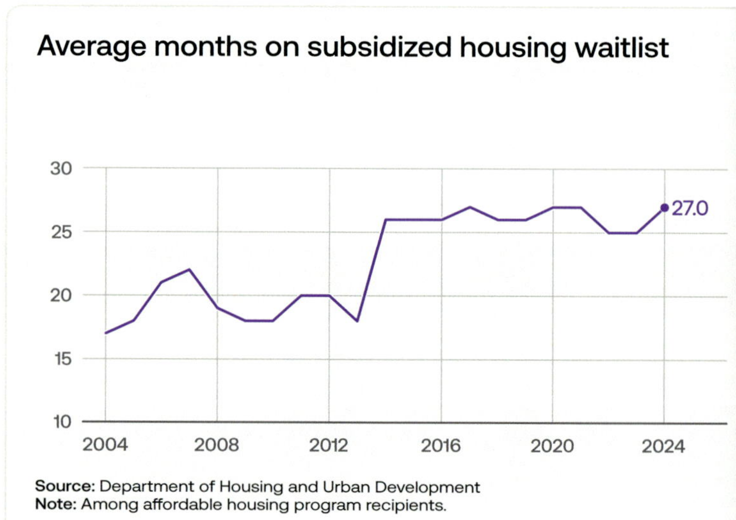

What share of households are food insecure?

In 2023, 13.5% of households were food insecure, meaning they were uncertain about having enough food or did not have enough food at some point in the year. This was 1.4 percentage points lower than the peak of 14.9% in 2011, but 0.7 points higher than in 2022. Food insecurity rates for households with children rose 0.6 percentage points compared to 2022. Seven Southern states had food insecurity rates significantly higher than the national average.

Share of households that are food insecure

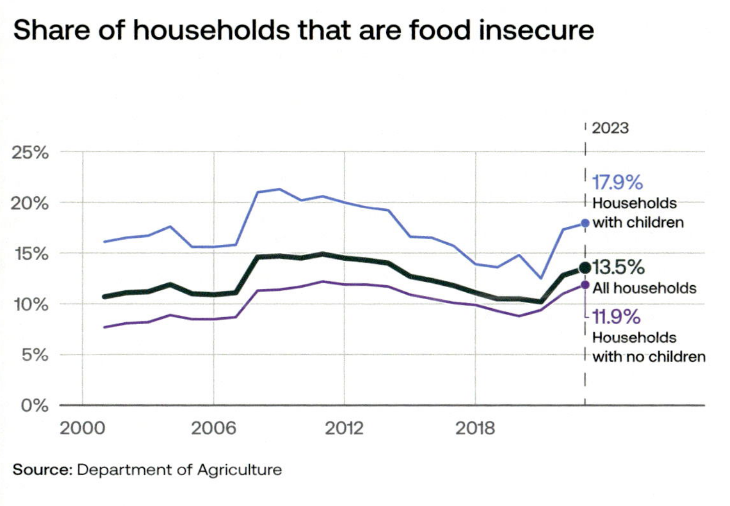

Source: Department of Agriculture

Share of households that are food insecure (2021-2023 average)

By state

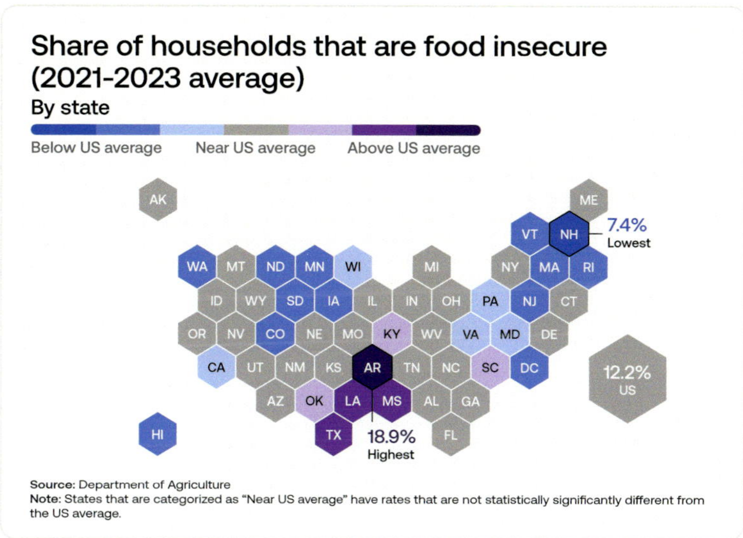

Source: Department of Agriculture
Note: States that are categorized as "Near US average" have rates that are not statistically significantly different from the US average.

How many people receive SNAP assistance? How much do they receive?

The Supplemental Nutrition Assistance Program (SNAP) is a federally funded program that provides food benefits to low-income families and individuals who meet certain work requirements. An average of more than 41.7 million people received benefits each month in fiscal year (FY) 2024, 17% more than in FY 2019, but less than the peak of 47.6 million in FY 2013.

The average monthly benefit was $187.54 per person, 18% higher than in FY 2019 but 14% lower than in FY 2023. Congress expanded SNAP benefits during the pandemic to combat food insecurity. These emergency allotments ended in March 2023.

Nutrition assistance (SNAP) average monthly recipients

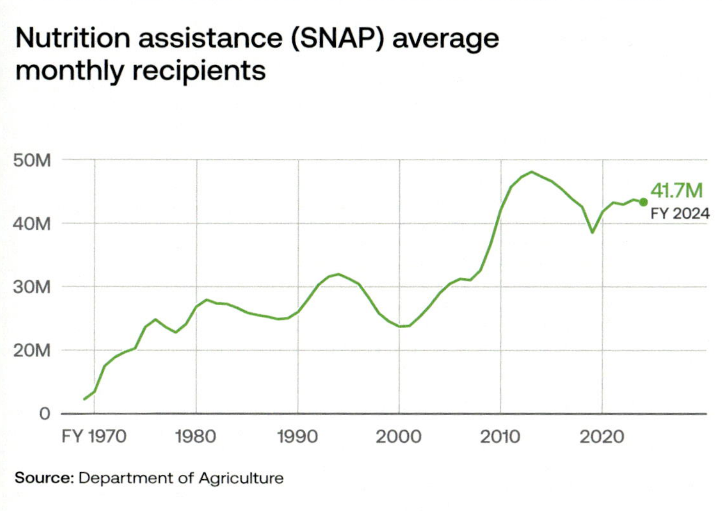

Source: Department of Agriculture

Nutrition assistance (SNAP) average monthly benefit per person

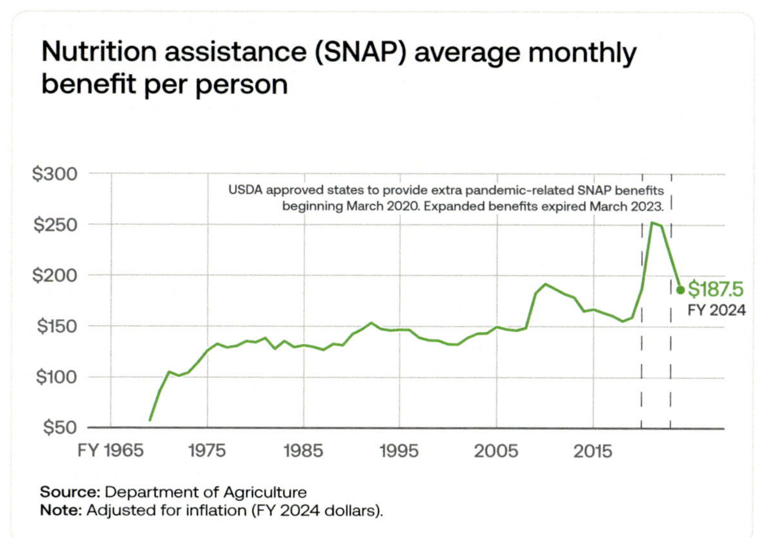

Source: Department of Agriculture
Note: Adjusted for inflation (FY 2024 dollars).

How many people receive nutrition assistance through WIC?

The Special Supplemental Nutrition Program for Women, Infants, and Children (WIC) provides nutrition benefits to qualifying low-income currently or recently pregnant women, and young children. In FY 2024, it served 6.7 million people at an average of $61 per person per month in food benefits. Program participation peaked at 9.2 million in FY 2010, declined to 6.2 million in FY 2021, and has increased for the last three years.

Average monthly WIC recipients

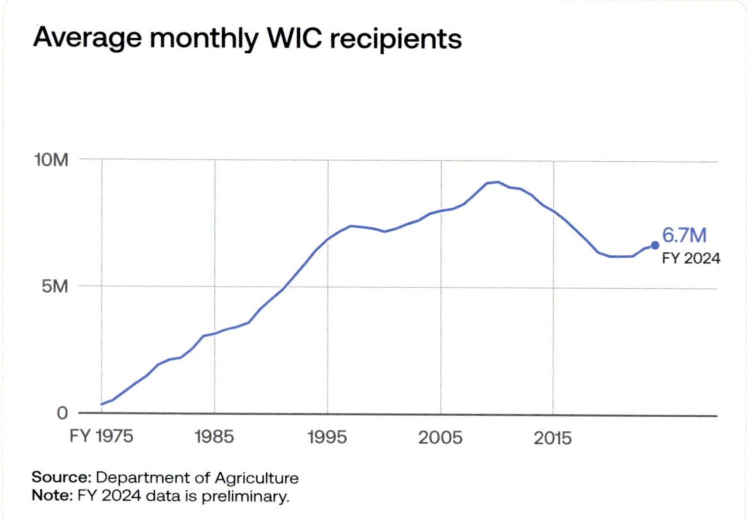

Source: Department of Agriculture
Note: FY 2024 data is preliminary.

WIC average monthly food cost per person

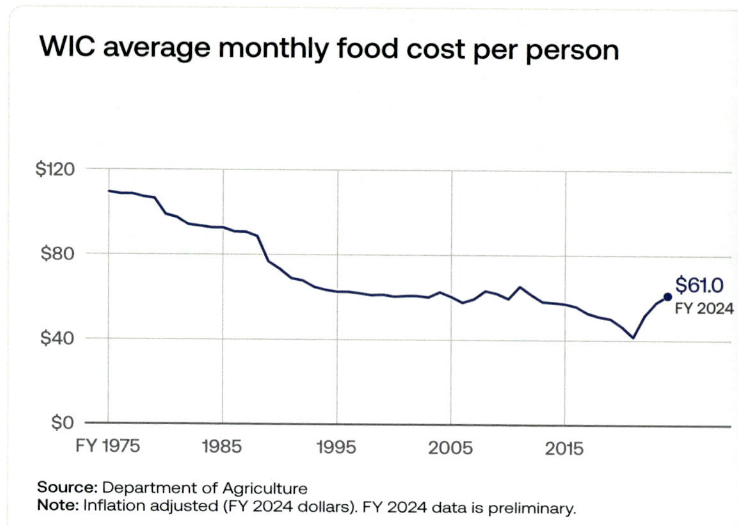

Source: Department of Agriculture
Note: Inflation adjusted (FY 2024 dollars). FY 2024 data is preliminary.

How many children use the free and reduced school lunch program?

Children from families earning below 130% of the federal poverty guidelines qualify for free school meals, while those between 130% and 185% qualify for reduced prices through the National School Lunch Program (NSLP). Schools in high-poverty areas may also serve all students regardless of eligibility. About 25.5 million students (53%) were eligible in the 2022–2023 school year.[iii]

The NSLP served free or reduced lunch to an average of 21.4 million children monthly in FY 2024. While the program also offers full-priced meals in the schools in which it operates, three of four meals it served were free or reduced.

Average monthly number of children receiving free or reduced lunch

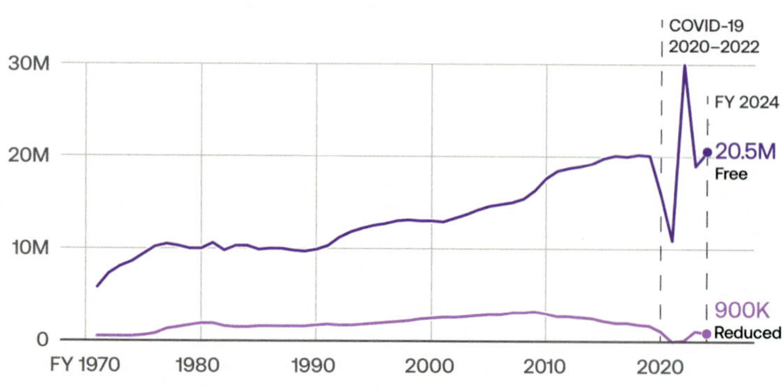

Share of school lunches served at free or reduced price

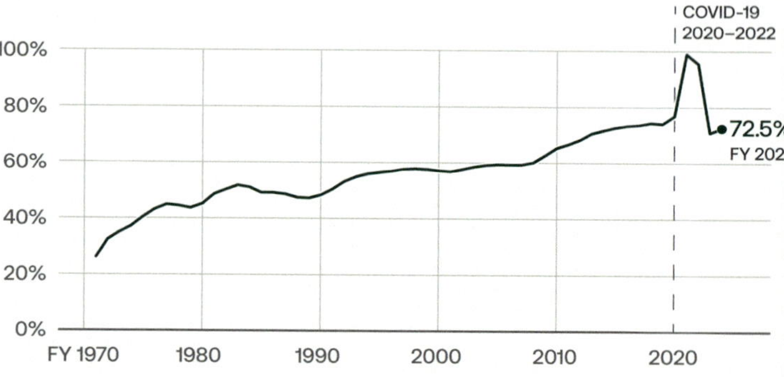

Source: Department of Agriculture
Note: In school year 2020-2021, many schools served meals through the Summer Food Service Program due to the COVID-19 waiver and are not captured here. FY 2021-2022 data includes meals served through the Seamless Summer Option. 2024 data is preliminary.

Chapter sources and data timeliness

Publishing agency	Program	Publication name	Release date	Most recent period in data
US Census Bureau	Current Population Survey	Annual Social and Economic Supplement, Historical poverty tables	Sep. 2024	2023
	Population Estimates Program	State population totals and components of change	Dec. 2024	2024
	American Community Survey	1-year estimates	Sep. 2024	2023
Bureau of Economic Analysis	National Income and Product Accounts	Gross domestic product	Updates quarterly for most recently completed quarter	
Bureau of Labor Statistics	Occupational Employment and Wage Statistics	OEWS tables	April 2025	2024
Department of Housing and Urban Development	Assisted Housing: National and Local	Picture of Subsidized Housing	Feb. 2025	2024
Department of Agriculture	Food Security in the US	National annual summary tables	Sep. 2024	2023
	Child nutrition programs	National annual summary tables	June 2025	FY 2024
	WIC	National level annual summary	June 2025	FY 2024
	SNAP	National level annual summary	June 2025	FY 2024
Internal Revenue Service	Statistics of Income	Public Use File	2023	2015
Employment and Training Administration	Unemployment Insurance	Weekly claims data	Updates weekly with data for about one month ago	

See sources and notes section at the end of this report for detailed citation information.

- There are many ways to define middle class. USAFacts defines it as those in the middle fifth of the family market income distribution — or the 40th–60th percentile. Families are defined in this analysis as tax filing units and can consist of one or more individuals.
- USAFacts combines IRS, Census, and other government sources for a closer look at how certain economic and demographic characteristics differ among family types and across the income spectrum. Charts in this section showing market income, taxes paid, and transfers received by income quintile rely upon this combined data. USAFacts uses a procedure similar to that used by the Congressional Budget Office and others, as explained in our methodology that can be found at: https://usafacts.org/methodology/.
- Our data on income quintiles makes use of the IRS's SOI public use microdata. The latest file, which provides detailed microdata on individual income tax returns, is from 2015.
- USAFacts notes when data is adjusted for inflation. Inflation adjustments use the Consumer Price Index for urban consumers (CPI-U), unless otherwise noted.

Economy

Economy facts

This chapter provides a foundation for understanding labor market, inflation, economic growth, and trade trends. As Congress weighs policies that influence the country's economy, the data here offers context for assessing the current outlook and the potential effects of legislation.

Inflation and interest rates

- Inflation was less than 4% year-over-year from mid-2023 through mid-2025 after peaking at 9.0% in June 2022.
- Housing has been the largest contributor to CPI increases due to both rising prices and its weight of 44% in household budgets.
- The Federal Reserve lowered the federal funds rate three times in 2024 after raising it 11 times from 2022–2023.
- When the Fed raises or lowers rates, it affects expectations in financial markets. This can change long-term interest rates like mortgage rates, which often move with the 10-year Treasury yield.

Jobs and labor market

- Employers added about 2.0 million jobs in 2024, higher than the 2000 to 2023 average annual increase of 1.1 million.
- The national unemployment rate was 4.0% in 2024. It ranged from 1.8% in South Dakota to 5.6% in Nevada.
- The labor force participation rate held steady at 62.6%, still below pre-pandemic highs but recovering from 2020 lows.
- Job openings declined to 4.7% in 2024 from a peak of 6.8% in 2022, while layoff rates remained at 1.1%.

Economic growth

- GDP reached $29.2 trillion in 2024.
- Real GDP, which is GDP adjusted for inflation, rose 2.8% in 2024, surpassing the 2000 to 2023 average growth rate of 2.2%.
- State-level growth varied, with Utah and South Carolina exceeding 4% growth while Iowa and North Dakota shrank by less than 1%.

International trade

- Imports totaled $4.1 trillion in 2024, led by capital goods (e.g., semiconductors) and services like international travel.
- Exports reached $3.2 trillion. Top categories included petroleum products and professional consulting services.
- The US had a $903.5 billion trade deficit in 2024, with a $1.2 trillion goods deficit and $311.9 billion services surplus.
- Mexico became the nation's top trading partner in 2024, followed by Canada and China. These countries made up 36% of imports and 32% of exports.
- In FY 2024, the US collected $77.0 billion in customs duties revenue, including revenue from tariffs and other import fees. It accounted for less than 2% of federal revenue.

How quickly are prices increasing? What's increasing the most?

The Consumer Price Index (CPI) is a common measure of price inflation. The 12-month percent change in CPI began rising in early 2021, peaking at 9.0% in June 2022. Year-over-year inflation has since cooled. It's been below 4.0% since June 2023 and 3.0% or less since June 2024. Compared to January 2021, transportation prices in June 2025 increased more than any other CPI category, about 28%. This was followed by housing (26%) and food and beverages (24%).

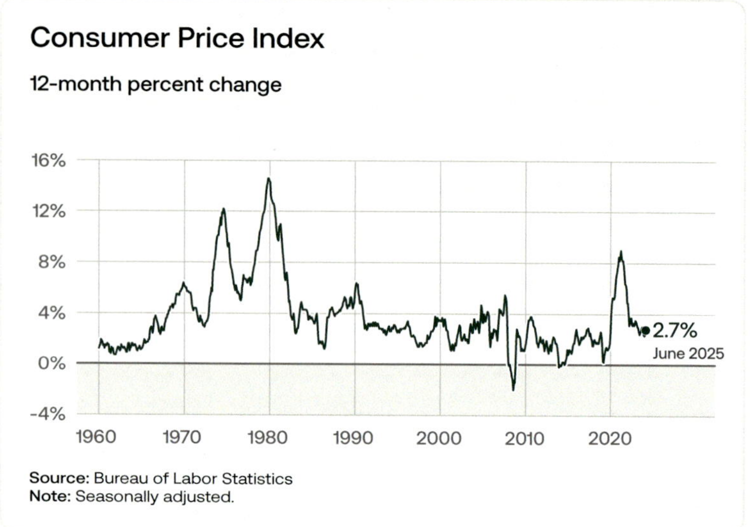

Source: Bureau of Labor Statistics
Note: Seasonally adjusted.

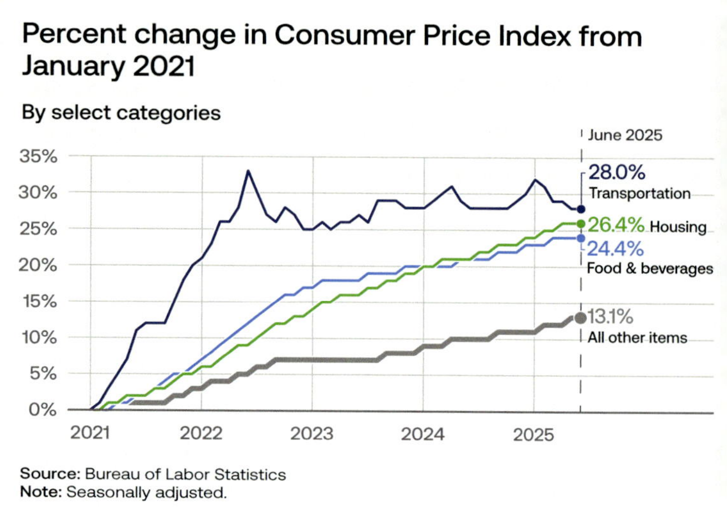

Source: Bureau of Labor Statistics
Note: Seasonally adjusted.

What contributes the most to increases in the CPI?

Housing has been the largest driver of CPI increases since mid-2022, surpassing transportation, which includes prices of motor vehicles and gasoline. Note that the items that contribute the most to inflation aren't always the ones with the biggest price jumps. The CPI is weighted based on how much people spend on each category. For example, transportation prices increased more sharply than housing from January 2021 to June 2025. Since transportation makes up a smaller part of household spending, it is given less weight in the CPI, therefore contributing less to the increase in the index.

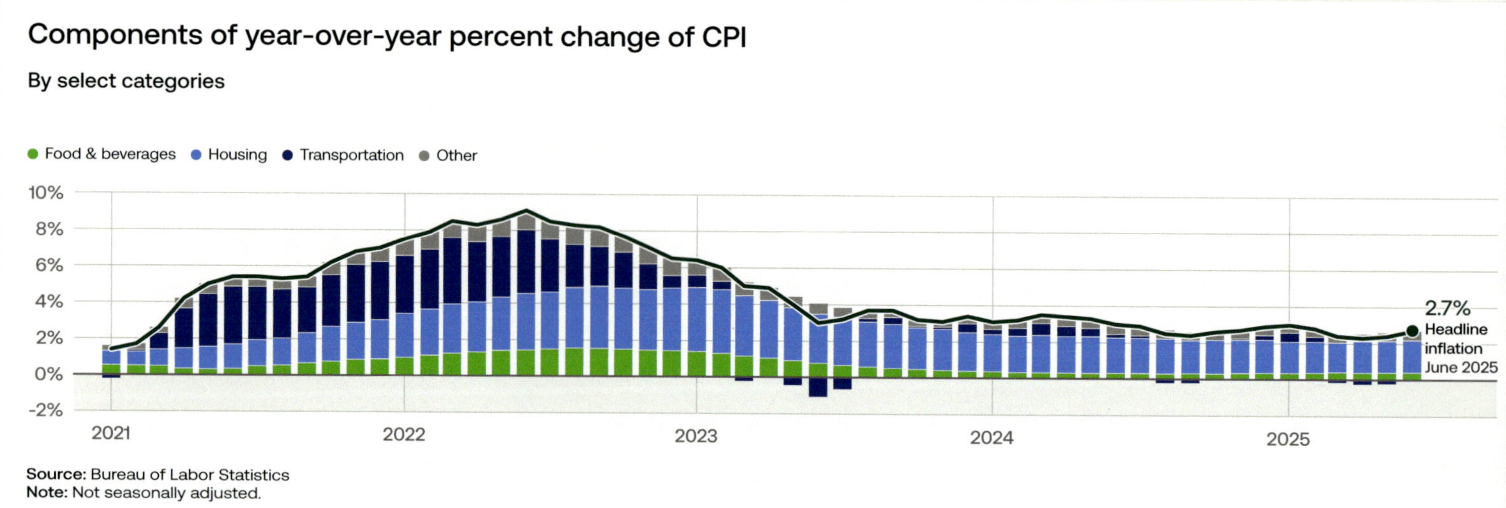

Source: Bureau of Labor Statistics
Note: Not seasonally adjusted.

How does the Federal Reserve aim to influence inflation?

The Federal Reserve (Fed) increases the federal funds rate to bring down inflation. It increased the target rate seven times in 2022 and four times in 2023. The Fed then lowered the target rate three times in 2024 to 4.25%–4.5%. The PCE price index measures the prices of goods and services consumers purchase and is the Fed's preferred inflation measure. Inflation inched toward the Fed's target rate of 2% year-over-year in 2023 through the beginning of 2025.

Federal funds rate

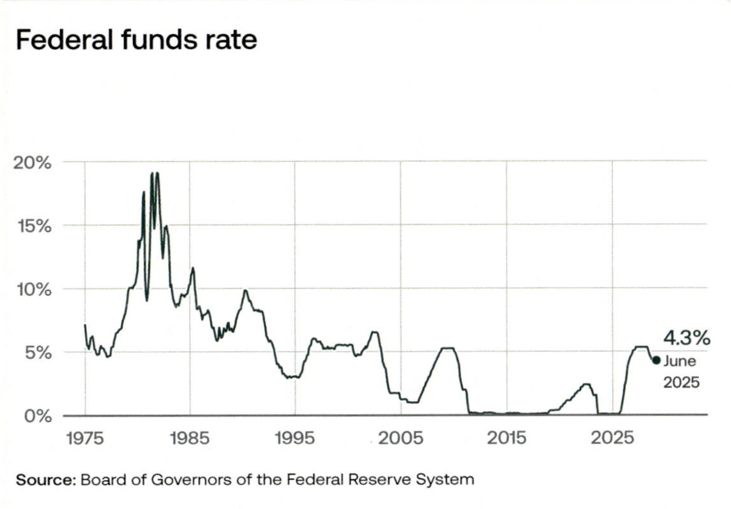

Source: Board of Governors of the Federal Reserve System

Personal Consumption Expenditures (PCE) price index

12-month percent change

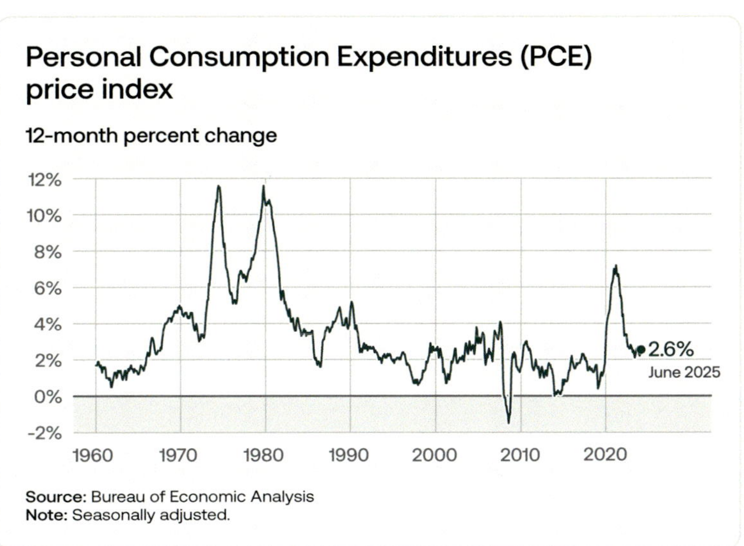

Source: Bureau of Economic Analysis
Note: Seasonally adjusted.

How does the Federal Reserve affect interest rates faced by consumers?

When the Federal Reserve raises the federal funds rate, it increases the rate banks use when lending to each other. Banks typically pass these increased borrowing costs to consumers by raising the interest rates on credit cards, business loans, and other products. Long-term rates are especially influenced by the 10-year Treasury yield, which reflects, among other things, investors' expectations about future Fed decisions. Expectations shift as the Fed raises or lowers its rate, moving many long-term interest rates as well. For example, the 30-year fixed mortgage rate closely tracks the 10-year Treasury yield.

Yield on 10-year Treasury securities vs. 30-year mortgage rate

Monthly average

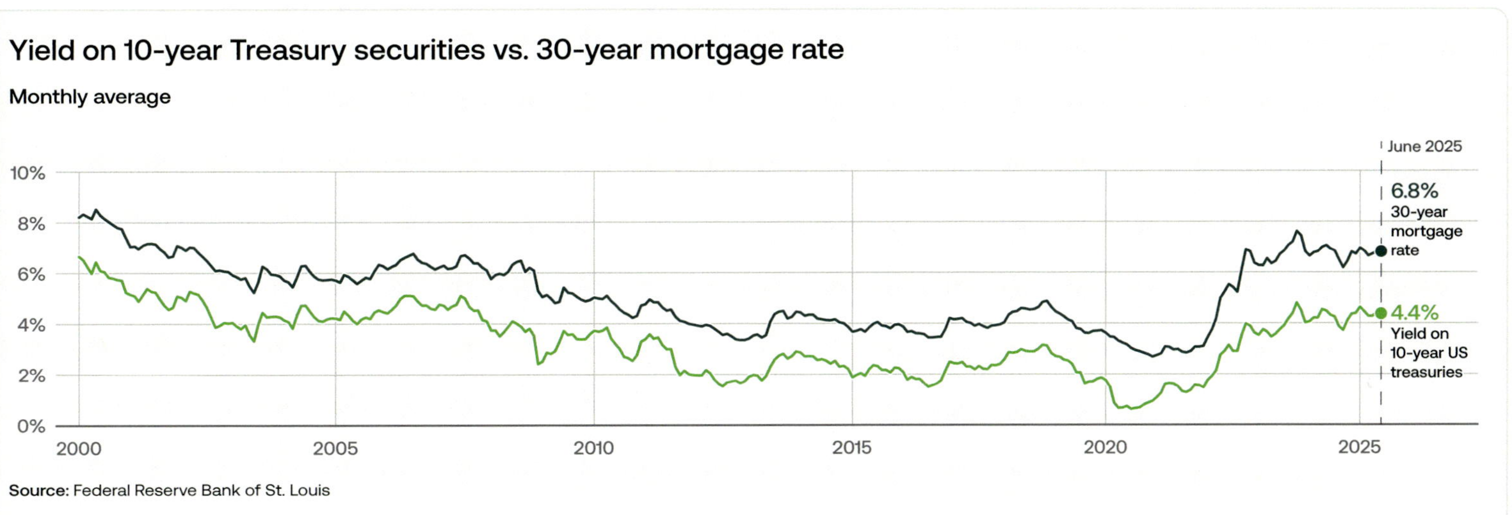

Source: Federal Reserve Bank of St. Louis

Is the economy growing?

In 2024, US GDP reached $29.2 trillion. Real GDP (rGDP), which accounts for inflation, increased 2.8%, which was above the 2000 to 2023 average annual rate of 2.2%. From 2023 to 2024, rGDP decreased in two states, Iowa and North Dakota. It increased by less than 1.0% in South Dakota, Nebraska, and Wyoming. It increased by more than 4.0% in Utah and South Carolina.

Annual percent change in real GDP

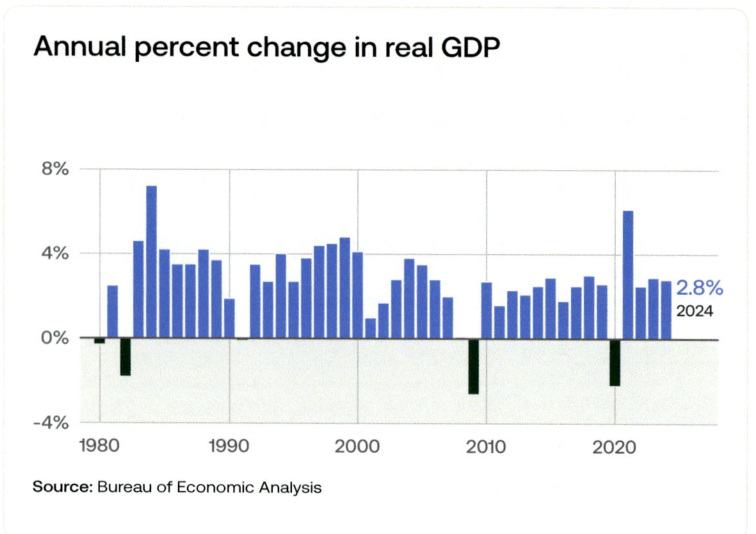

Source: Bureau of Economic Analysis

Percent change in real GDP (2023 vs. 2024)

By state

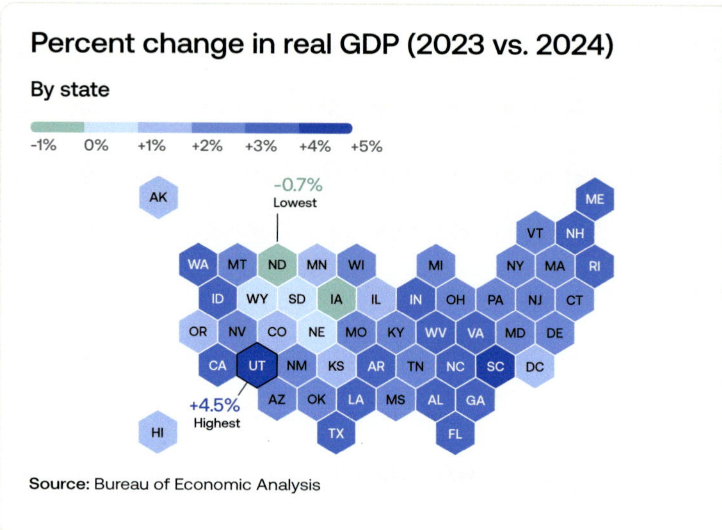

Source: Bureau of Economic Analysis

How many more people are employed compared to 2023?

US employers added about 2.1 million jobs in 2024. From 2000 to 2023, employment increased by 1.1 million each year, on average. Change in 2024 was higher than this average, but lower than the annual increases from the past three years. From 2023 to 2024, Alaska had the highest employment increase at 2.1%, and Massachusetts and Iowa had the lowest, less than 0.2% each.

Net change in employment (jobs)

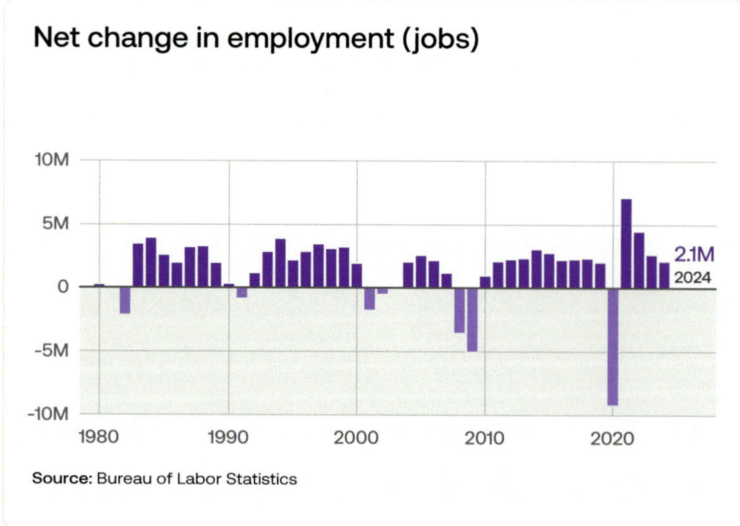

Source: Bureau of Labor Statistics

Percent change in annual average employment (2023 vs. 2024)

By state

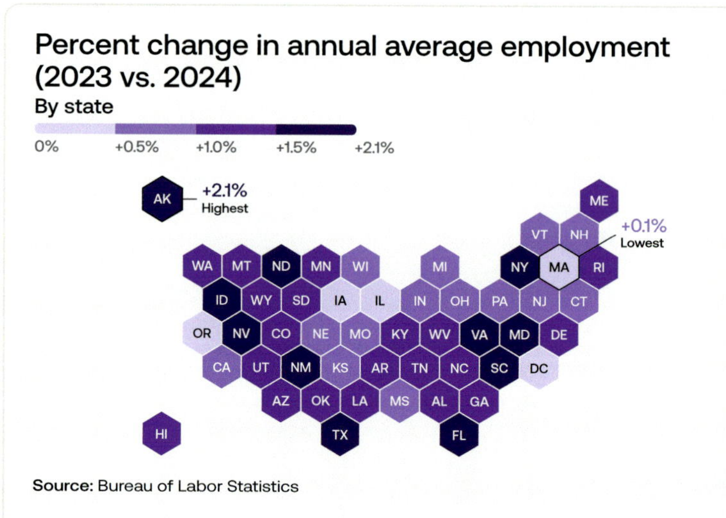

Source: Bureau of Labor Statistics

What is the unemployment rate and how does it vary by state?

The average unemployment rate was 4.0% in 2024, 0.4 percentage points above the 2022 and 2023 rates. State rates ranged from a low of 1.8% in South Dakota to a high of 5.6% in Nevada.

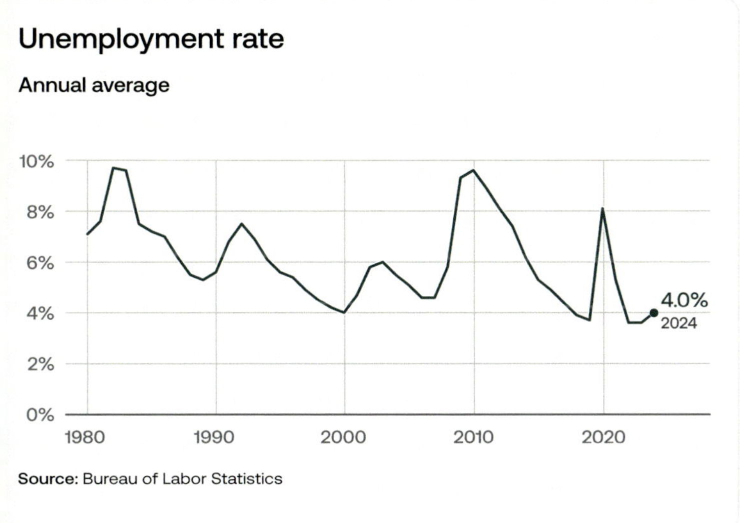

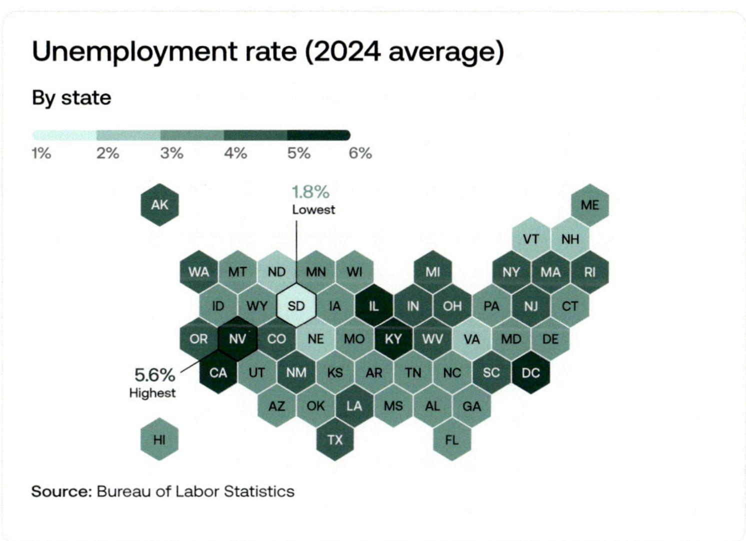

What is the labor force participation rate and how does it vary by state?

The labor force participation rate is the share of the population age 16 and older that is either employed or looking for work. It peaked between 1997 and 2000. It hit a low of 61.7% during the pandemic and reached 62.6% in 2023, remaining unchanged in 2024. The rate was higher than 68% in six states and lower than 58% in five states.

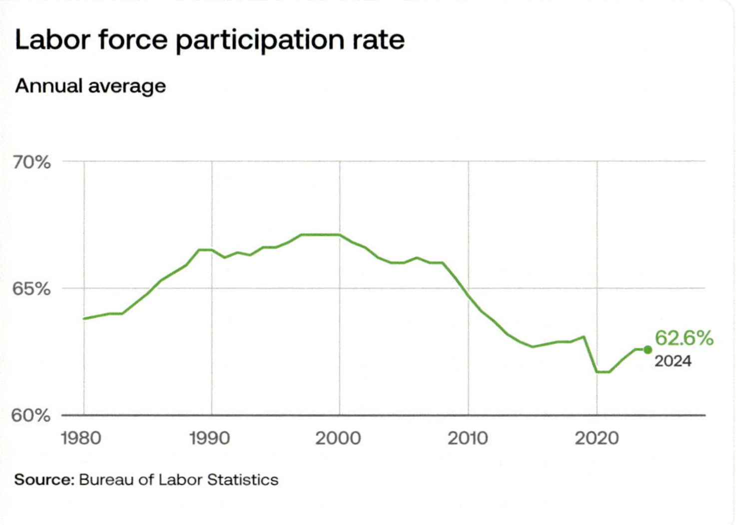

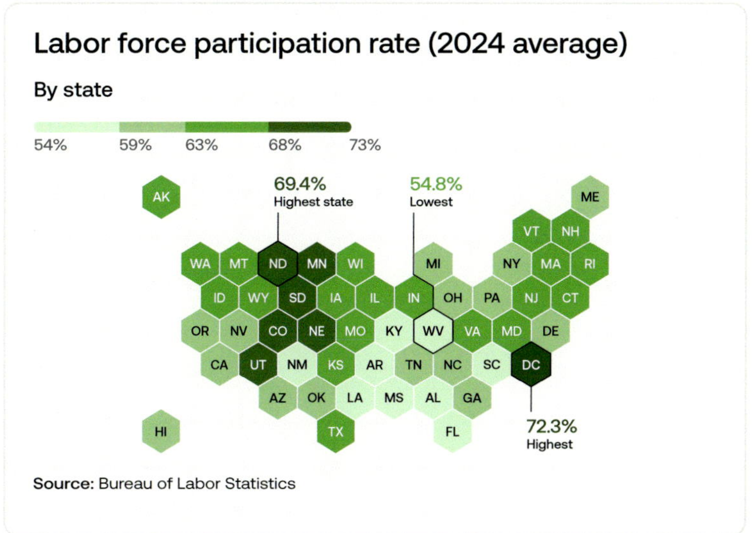

Are employers hiring?

The average job openings rate in 2024 was 4.7% of all jobs, both filled and unfilled, equal to 7.78 million job openings. This is down 2.1 percentage points from the 2022 peak of 6.8%, but higher than any other year prior to 2021. The job openings rate ranged from 3.7% in California to 6.6% in Alaska.

Job openings rate

Annual average

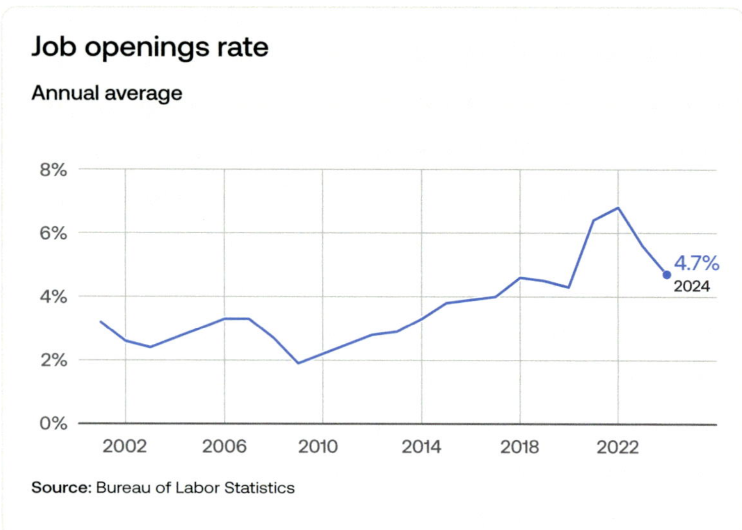

Source: Bureau of Labor Statistics

Job openings rate (2024 average)

By state

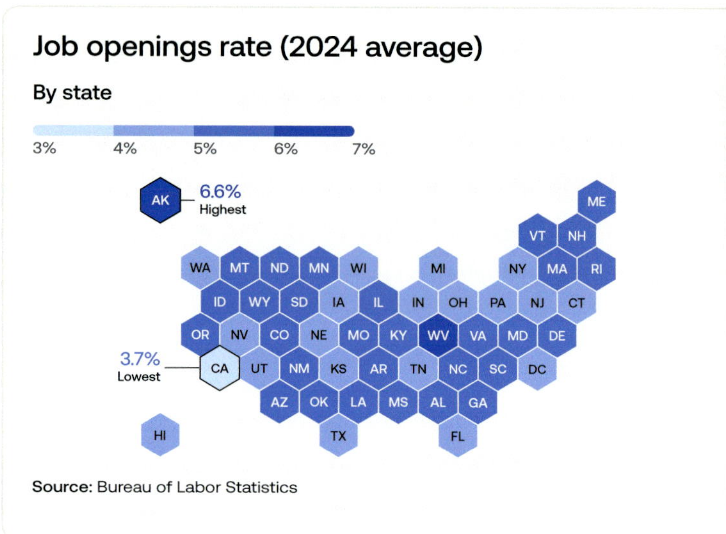

Source: Bureau of Labor Statistics

How many people are laid off?

The average layoff and discharge rate in 2024 was 1.1%, the same as in 2023. The rate was lower than in any other year prior to 2020. Four states had rates higher than 1.5%: Alaska, Rhode Island, Montana, and Wyoming. Washington, DC, had the lowest rate at 0.8%. The 2024 data does not reflect the reductions in the federal workforce that began in January 2025.

Layoff and discharge rate

Annual average

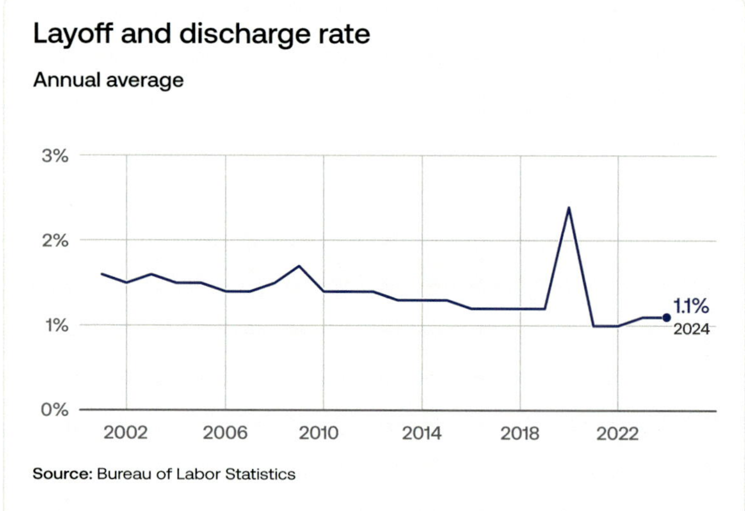

Source: Bureau of Labor Statistics

Layoff and discharge rate (2024 average)

By state

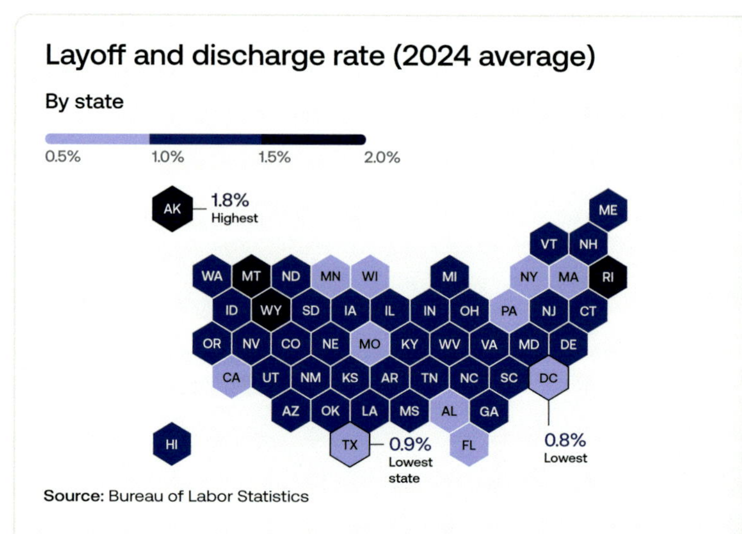

Source: Bureau of Labor Statistics

What does US international trade look like?

US sales abroad are exports, and US purchases from abroad are imports. When a nation imports more than it exports, it's called a trade deficit. The US has had a trade deficit from 1976 to 2024. In 2024, the US imported $4.1 trillion and exported $3.2 trillion, leading to a $903.5 billion trade deficit.

Trade balance

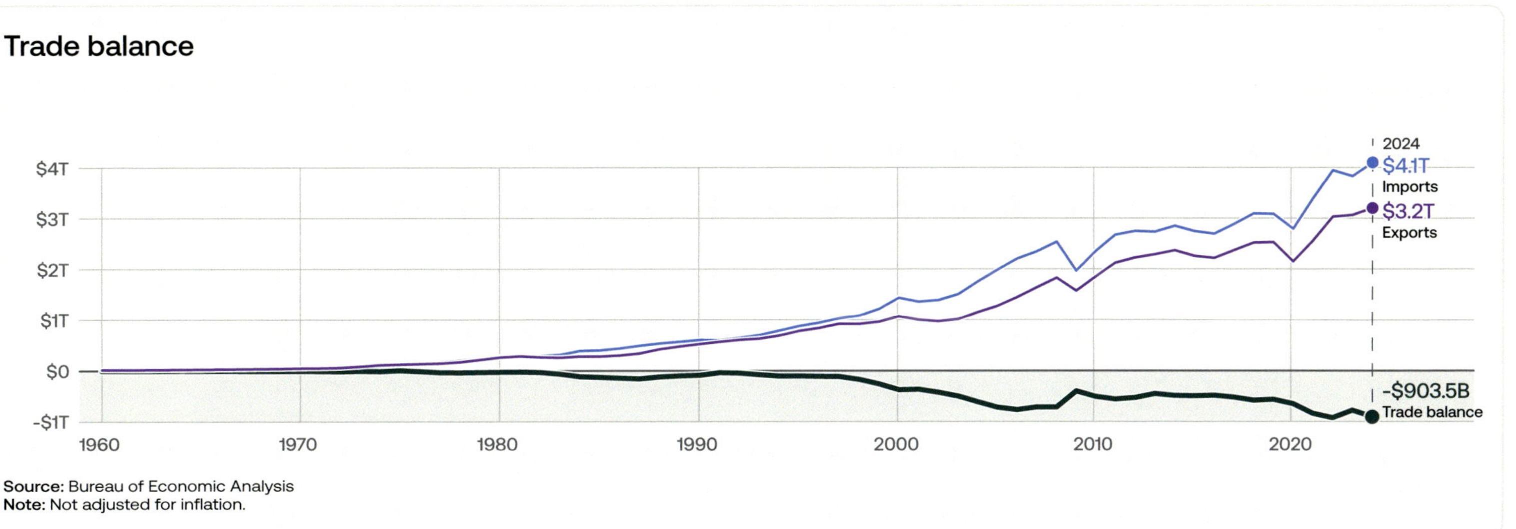

Source: Bureau of Economic Analysis
Note: Not adjusted for inflation.

How much does the US trade in goods and services?

Trade can also be divided into goods and services. Net trade in services has been positive since 1971, meaning the US exported more services than it imported each year. On the other hand, the nation imports more goods than it exports, leading to a negative net goods trade. The US goods deficit has exceeded $1 trillion in the last four years, not adjusted for inflation. In 2024, the US had a $311.9 billion services surplus and a $1.2 trillion goods deficit.

Net trade of goods and services

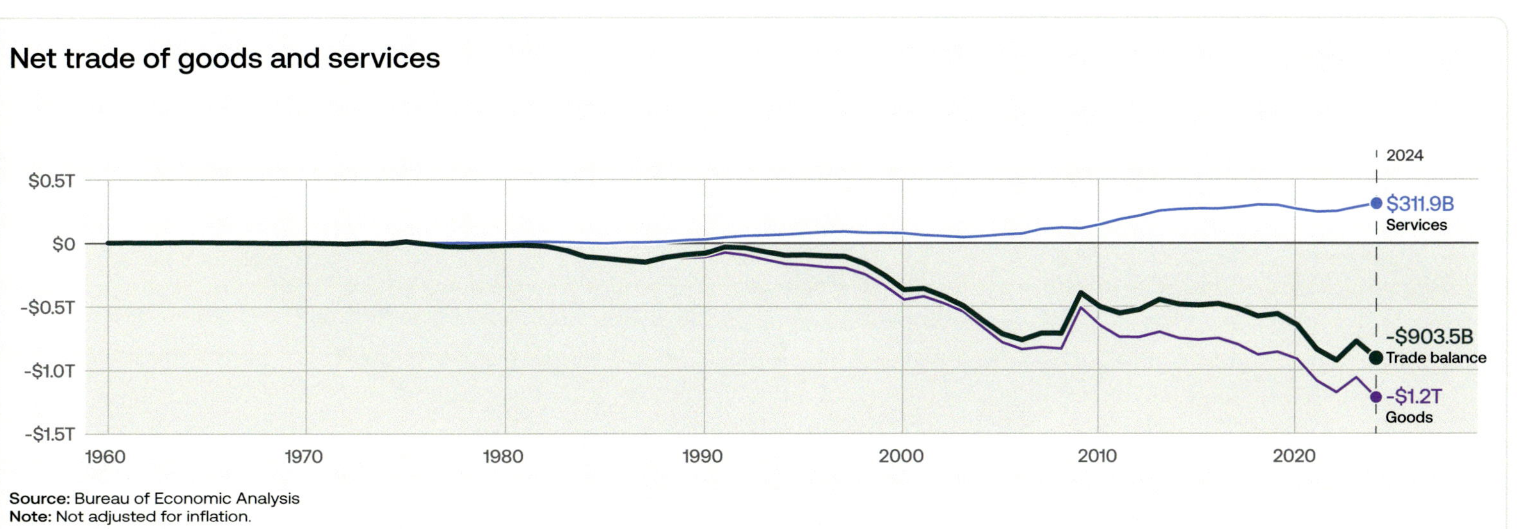

Source: Bureau of Economic Analysis
Note: Not adjusted for inflation.

What does the US import?

In 2024, $3.3 trillion (80%) of imports to the US were goods. The other $840.9 billion (20%) were services. The largest categories of imports were capital goods (goods used to produce other goods, as opposed to goods purchased by consumers), mainly comprised of machinery and equipment, like semiconductors and scientific equipment. It was followed by consumer goods, composed of medical products, household appliances, and other goods for personal use. Travel was the predominant imported service, including what US residents spent abroad for accommodation, food, and other expenses.

Imports (2024)

By goods and services

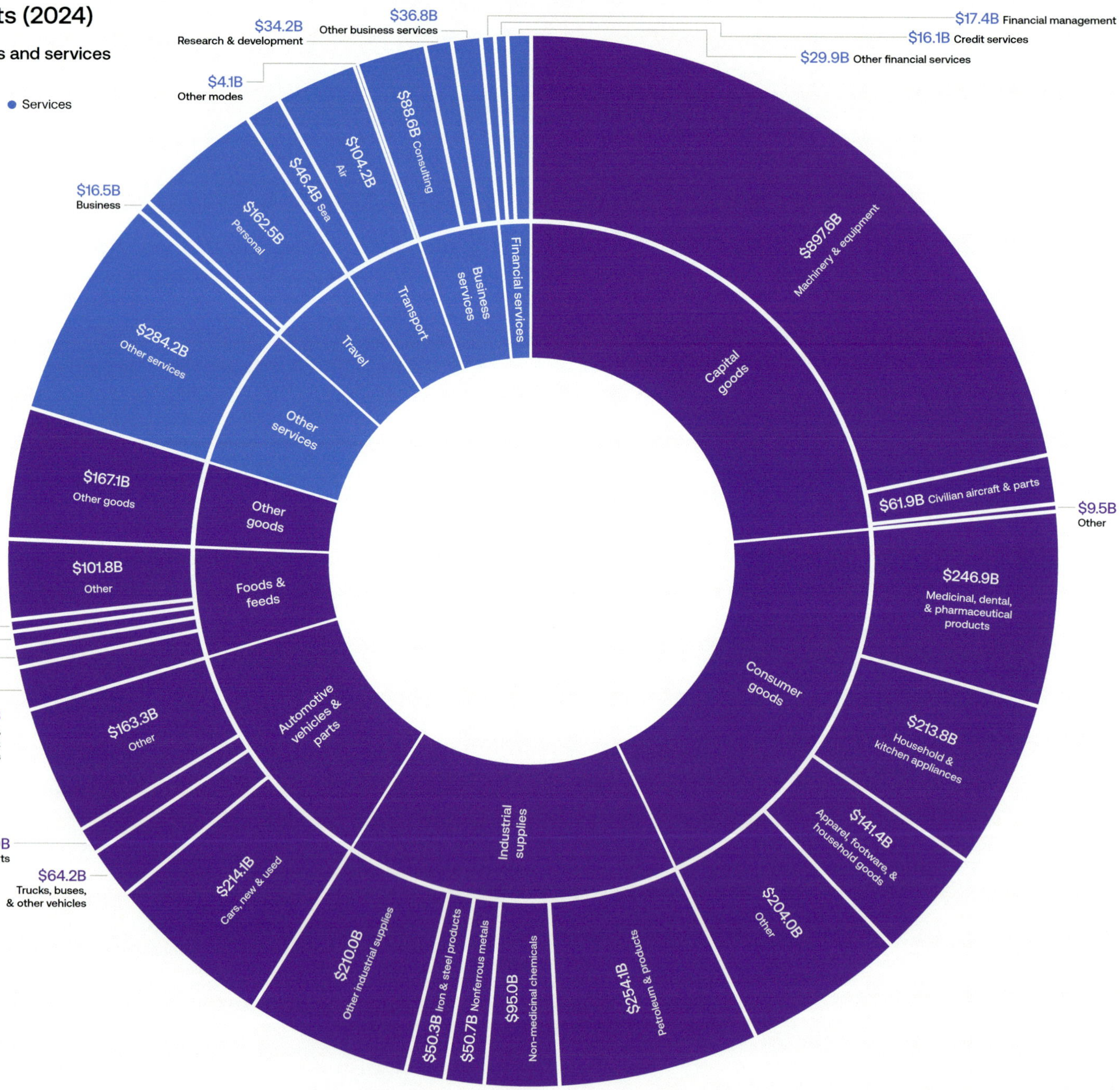

Source: Bureau of Economic Analysis

What does the US export?

In 2024, $2.1 trillion (64%) of exports from the US were goods, while the other $1.2 trillion (36%) were services. The largest categories of exports were industrial supplies, mainly comprised of petroleum products and non-medicinal chemicals. It was followed by capital goods, including machinery and civilian aircraft. The largest service exported was business services, primarily professional and management consulting.

Exports (2024)

By goods and services

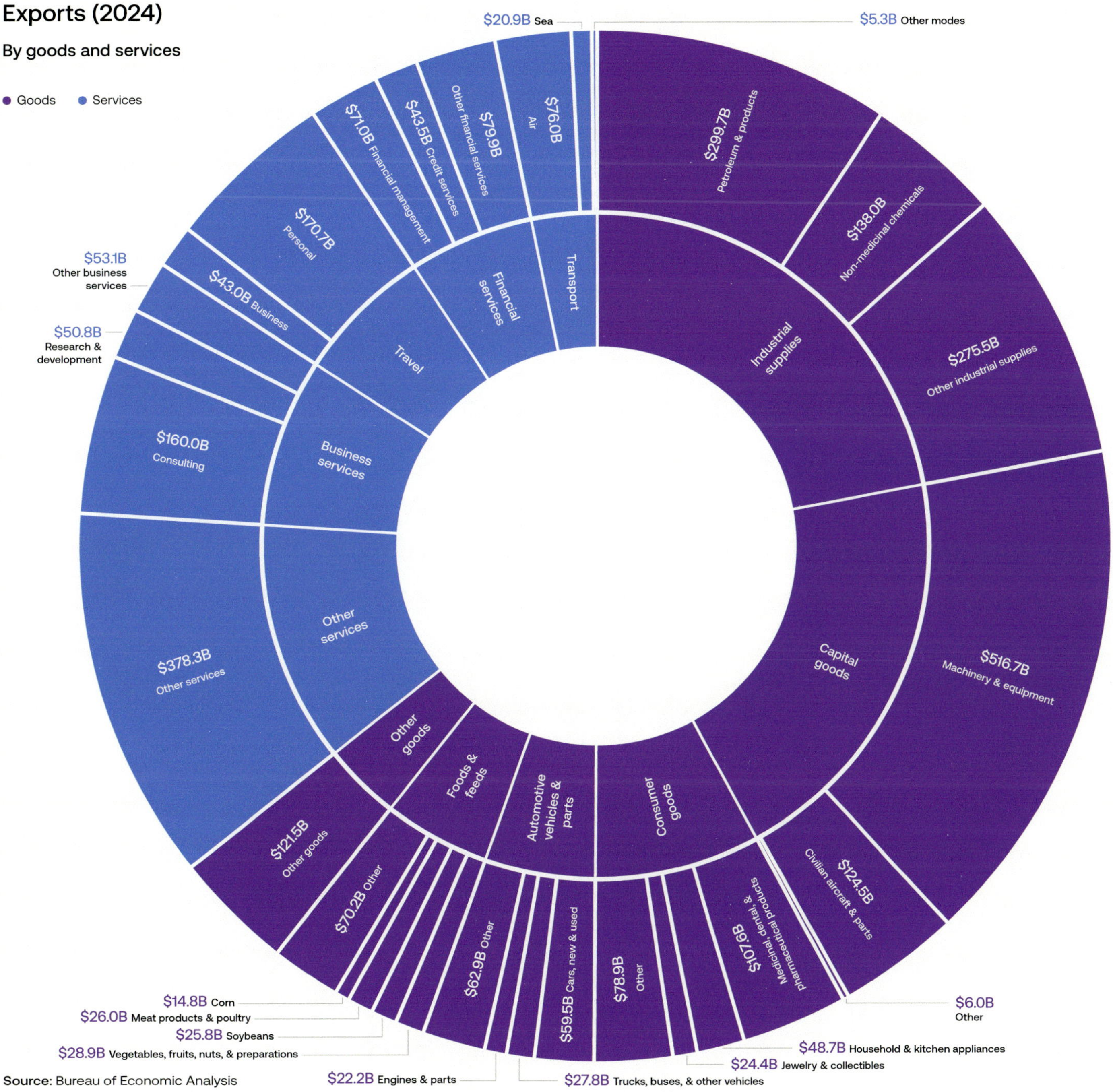

Goods | Services

Industrial supplies
$299.7B Petroleum & products
$138.0B Non-medicinal chemicals
$275.5B Other industrial supplies

Capital goods
$516.7B Machinery & equipment
$124.5B Civilian aircraft & parts
$6.0B Other

Consumer goods
$107.6B Medicinal, dental, & pharmaceutical products
$48.7B Household & kitchen appliances
$24.4B Jewelry & collectibles
$78.9B Other

Automotive vehicles & parts
$59.5B Cars, new & used
$27.8B Trucks, buses, & other vehicles
$22.2B Engines & parts
$62.9B Other

Foods & feeds
$28.9B Vegetables, fruits, nuts, & preparations
$25.8B Soybeans
$26.0B Meat products & poultry
$14.8B Corn
$70.2B Other

Other goods
$121.5B Other goods

Other services
$378.3B Other services

Business services
$160.0B Consulting
$50.8B Research & development
$53.1B Other business services

Travel
$43.0B Business
$170.7B Personal

Financial services
$71.0B Financial management
$43.5B Credit services
$79.9B Other financial services

Transport
$76.0B Air
$20.9B Sea
$5.3B Other modes

Source: Bureau of Economic Analysis

Who does the US trade with?

In 2024, the US imported the most from the Asia and Pacific region and Europe, at values over $1 trillion each. The countries the US imported most from were Mexico, Canada, China, Germany, and Japan, each valued at over $190 billion. Combined, these five countries accounted for 46% of imports to the US.

Imports and exports (2024)

By area

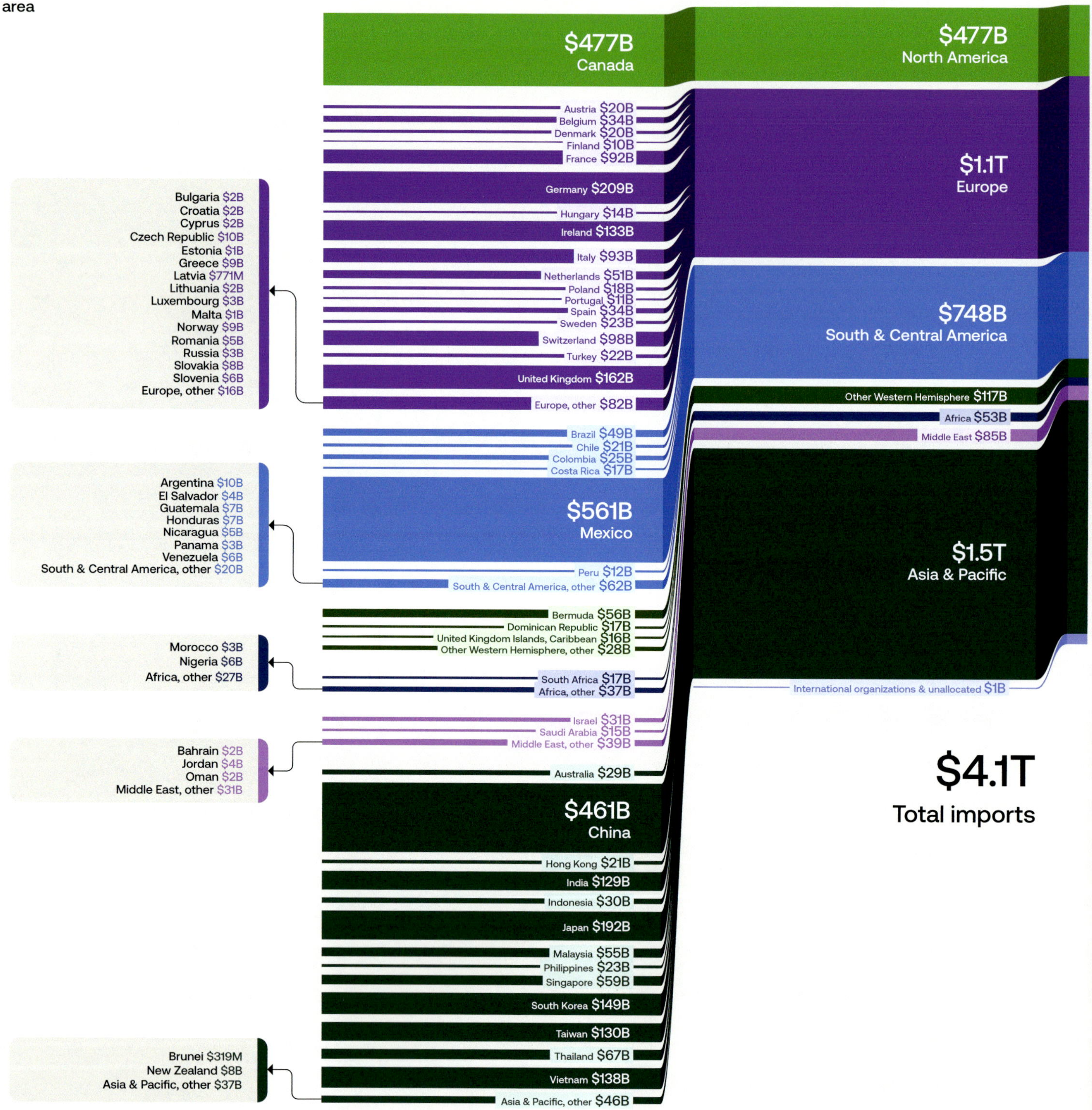

Source: Bureau of Economic Analysis
Note: Source classifies Mexico as part of South & Central America.

In 2024, the US exported the most to Europe and the Asia and Pacific region, $998.0 billion and $875.5 billion, respectively. The countries receiving the most US exports were Canada, Mexico, China, the United Kingdom, and Japan, each valued over $129 billion. Combined, these five countries accounted for 41% of exports.

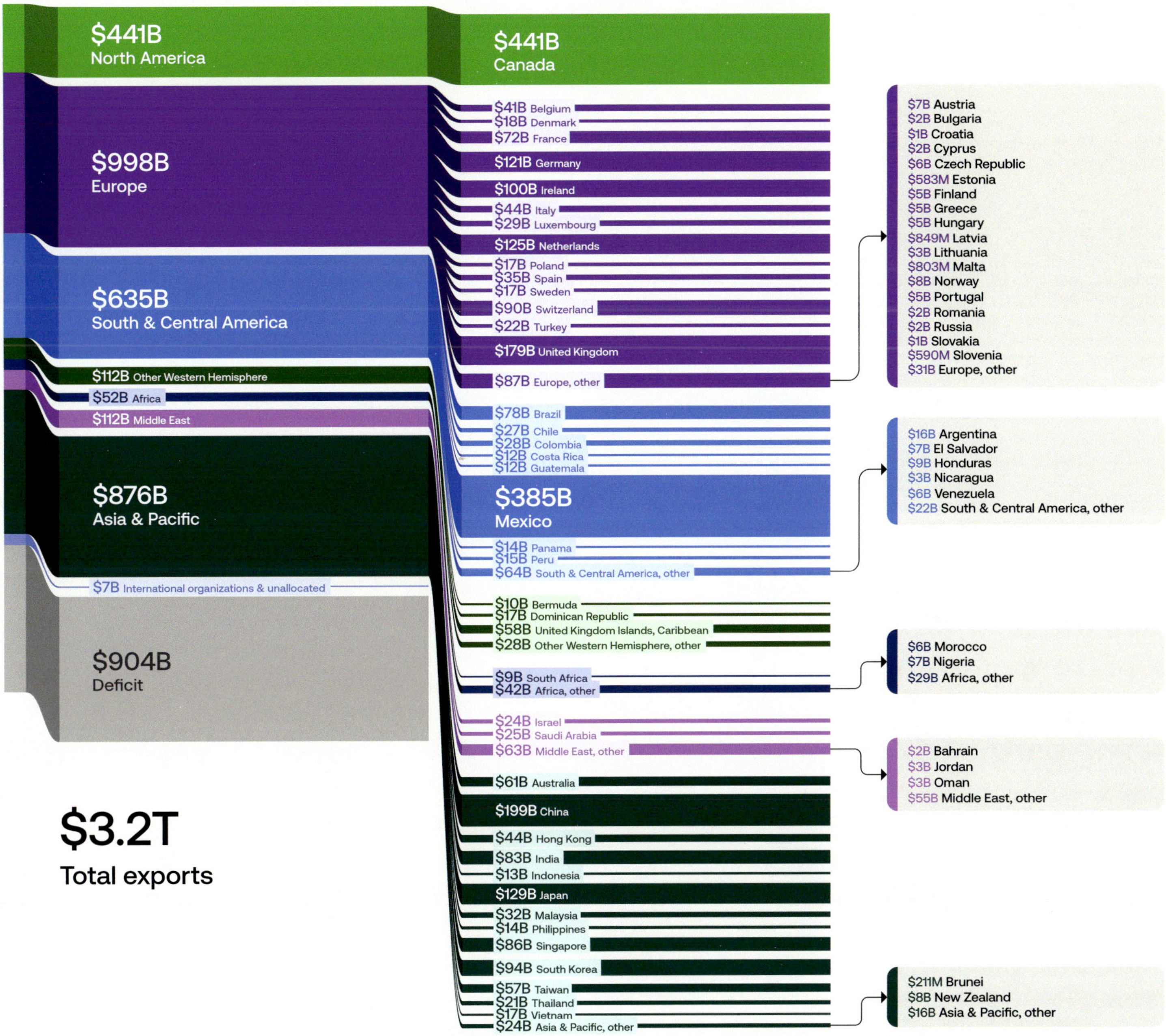

$441B North America
$998B Europe
$635B South & Central America
$112B Other Western Hemisphere
$52B Africa
$112B Middle East
$876B Asia & Pacific
$7B International organizations & unallocated
$904B Deficit

$441B Canada
$41B Belgium
$18B Denmark
$72B France
$121B Germany
$100B Ireland
$44B Italy
$29B Luxembourg
$125B Netherlands
$17B Poland
$35B Spain
$17B Sweden
$90B Switzerland
$22B Turkey
$179B United Kingdom
$87B Europe, other
$78B Brazil
$27B Chile
$28B Colombia
$12B Costa Rica
$12B Guatemala
$385B Mexico
$14B Panama
$15B Peru
$64B South & Central America, other
$10B Bermuda
$17B Dominican Republic
$58B United Kingdom Islands, Caribbean
$28B Other Western Hemisphere, other
$9B South Africa
$42B Africa, other
$24B Israel
$25B Saudi Arabia
$63B Middle East, other
$61B Australia
$199B China
$44B Hong Kong
$83B India
$13B Indonesia
$129B Japan
$32B Malaysia
$14B Philippines
$86B Singapore
$94B South Korea
$57B Taiwan
$21B Thailand
$17B Vietnam
$24B Asia & Pacific, other

$7B Austria
$2B Bulgaria
$1B Croatia
$2B Cyprus
$6B Czech Republic
$583M Estonia
$5B Finland
$5B Greece
$5B Hungary
$849M Latvia
$3B Lithuania
$803M Malta
$8B Norway
$5B Portugal
$2B Romania
$2B Russia
$1B Slovakia
$590M Slovenia
$31B Europe, other

$16B Argentina
$7B El Salvador
$9B Honduras
$3B Nicaragua
$6B Venezuela
$22B South & Central America, other

$6B Morocco
$7B Nigeria
$29B Africa, other

$2B Bahrain
$3B Jordan
$3B Oman
$55B Middle East, other

$211M Brunei
$8B New Zealand
$16B Asia & Pacific, other

$3.2T

Total exports

Who are the US' top trading partners?

How have they changed over time?

When adding the value of imports and exports, Mexico, Canada, and China have been the US' top trading partners since 2004. In 2024, Mexico became the nation's top trading partner for the first time since data became available in 1999. China went from being the sixth top trading partner in 1999 to the first throughout 2016 to 2018. As of 2024, it was third after Mexico and Canada.

Total trade value with top trading partners

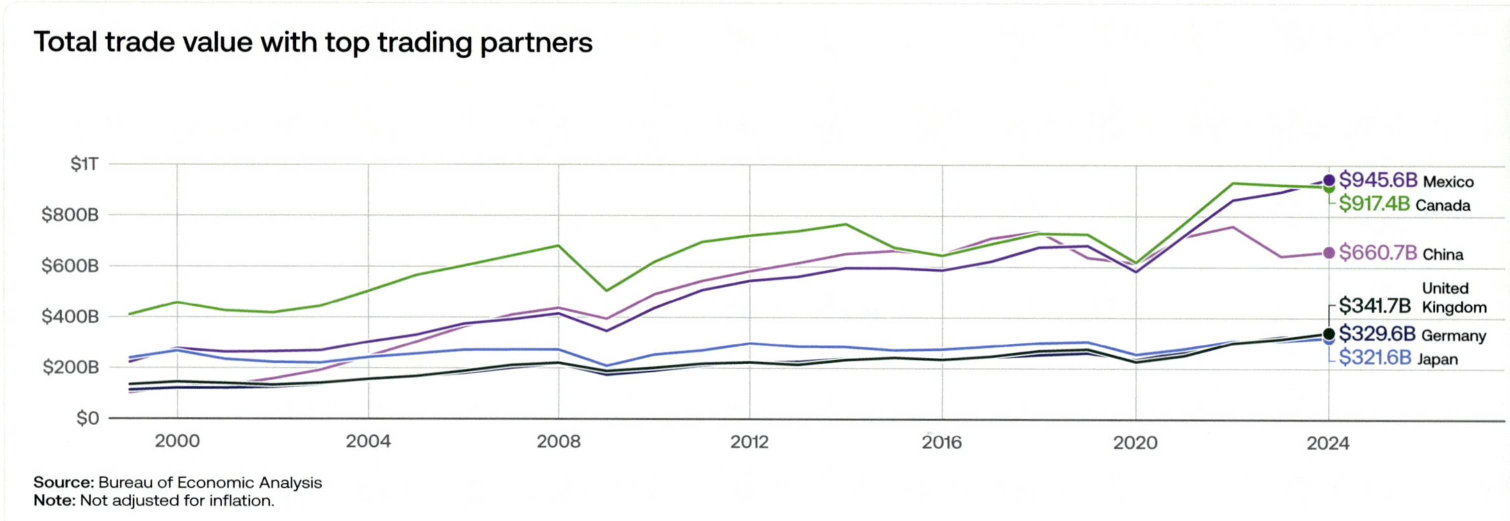

Source: Bureau of Economic Analysis
Note: Not adjusted for inflation.

Does the US import more from or export more to its top trading partners?

The US had a trade deficit with five of its six top trading partners in 2024. The largest deficit was with China at $262.2 billion, followed by Mexico at $175.9 billion. From 2023 to 2024, the US trade deficit grew most with Mexico (up 13%) and fell most with Canada (down 11%).

Net trade balance with top trading partners

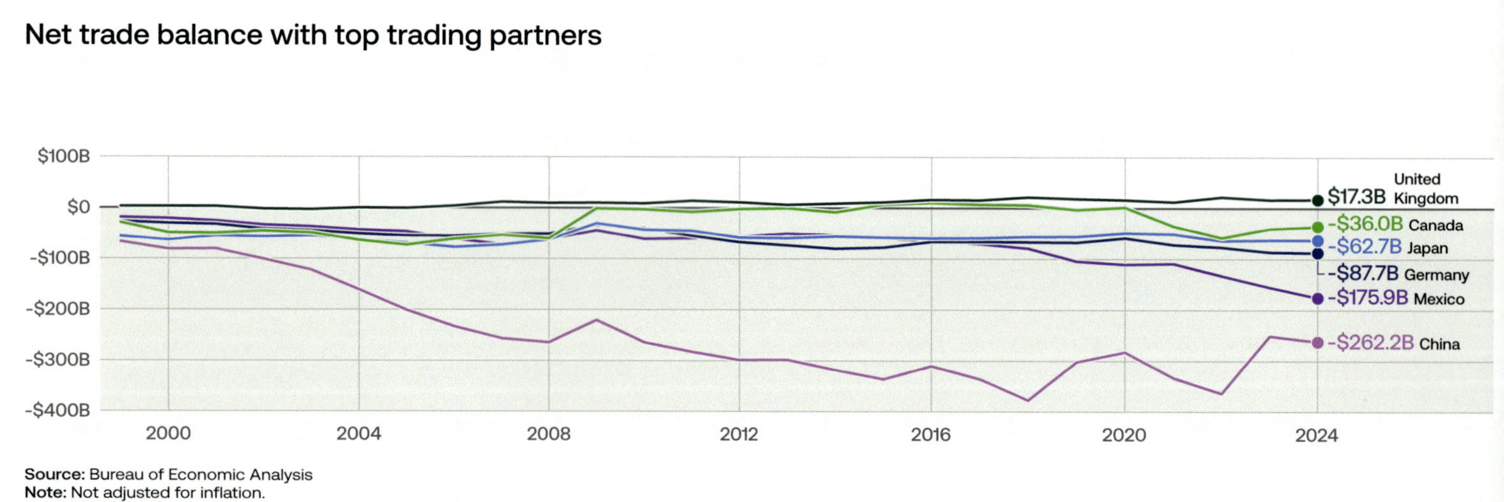

Source: Bureau of Economic Analysis
Note: Not adjusted for inflation.

Where does the US get the most imports from?

In 2024, Mexico accounted for nearly 14% of all imports to the US, the most of any nation. Canada was second, followed by China. Together, these countries accounted for 36% of total US imports. Capital goods were the top US import category; Mexico accounted for 18% of these goods and China another 15%.

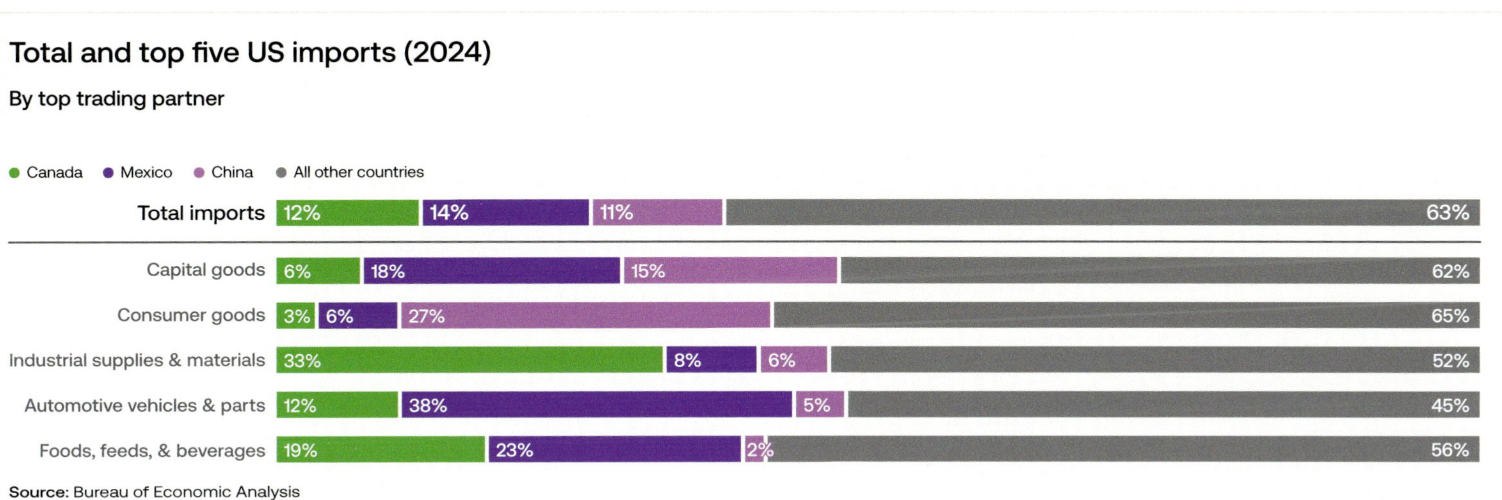

Which countries receive the most US exports?

In 2024, Canada received nearly 14% of all US exports, the most of any nation. Mexico was the second largest destination, followed by China. Together, these countries accounted for about one-third of total US exports. The leading US export category was industrial supplies; Mexico purchased 17% of these goods. Canada bought another 14%.

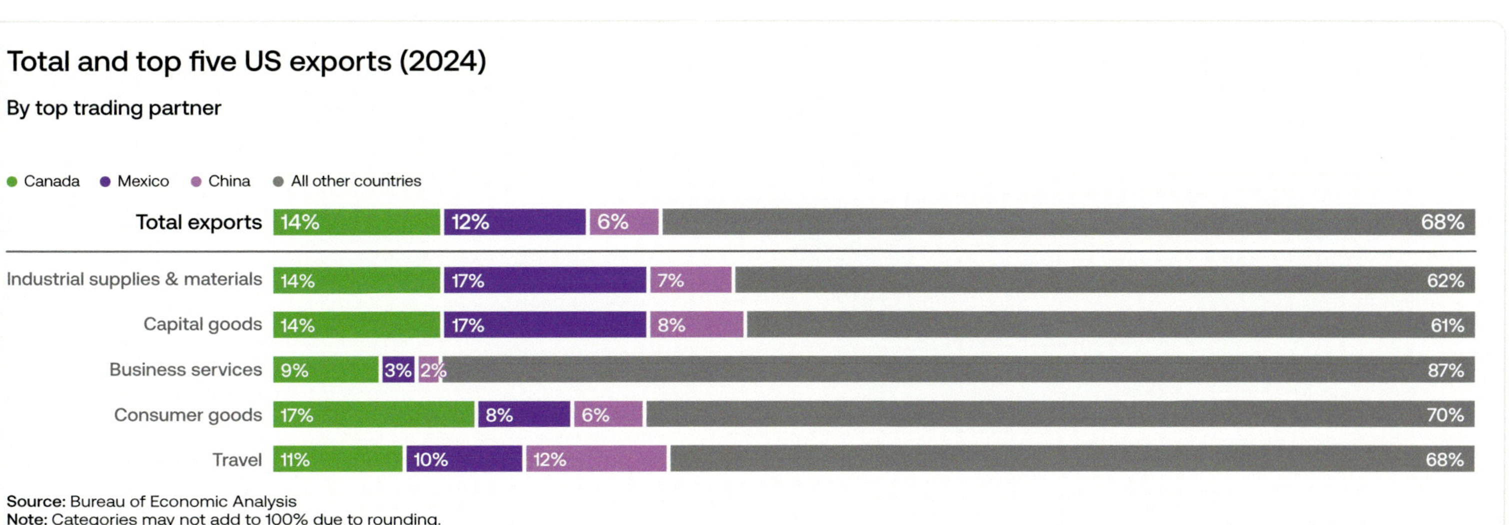

At what rate are imports taxed?

The average effective tariff rate shows how much the US collects in customs duties as a percentage of the total value of imported goods. Customs duties include tariffs on goods and other import fees. It estimates how much tariffs cost, on average, across all goods brought into the country. Imports may have different tariff rates (or none at all) depending on a range of factors, including country of origin, product type, trade agreements, value, and quantity.

From 1891 to 1933, the average effective tariff rate was about 19%. The rate mostly decreased over the next several decades, until it increased from 2018 to 2021. In 2024, the rate decreased to 2.3% from 2.4% in 2023. The data does not yet reflect recent changes in tariff policy.

Average effective tariff rate

Customs duty revenue as a share of good imports

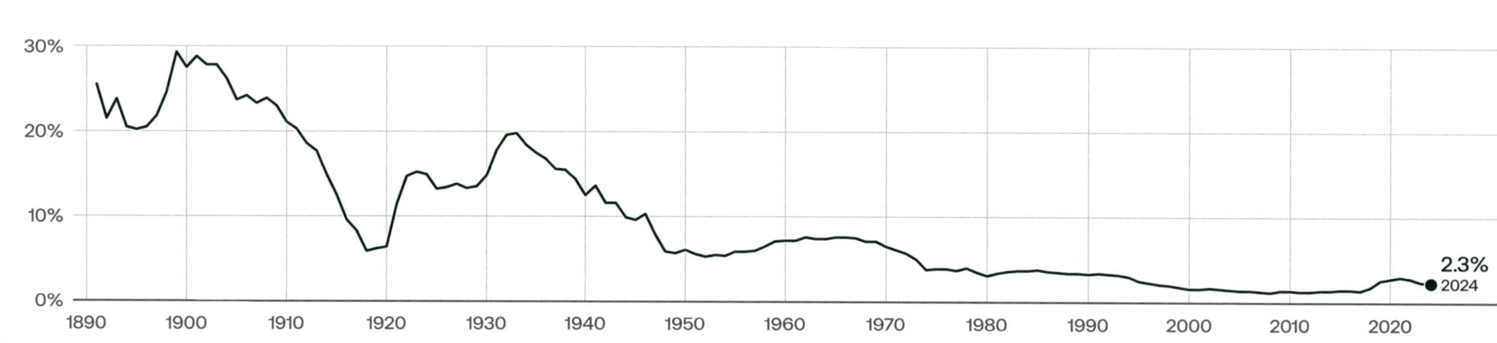

Source: US International Trade Commission

How much tariff revenue does the US collect?

In FY 2024, the federal government collected $77.0 billion in customs duties (1.6% of total federal revenue). This was down 29% from the peak of $108.2 billion in FY 2022. Since 1980, customs duties have not exceeded 2% of revenue.

Customs duties revenue

As a share of federal revenue

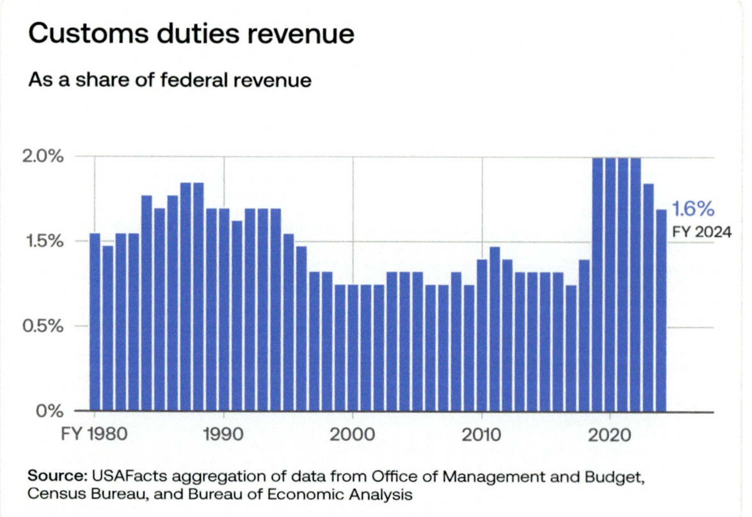

Source: USAFacts aggregation of data from Office of Management and Budget, Census Bureau, and Bureau of Economic Analysis

Customs duties revenue

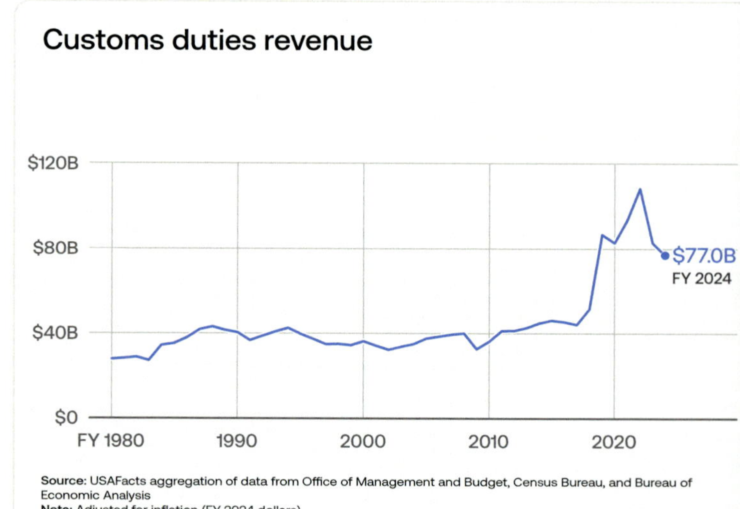

Source: USAFacts aggregation of data from Office of Management and Budget, Census Bureau, and Bureau of Economic Analysis
Note: Adjusted for inflation (FY 2024 dollars).

Chapter sources and data timeliness

Economic activity is among the most consistently and rigorously measured areas of American life and several federal agencies produce timely, detailed economic data. The Bureau of Labor Statistics, for example, releases monthly reports on inflation, employment, and job openings — core economic indicators. However, there are still gaps in the data. One notable limitation is that the federal government does not separately report revenue collected from tariffs. Instead, it combines tariff revenue with other customs-related collections under the broader category of "customs duties," making it difficult to assess the fiscal impact of specific trade policies.

Publishing agency	Program	Publication name	Data updates
Bureau of Labor Statistics	Consumer Price Index	CPI news release	Updates monthly for most recently completed month
	Current Employment Statistics	Employment Situation Summary	
	Local Area Unemployment Statistics		
	Current Population Survey		
	Job Openings and Labor Turnover Survey (JOLTS)	JOLTS news release	Updates monthly for data from two months prior
Bureau of Economic Analysis	National Income and Product Accounts	Gross domestic product	Updates quarterly for most recently completed quarter
	Regional Economic Accounts	Gross domestic product by state	
	International Transactions Accounts	US international trade in goods and services	
Federal Reserve Bank of St. Louis	FRED Economic Data	Market yield on US Treasury securities at 10-year constant maturity	Updates daily for most recently completed business day
		30-year fixed rate mortgage average in the United States	Updates weekly for most recently completed Thursday
		Personal consumption expenditures: Chain-type price index	Updates monthly for most recently completed month
Board of Governors of the Federal Reserve System	Federal Reserve Board Data	Federal funds effective rate	Updates monthly for most recently completed month
US International Trade Commission	DataWeb	US Ad Valorem Equivalent (AVE) duties & preference programs	Annually for the most recently completed year
Office of Management and Budget	President's Budget	Historical tables	Annually for the most recently completed fiscal year

See sources and notes section at the end of this report for detailed citation information.

CHAPTER 05

Immigration & border security

Immigration facts

This chapter provides the numbers to understand the foreign-born people who come to the US and the different pathways they follow. It brings together the best public data available from the agencies charged with administering and reporting on different parts of the complex immigration system.

Incoming authorized immigrants

- About 2.9 million authorized immigrants entered the US in FY 2023, up 15% from FY 2022 and a record high since at least FY 1997.
- Work is the most common reason for authorized immigration to the US (42% of immigrants in FY 2023). Of all authorized work-related entries, 36% were from Mexico.
- More than half of all authorized immigrants come either to join family (27% of all authorized immigration in FY 2023) or for education (27%). More than half of these come from Asian countries.
- Refugee admissions reached 100,000 in FY 2024, the highest level since at least FY 2001. This was 25,000 below the annual refugee cap set by the Biden administration.

Unauthorized immigration and courts

- Though asylum is a recognized process, asylum seekers are typically counted as unauthorized immigrants until their claims are approved. There were about 945,000 new asylum applications in FY 2023. About 17% of asylum decisions were approvals in FY 2023.
- The number of pending immigration court cases has increased every year since at least FY 2009, reaching a record 3.9 million in FY 2024.
- Border enforcement actions occur when people are deemed inadmissible at ports of entry or are apprehended after illegal crossings. There were 2.9 million of these actions in FY 2024, down from FY 2023's record high of 3.2 million.
- The US removed about 330,000 people in FY 2024, an 86% increase from FY 2023 but still 24% below the FY 2013 peak of 432,000.

Immigrants in the US

- About 48 million foreign-born individuals lived in the US in 2023, comprising 14.3% of the population. More than half were naturalized citizens.
- An estimated 23% of the foreign-born population were unauthorized immigrants in 2023.

Immigrants in the workforce

- The share of the US labor force that was foreign-born reached its highest level since at least 2007, at 19.2% of all workers in 2024.
- Foreign-born workers were most common in the construction industry, making up 29% of those employed.
- Work visas granted fell to 1.1 million in FY 2024 from their 25-year peak in FY 2023. Around 29% were for temporary agricultural (H-2A) workers. There were also 220,000 H-1B visas (20% of all work visas) for workers in specialty occupations, a decline of 17% from the record-high numbers of FY 2023.

How many authorized immigrants come to the US each year?

About 2.9 million new authorized immigrants entered the US in FY 2023. Since FY 1997, about 76% of all new authorized immigrants have entered on non-tourist visas.

New authorized immigrant arrivals

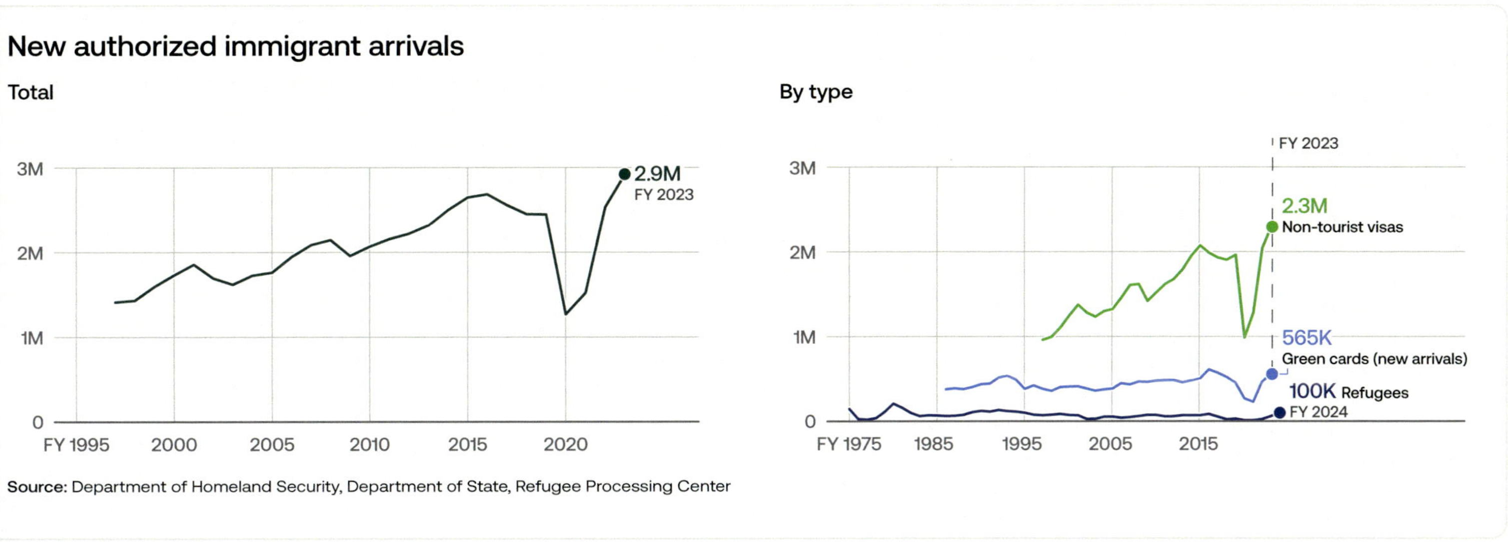

Source: Department of Homeland Security, Department of State, Refugee Processing Center

Where do authorized immigrants come from?

People from Mexico and India accounted for 41% of all authorized arrivals, outnumbering all immigrants from Africa, Europe, and South America combined. A plurality of new authorized immigrants in FY 2023 came to the US for work.

New authorized immigrant arrivals (FY 2023)

By region of birth/nationality

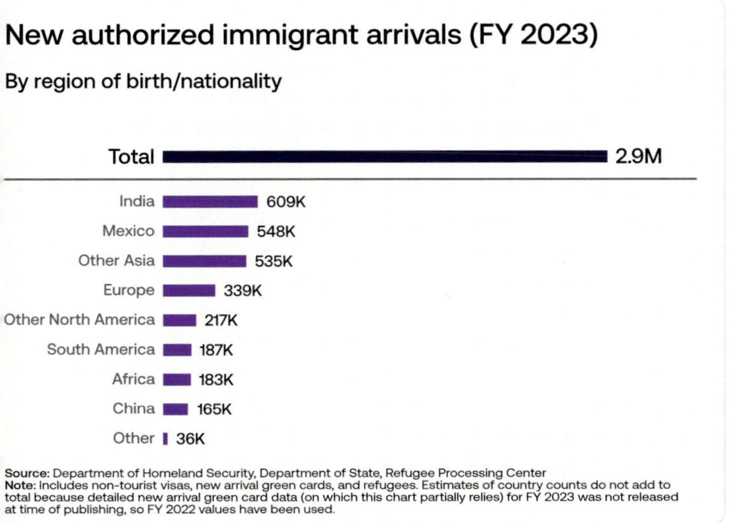

Source: Department of Homeland Security, Department of State, Refugee Processing Center
Note: Includes non-tourist visas, new arrival green cards, and refugees. Estimates of country counts do not add to total because detailed new arrival green card data (on which this chart partially relies) for FY 2023 was not released at time of publishing, so FY 2022 values have been used.

New authorized immigrant arrivals (FY 2023)

By reason for granted entry

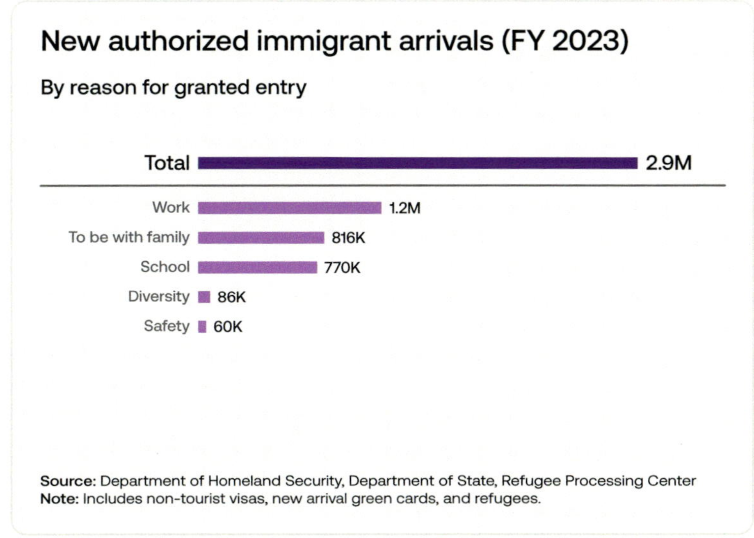

Source: Department of Homeland Security, Department of State, Refugee Processing Center
Note: Includes non-tourist visas, new arrival green cards, and refugees.

Authorized immigration includes people coming to the US on temporary visas that offer no path to citizenship and allow time-limited entry for work, school, or to visit family. It also includes people sponsored for visas by a relative or employer, refugees, and winners of the diversity visa lottery. Tourists, while authorized to enter the US, are not immigrants and are excluded from this analysis.

Where do authorized immigrant workers and students come from?

In FY 2023, 1.2 million people, or 42% of all authorized immigrants, came to the US for work. A plurality of these were of Mexican nationality (36%).[iv] The number of workers arriving from Mexico quadrupled between FY 2010 (when they were at a low) and FY 2023, compared to the 64% growth in workers coming from all other countries over the same period.

About 27% of all authorized immigrants, or 770,000 people, came to the US to study in FY 2023. The US issued 10% more education visas in FY 2023 than the prior year. Most were issued to people from Asia, who made up 55% of people entering the US to study. Thirty-one percent of education visas were issued to people from just two countries: India (19% of all education visas, up 14% from FY 2022) and China (13%, up 40%).

New authorized immigrant arrivals, by country of birth/nationality

Immigrants coming for work

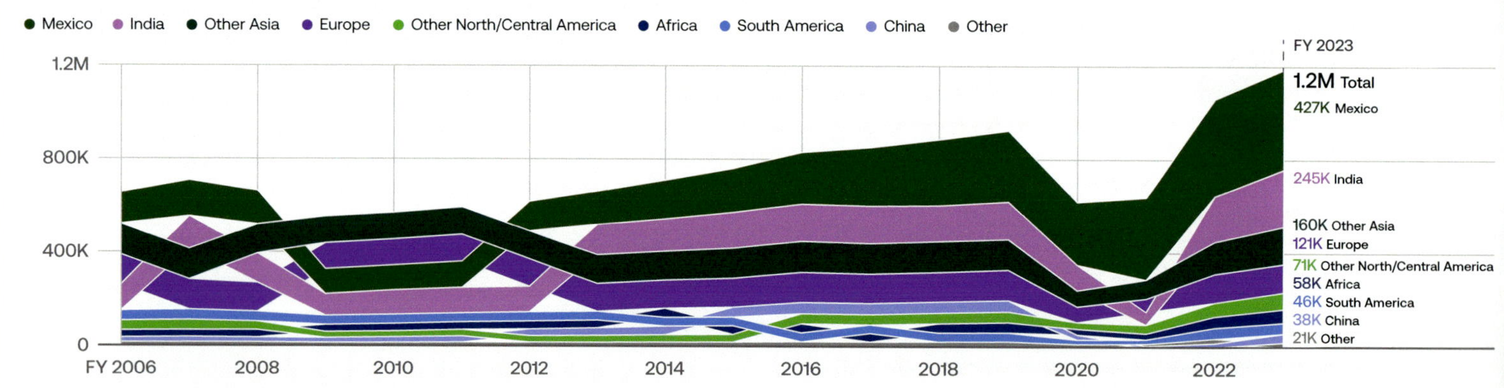

Immigrants coming for school

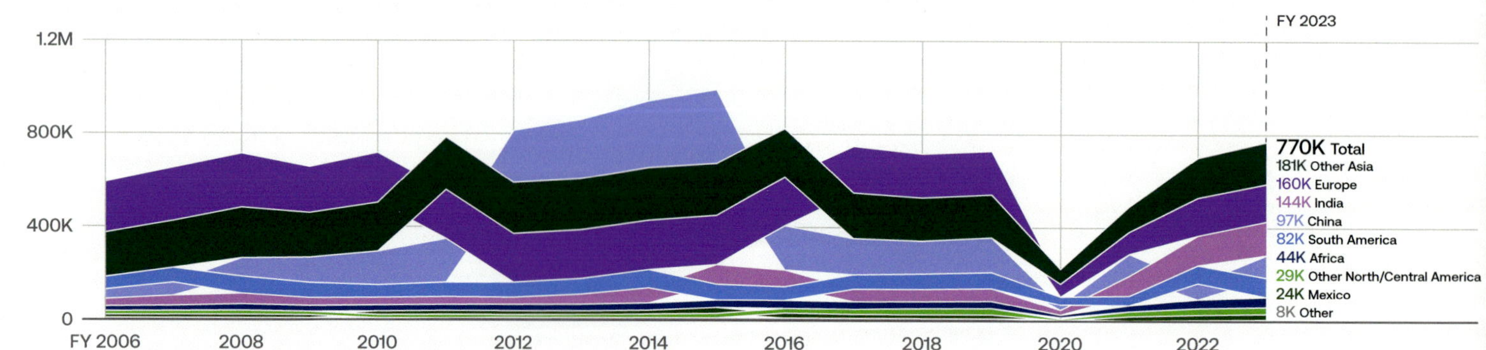

Source: Department of Homeland Security and Department of State
Note: Data includes non-tourist visas, new arrival green cards, and refugees. A change in policy in 2014 made Chinese students eligible for five-year student visas rather than one.

How has authorized family immigration changed over time?

Why else do immigrants come to the United States via authorized channels, and where do they come from?

In FY 2023, 751,000 people (about 27% of all authorized immigrants) came to the US to be with family, up 8% from FY 2022. Indians accounted for 29% of these immigrants; the 220,000 authorized Indian immigrants were the most of any nationality and up 33% from FY 2022. People from Asian countries besides India and China (19% of all family visas), Mexico (13%), and elsewhere in North and Central America (15%) also came to be with family. Immigrants from Europe and South America fell by 7% and 6%, respectively.

Four percent of all authorized immigrants, or 113,000 people, came to the US for reasons other than work, family, or school in FY 2023. Nearly half came from Asian countries besides China and India and 24% were refugees from this region. African immigrants accounted for a third of this group; 66% came as refugees and 34% entered with diversity visas.

2023 green card data from the Department of Homeland Security describing new arrivals, countries of origin, and reasons for migration was not available as of publishing in August 2025, so these charts replicate the 2022 data for 2023. See chart notes on page 105 for more detail.

Immigrants coming for family

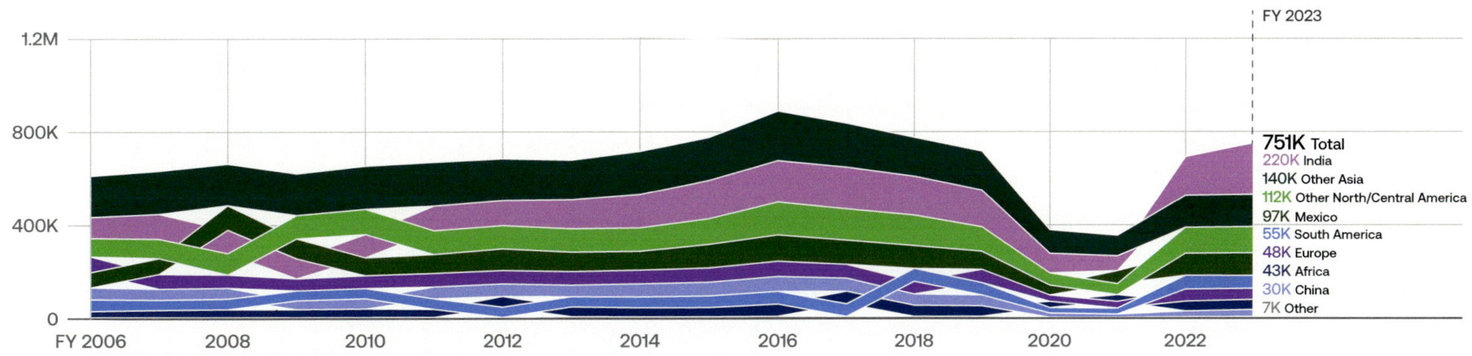

FY 2023
751K Total
220K India
140K Other Asia
112K Other North/Central America
97K Mexico
55K South America
48K Europe
43K Africa
30K China
7K Other

Immigrants coming for reasons other than work, family, or school

Please note difference in chart Y-axis scale (for legibility)

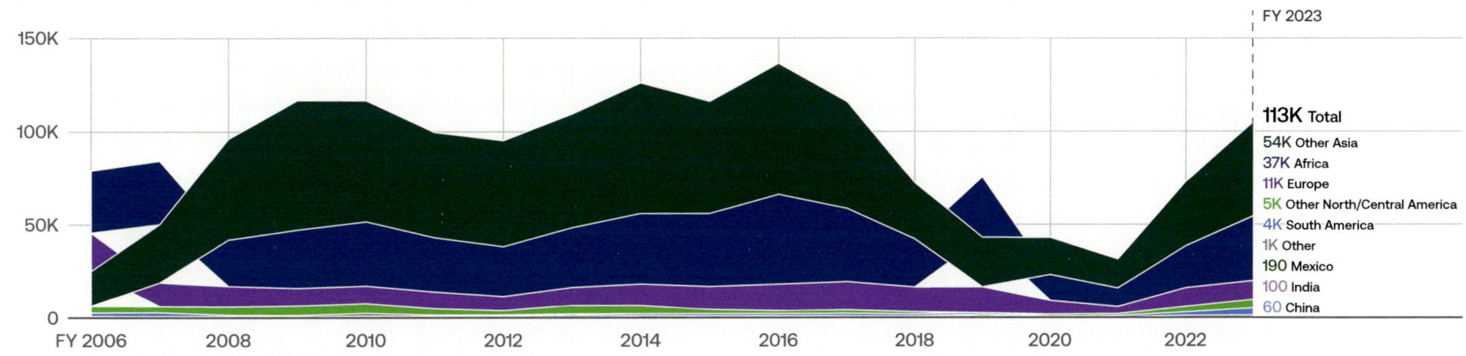

FY 2023
113K Total
54K Other Asia
37K Africa
11K Europe
5K Other North/Central America
4K South America
1K Other
190 Mexico
100 India
60 China

How have reasons for authorized immigration changed over time?

Employment has been the largest driver of authorized immigration to the US since FY 2017, accounting for 42% of admissions in FY 2023. This hasn't always been the case: from FY 2008 to FY 2015, work was the third most common reason for admission, trailing both entries granted for education and to be with family. A 2014 policy change made Chinese students eligible for five-year (rather than one-year) student visas, which explains at least part of the decline in new student visas issued between 2015 and 2016.

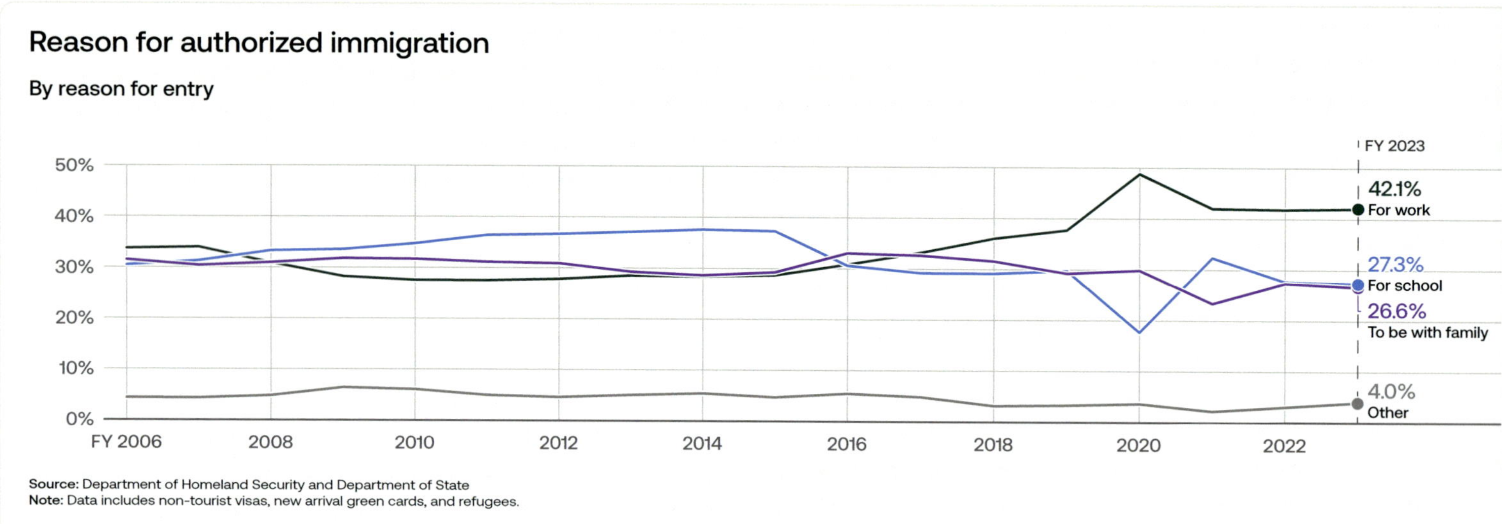

How many refugees come to the US each year?

About 100,000 refugees were admitted in FY 2024, the most since at least FY 2001. Refugees are people who have left their homes due to persecution or fear of it to seek safety elsewhere; they must apply and be accepted for admission to the US before arrival.[v] In FY 2023, 45% of refugees came from Asia and 41% from Africa. Each year, the president caps the number of refugees who can enter the US. In October 2024, President Biden officially set the refugee ceiling for FY 2025 at 125,000.[vi] However, in January 2025, President Trump issued an executive order temporarily suspending all refugee resettlement.[vii]

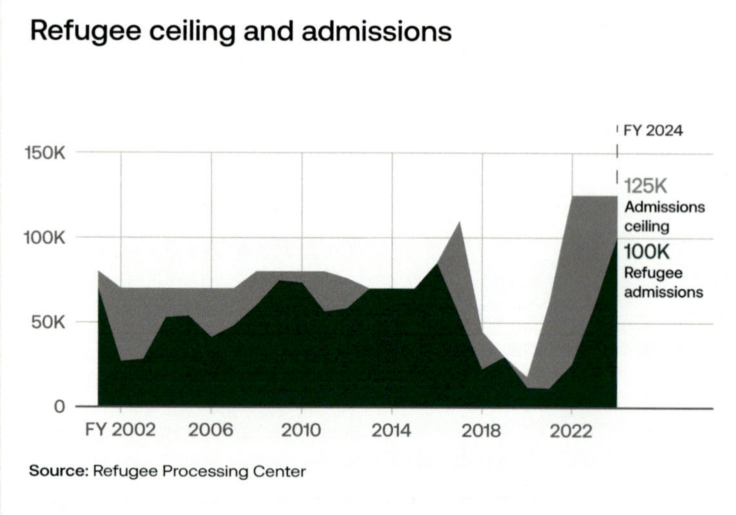

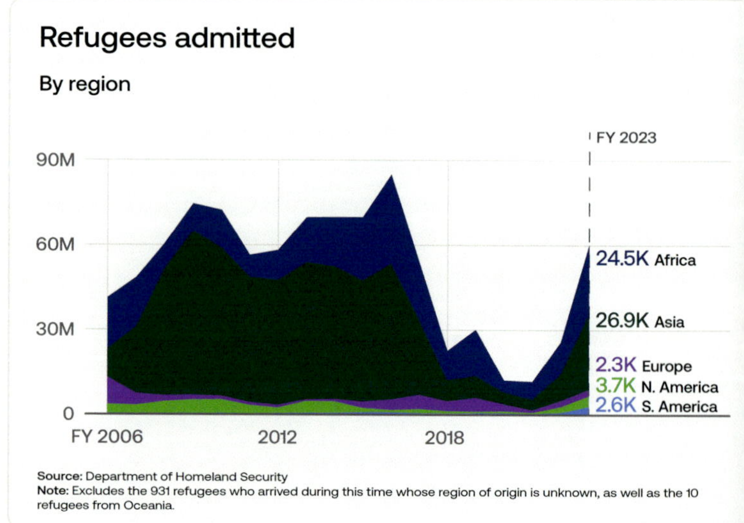

How many people are encountered by US Customs and Border Protection (CBP)?

Border enforcement actions fell to 2.9 million in FY 2024, down from a record high 3.2 million in FY 2023. In June 2025, there were about 25,000 enforcement actions, down 88% from June 2024. Total enforcement actions are the sum of individuals deemed inadmissible at ports of entry by the Office of Field Operations (OFO) and people who are apprehended after crossing the border between legal ports of entry by US Border Patrol (USBP). Between 2020 and 2023, enforcement also included people expelled during the pandemic under Title 42 of the US code.

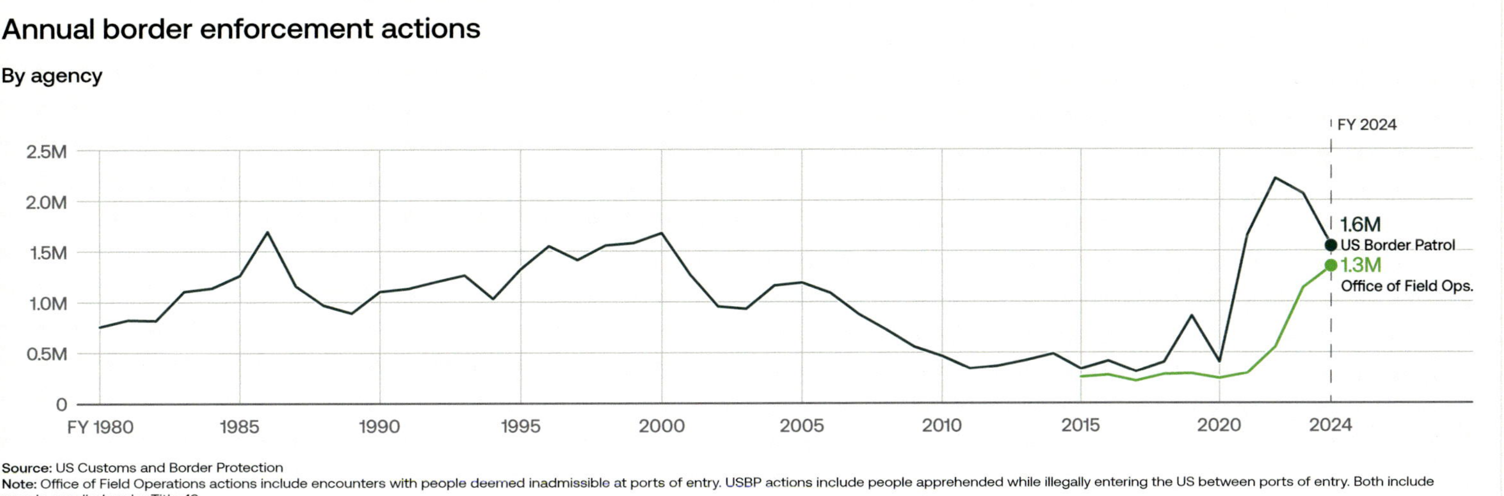

Source: US Customs and Border Protection
Note: Office of Field Operations actions include encounters with people deemed inadmissible at ports of entry. USBP actions include people apprehended while illegally entering the US between ports of entry. Both include people expelled under Title 42.

Monthly border enforcement actions

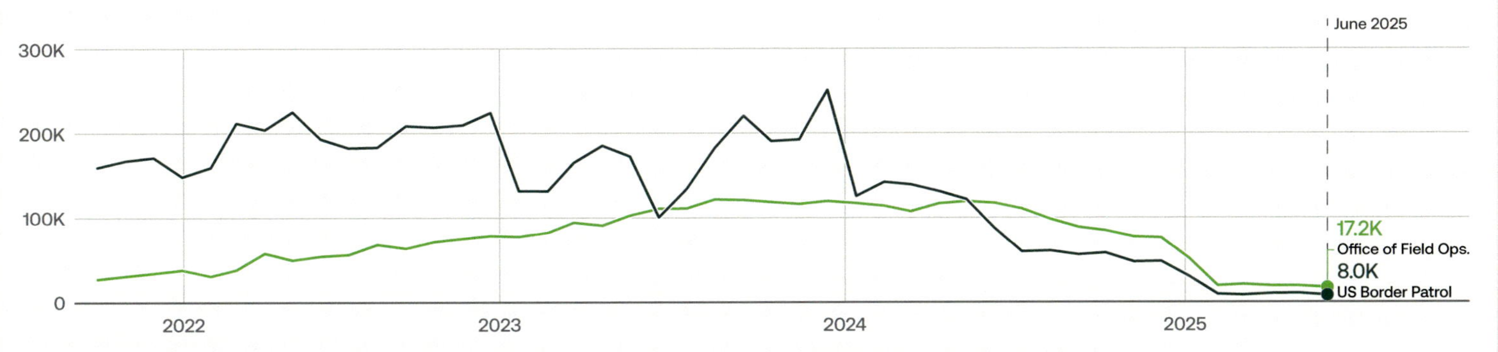

Source: US Customs and Border Protection
Note: Office of Field Operations actions include encounters with people deemed inadmissible at ports of entry. USBP actions include people apprehended while illegally entering the US between ports of entry. Both include people expelled under Title 42.

Unauthorized immigrants include: 1) Foreign-born people who are here in violation of our laws, like people who have crossed into the US undetected or have overstayed their temporary visas; 2) Noncitizens, referred to as *aliens* in US immigration law, lawfully released into the US while waiting for their asylum cases to be heard; 3) Noncitizens who are not otherwise eligible for admission but are paroled into the country for urgent humanitarian reasons or for the public benefit; and 4) People granted temporary relief from removal under programs like Temporary Protected Status (TPS) or Deferred Action for Childhood Arrivals (DACA).

What happens to unauthorized immigrants encountered by CBP along the southwest border?

In FY 2024, 2.1 million enforcement actions — 74% of the total — happened along the southwest land border. Of the 1.5 million people encountered by USBP and the 600,000 deemed inadmissible by OFO at border posts, 66% were released or paroled[viii] into the US and 14% were removed. The remaining 20% were transferred to Immigration and Customs Enforcement (ICE) or the Department of Health and Human Services for further processing. Enforcement actions away from the southwest border took place at airports (15%), the northern land border (7%), and coastal borders (4%).

Outcomes of southwest border encounters (FY 2024)

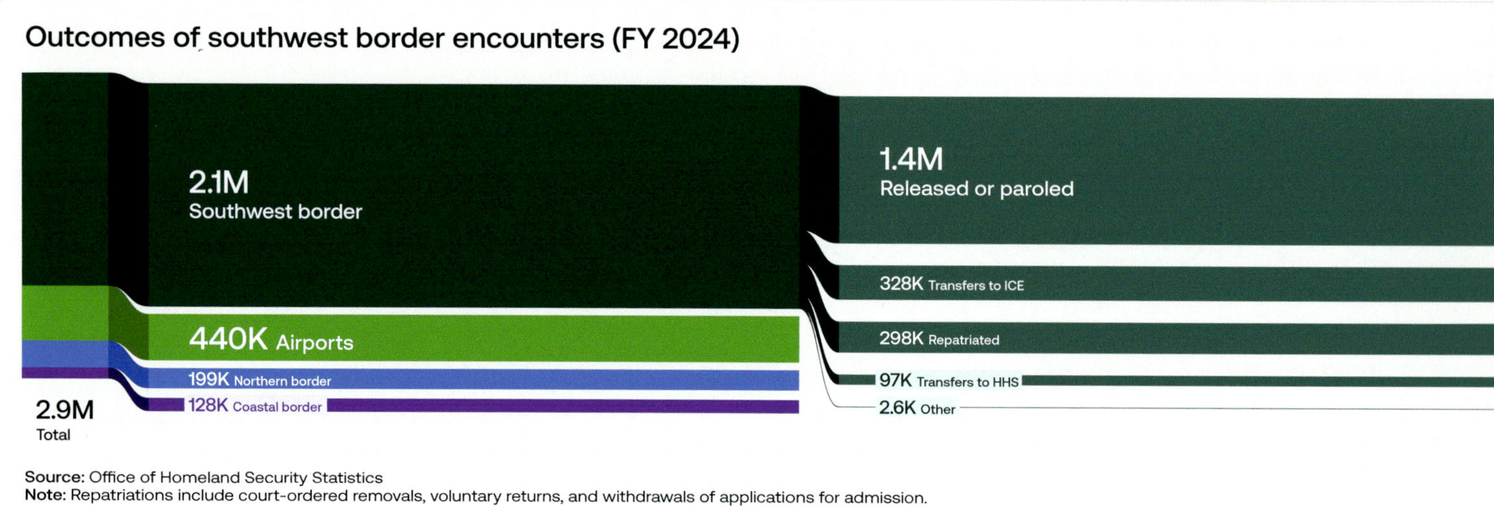

Source: Office of Homeland Security Statistics
Note: Repatriations include court-ordered removals, voluntary returns, and withdrawals of applications for admission.

Why are unauthorized immigrants sometimes permitted to enter the US?

People who would otherwise not be legally permitted to enter the US may sometimes be allowed into the country on a temporary basis and are counted amongst the unauthorized immigrant population. For example, people presenting at ports of entry or encountered at the border who may be eligible for asylum can be released into the country while waiting for their cases to be heard in immigration court.

People may also be let into the US through the parole process. Parolees are permitted to enter for urgent humanitarian reasons (e.g., medical treatment or family reunification); when their presence is a significant public benefit (e.g., testifying in criminal trial proceedings); through special programs offered to certain populations (e.g., the Central American Minors program); or when they're from specially designated countries in turmoil like Ukraine (through the U4U program) or Cuba, Haiti, Nicaragua, and Venezuela (through the CHNV program).[ix] Parole is granted at the discretion of immigration authorities, typically for a set period, and does not confer legal status (although parolees can pursue legal status through other channels). In January 2025, President Trump issued an executive order requiring a review of existing parole programs and policies.[x]

What is the asylum process?

Asylees are people who are unwilling or unable to return to their country of origin, either due to persecution or fear of it. Unlike refugees who must obtain permission to enter the US before arrival, asylum seekers must already be present in the country or seeking admission at a port of entry and must request asylum within one year of arriving.

There are two kinds of asylum applications: affirmative and defensive.[xi] Affirmative asylum claims are filed proactively by both authorized and unauthorized immigrants who are not in removal proceedings and are handled by US Citizenship and Immigration Services asylum officers. Defensive asylum may be claimed by people in removal proceedings as a defense against deportation. A defensive asylum filer may remain in the US as an unauthorized immigrant while waiting for their case to be resolved in immigration court and can receive a temporary work permit once their application has been pending for 180 days.

Asylum process explained

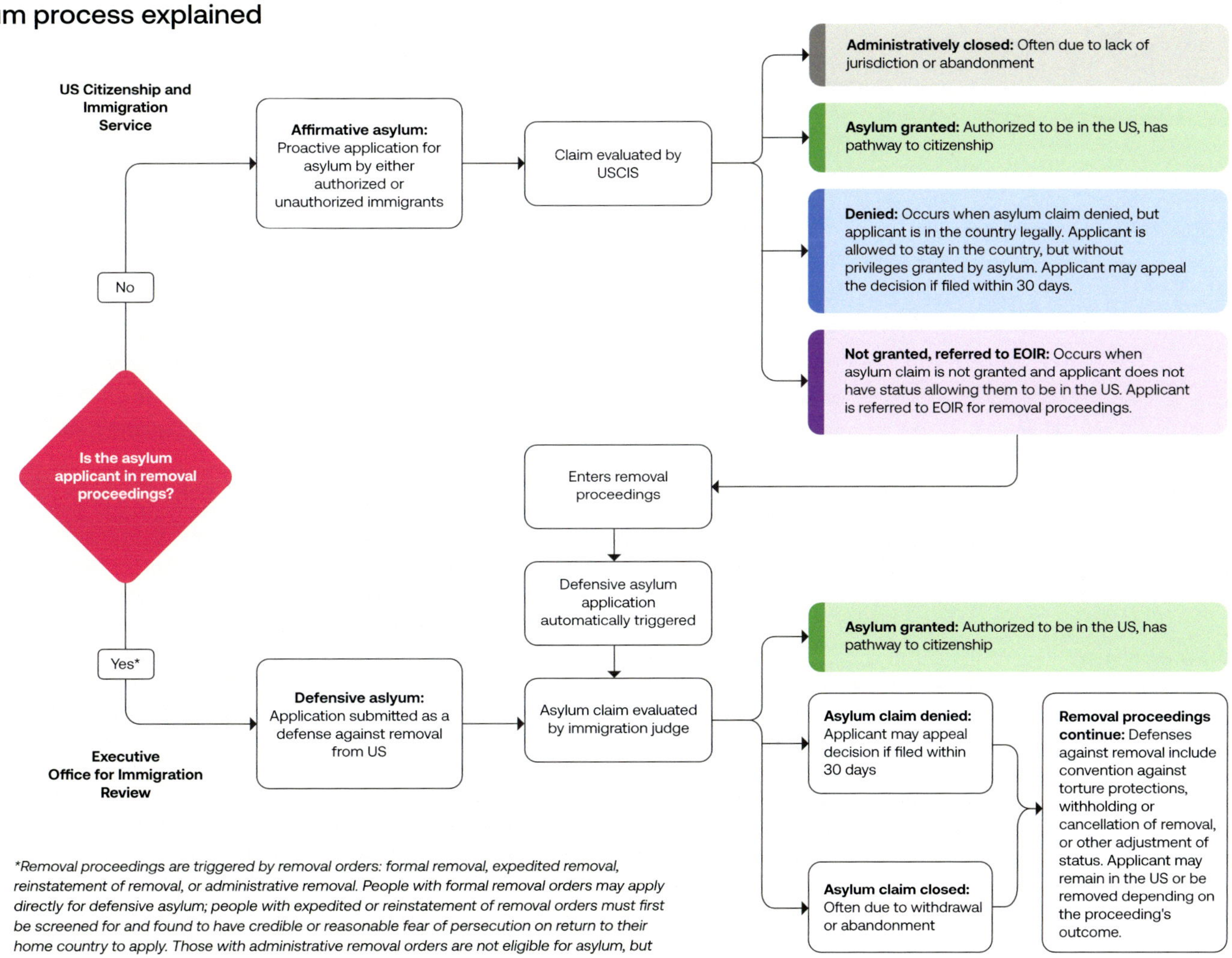

Is the asylum applicant in removal proceedings?

No → US Citizenship and Immigration Service

Affirmative asylum: Proactive application for asylum by either authorized or unauthorized immigrants

Claim evaluated by USCIS

- **Administratively closed:** Often due to lack of jurisdiction or abandonment
- **Asylum granted:** Authorized to be in the US, has pathway to citizenship
- **Denied:** Occurs when asylum claim denied, but applicant is in the country legally. Applicant is allowed to stay in the country, but without privileges granted by asylum. Applicant may appeal the decision if filed within 30 days.
- **Not granted, referred to EOIR:** Occurs when asylum claim is not granted and applicant does not have status allowing them to be in the US. Applicant is referred to EOIR for removal proceedings.

Enters removal proceedings

Defensive asylum application automatically triggered

Yes* → Executive Office for Immigration Review

Defensive asylum: Application submitted as a defense against removal from US

Asylum claim evaluated by immigration judge

- **Asylum granted:** Authorized to be in the US, has pathway to citizenship
- **Asylum claim denied:** Applicant may appeal decision if filed within 30 days
- **Asylum claim closed:** Often due to withdrawal or abandonment

Removal proceedings continue: Defenses against removal include convention against torture protections, withholding or cancellation of removal, or other adjustment of status. Applicant may remain in the US or be removed depending on the proceeding's outcome.

**Removal proceedings are triggered by removal orders: formal removal, expedited removal, reinstatement of removal, or administrative removal. People with formal removal orders may apply directly for defensive asylum; people with expedited or reinstatement of removal orders must first be screened for and found to have credible or reasonable fear of persecution on return to their home country to apply. Those with administrative removal orders are not eligible for asylum, but may have other defenses available.*

How many asylum applications does the US receive?

FY 2023 asylum applications totaled about 945,000, up 88% from FY 2022 and more than six times higher than in FY 2015, the earliest year of available data from the Department of Homeland Security (DHS).

Asylum application cases received

By type

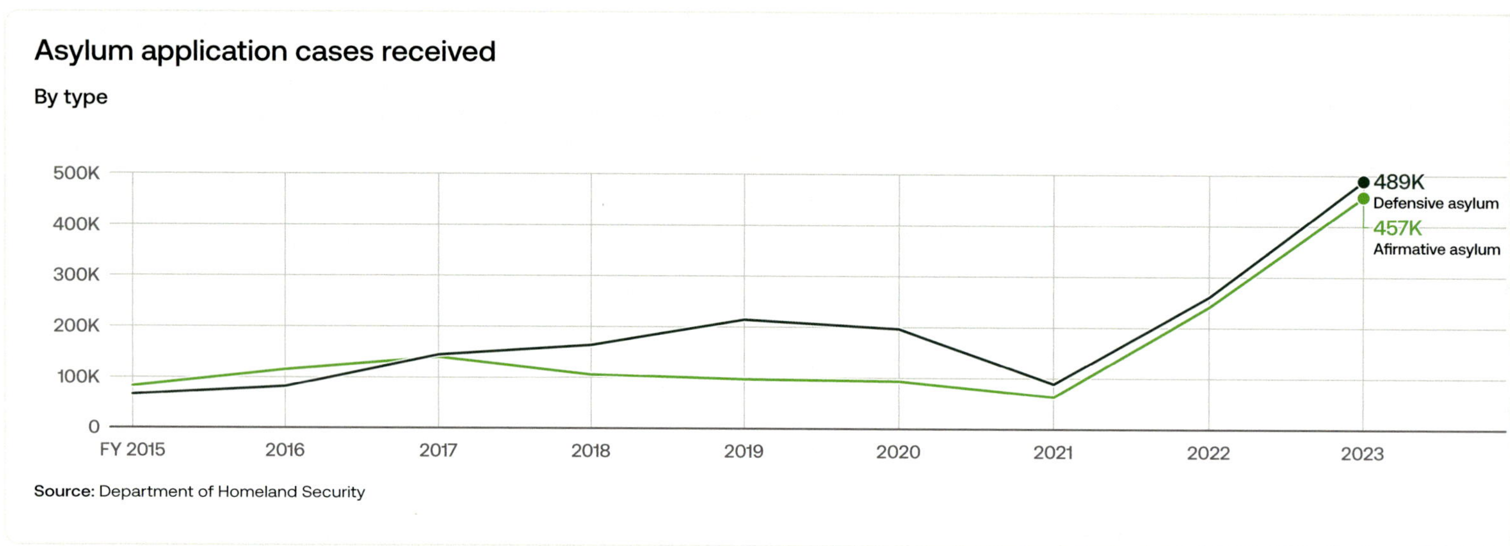

Source: Department of Homeland Security

How many people are granted asylum?

About 54,000 people were granted asylum in FY 2023, the most of any year since at least FY 2006, and a 52% increase from FY 2022. About 53% of asylees were from Asia, and 20% were from North America. Among countries, the increase in Afghan asylees in the aftermath of the US withdrawal is notable: from 110 asylees in FY 2021 to 1,240 in FY 2022 to 14,470 in FY 2023, the most of any single country and nearly triple the number from China, the second most common country for asylees. Of all asylum applications that were decided in FY 2023, 17% were granted, down from the high of 28% in FY 2014.

Individuals granted affirmative or defensive asylum

By region

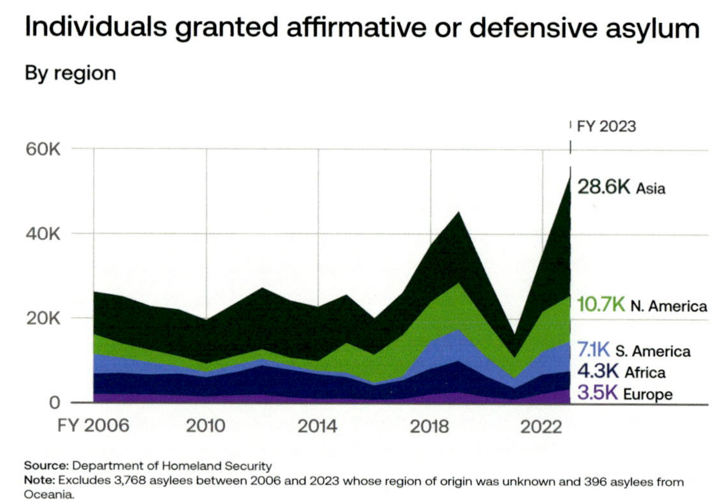

Source: Department of Homeland Security
Note: Excludes 3,768 asylees between 2006 and 2023 whose region of origin was unknown and 396 asylees from Oceania.

Decisions for asylum cases

Among affirmative and defensive asylum cases closed each year

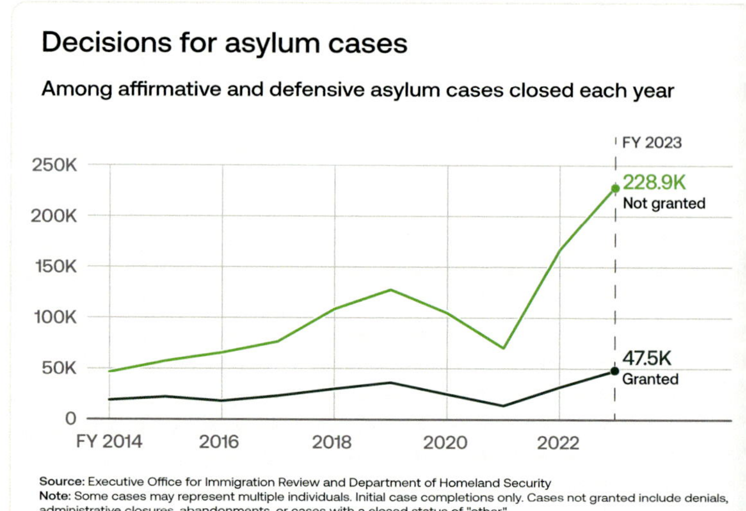

Source: Executive Office for Immigration Review and Department of Homeland Security
Note: Some cases may represent multiple individuals. Initial case completions only. Cases not granted include denials, administrative closures, abandonments, or cases with a closed status of "other".

How many immigration cases are received and completed?

Starting in FY 2009 and for each year since, immigration courts have received more new cases than they completed. The largest gap was recorded in FY 2024, when 1.1 million more cases were received than completed.

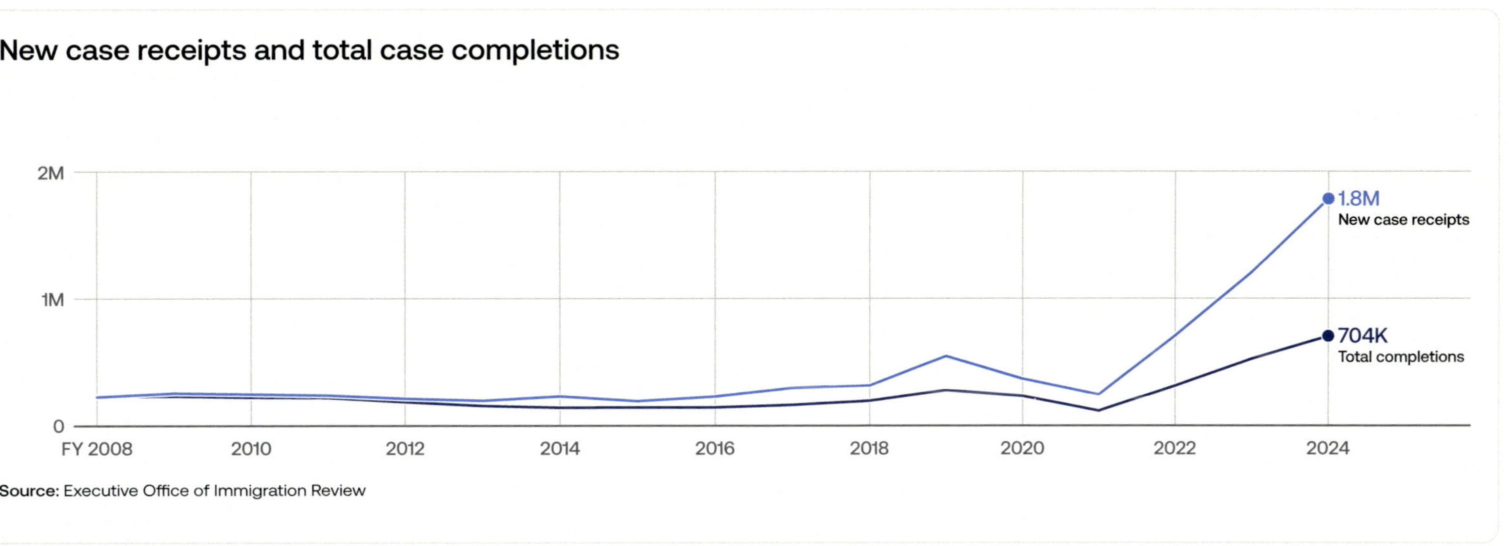

Are immigration courts keeping up with their caseloads?

In FY 2024, the backlog of pending immigration court cases grew to 3.9 million, up 40% from the prior year. The number of pending cases per judge reached a record high of 5,331 in FY 2024, more than double the number in FY 2015 (the earliest available data).

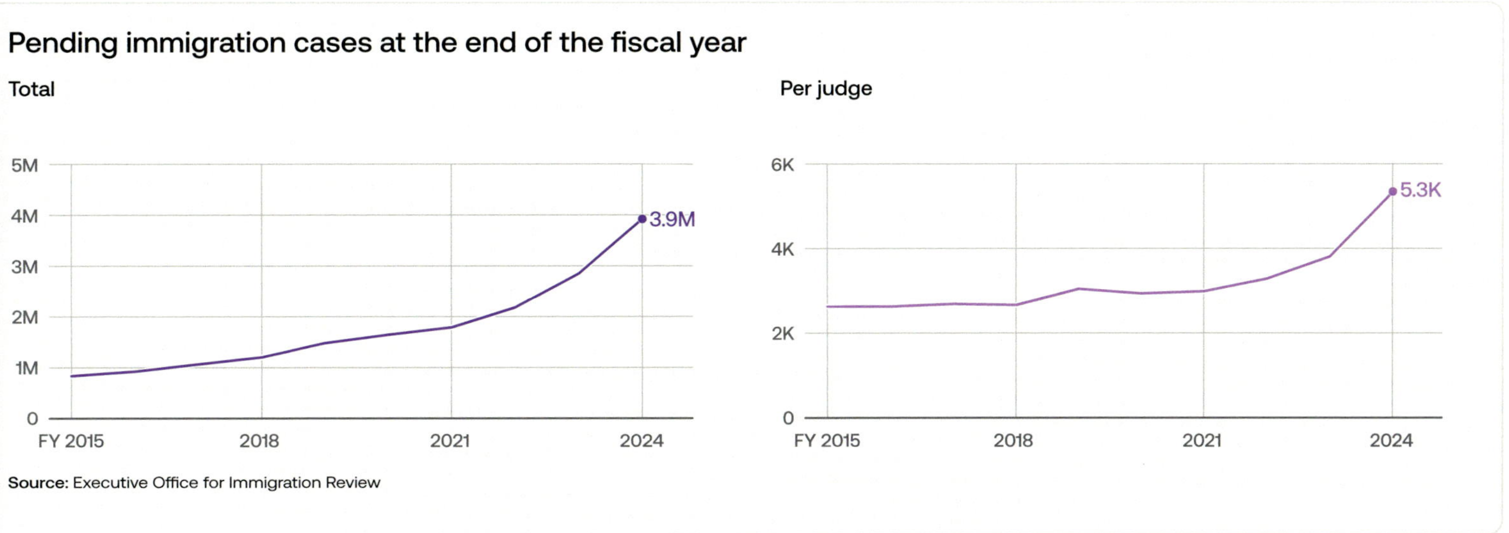

Immigration courts handle cases of people charged with violating federal immigration law. Their proceedings are civil rather than criminal. The system is administered by the Executive Office of Immigration Review (EOIR). Judges determine whether an immigrant may remain or must leave the US, with cases ranging from asylum protections to credible fear reviews to adjustments of or loss of immigration status to detention and bond decisions.[xii]

How many people does Immigration and Customs Enforcement (ICE) arrest?

The Enforcement and Removal Operations (ERO) division of ICE is charged with enforcing immigration law in the US interior. In FY 2024, ERO administratively arrested about 113,000 people for violating immigration law, down 34% from FY 2023. Administrative arrests are based on civil violations of immigration law and are independent of the arrestee's criminal history.

Administrative arrests by ICE Enforcement and Removal Operations

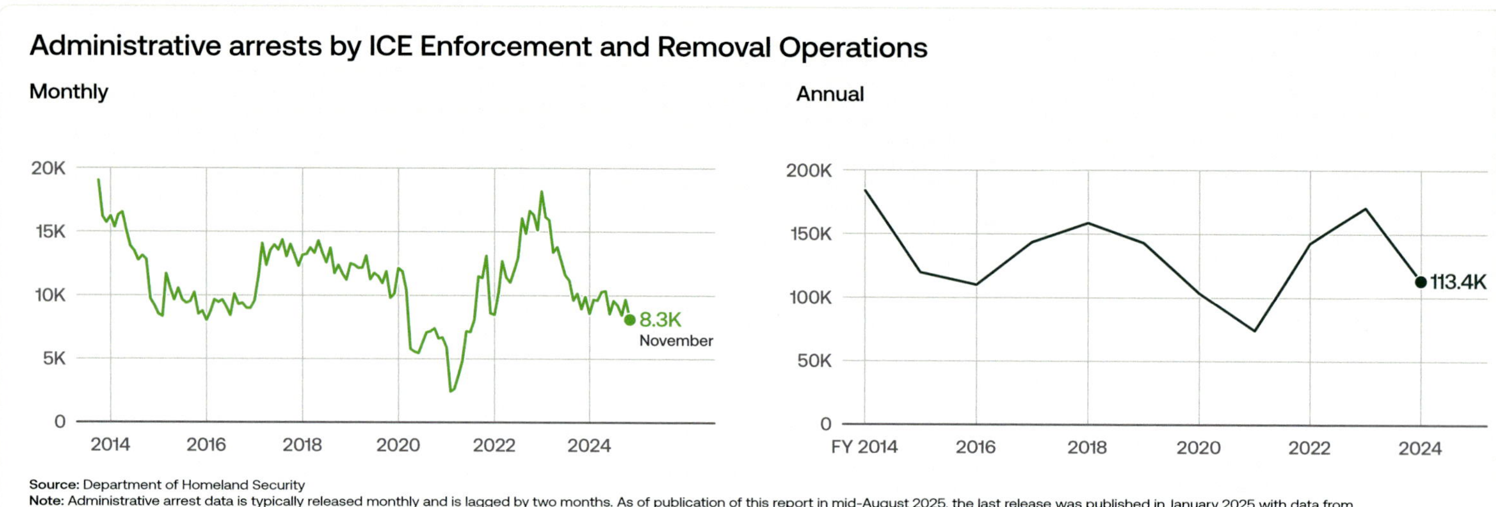

Source: Department of Homeland Security
Note: Administrative arrest data is typically released monthly and is lagged by two months. As of publication of this report in mid-August 2025, the last release was published in January 2025 with data from November 2024.

How many immigrants are removed or returned from the US?

Removal (also called "deportation") proceedings occur when a noncitizen, referred to as an *alien* in US immigration law, violates US immigration law and receives a removal order from an immigration judge. About 330,000 people were removed from the US in FY 2024, up 86% from FY 2023 but 24% below the 2013 peak. Returns count people who leave the US voluntarily and do not carry the same legal penalties as removals. Returns increased by less than 1% in FY 2024 to 448,000 after a post-1950 record increase of 70% in 2023, but they remain 73% below the 2000 peak of 1.7 million.

Noncitizen removals

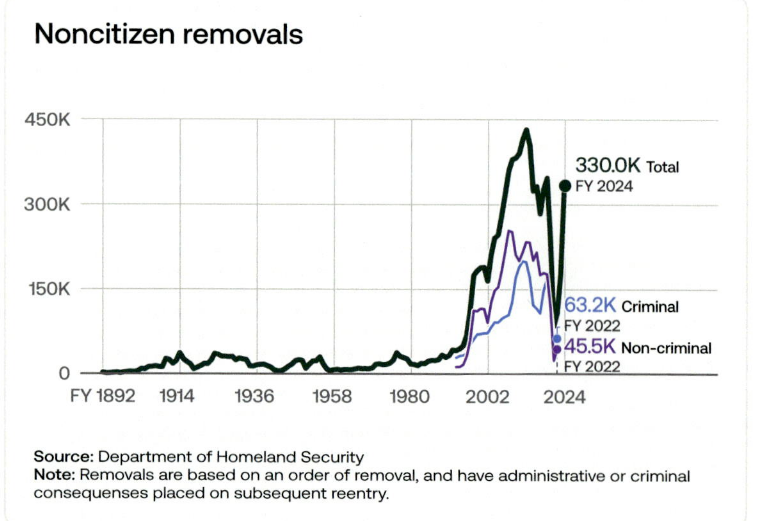

Source: Department of Homeland Security
Note: Removals are based on an order of removal, and have administrative or criminal consequenses placed on subsequent reentry.

Noncitizen returns

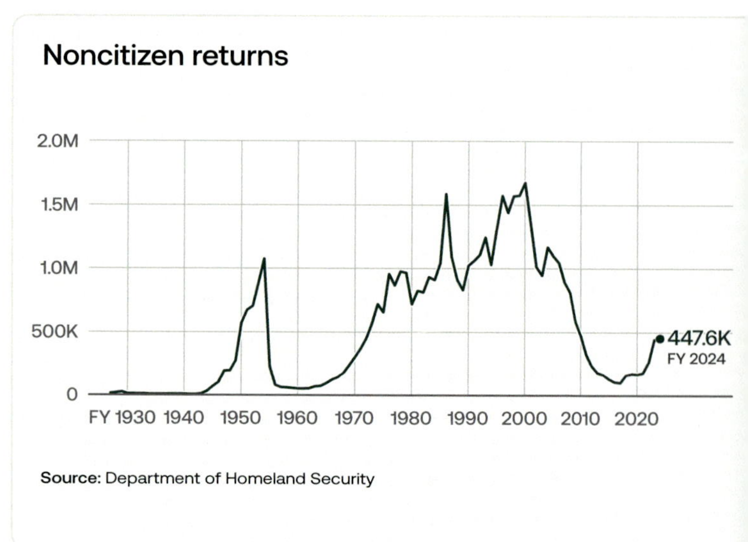

Source: Department of Homeland Security

How many immigrants live in the US?

In 2023, about 48 million people living in the US had been born in another country. Of these, more than half were naturalized citizens. Numbers on unauthorized immigrants — a subset of the non-naturalized population — are less recent: the Department of Homeland Security estimated 11.0 million unauthorized immigrants lived in the US in 2022.

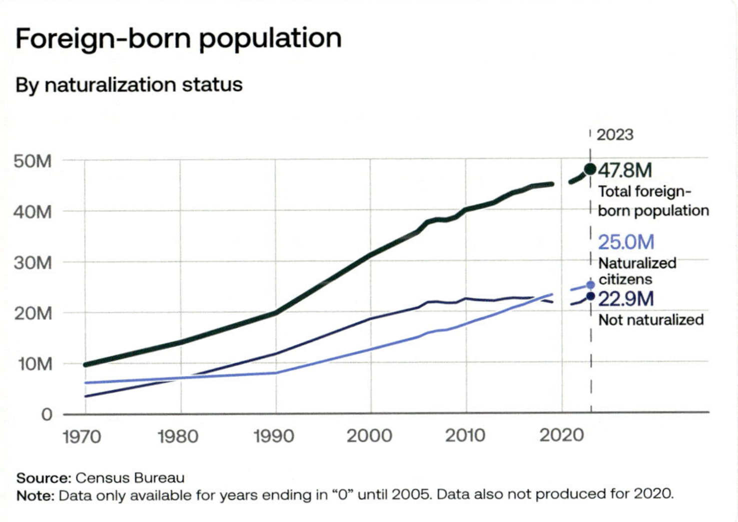

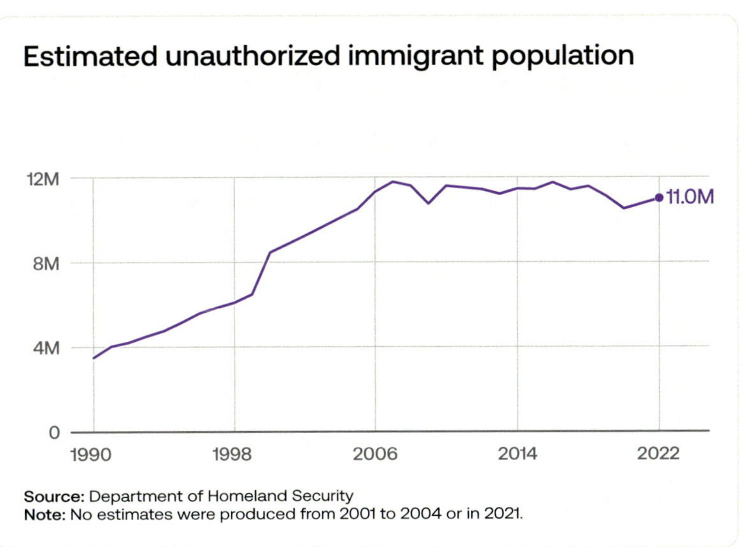

How does the immigrant population compare to the native-born population?

Immigrants made up 14.3% of the population in 2023. Immigrants were more likely than the native-born population to be of prime working age (25–54), 54.2% to 36.4%, and were less likely to be in school, 11.7% to 25.9%.

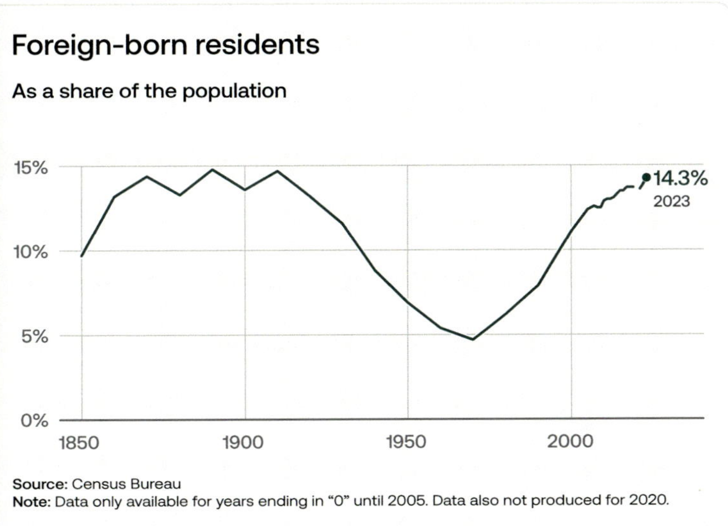

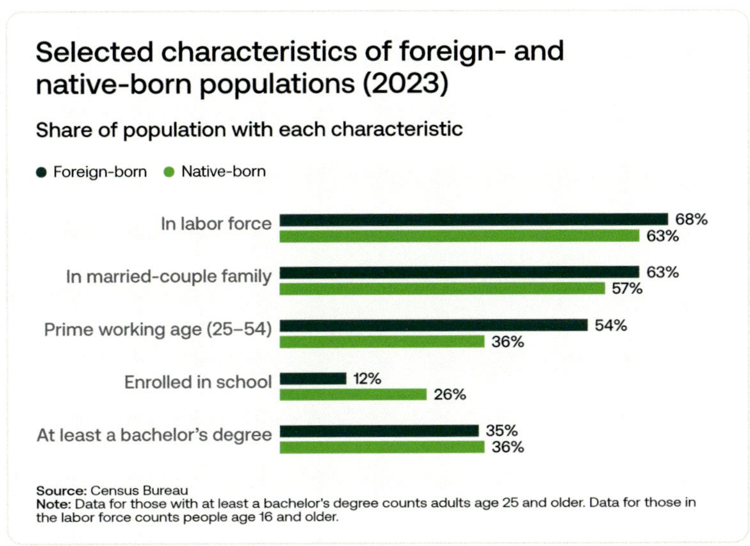

How does workforce participation compare between native-born and foreign-born people?

In 2024, the labor force participation rate (the share of people who are employed or looking for work) averaged 66.5% for foreign-born people and 61.7% for native-born people. Unemployment rates have historically been similar — 2024 averages were 4.0% for native-born people and 4.2% for foreign-born people. From January through July 2025, the average unemployment rate for native-born people was 4.3% and 4.1% among foreign-born people.

Annual average labor force participation rate

By nativity

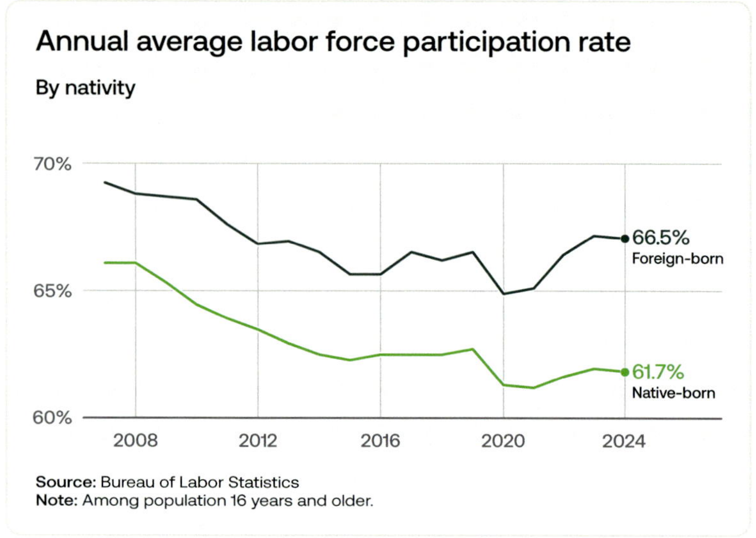

Source: Bureau of Labor Statistics
Note: Among population 16 years and older.

Annual average unemployment rate

By nativity

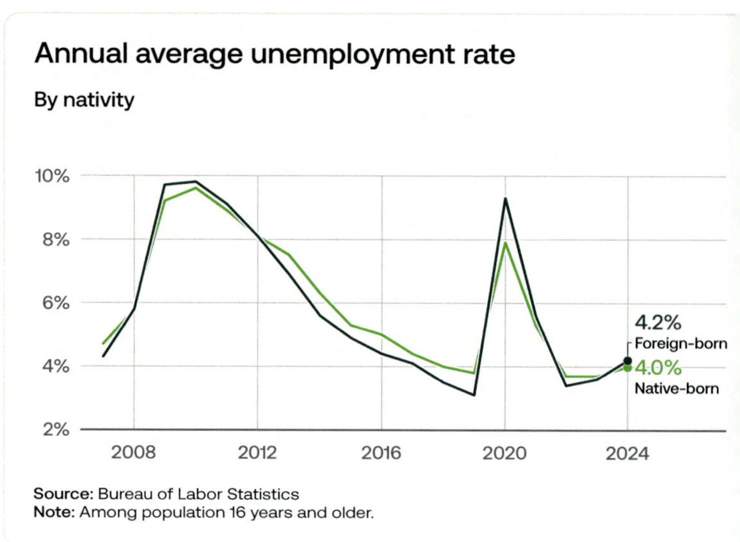

Source: Bureau of Labor Statistics
Note: Among population 16 years and older.

How many foreign-born workers are there?

The US had about 32 million foreign-born workers in 2024, making up 19.2% of the total labor force, both highs since at least 2007. The share of the labor force that's foreign-born varies across states, from a low of 2.6% in West Virginia to 32.9% in California in 2023.

Annual average civilian labor force level

Total and foreign-born

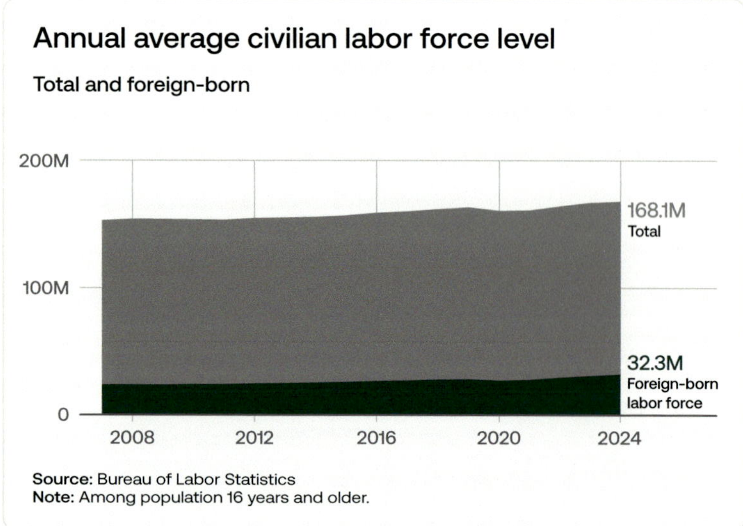

Source: Bureau of Labor Statistics
Note: Among population 16 years and older.

Percent of the civilian labor force that is foreign-born (2023)

By state

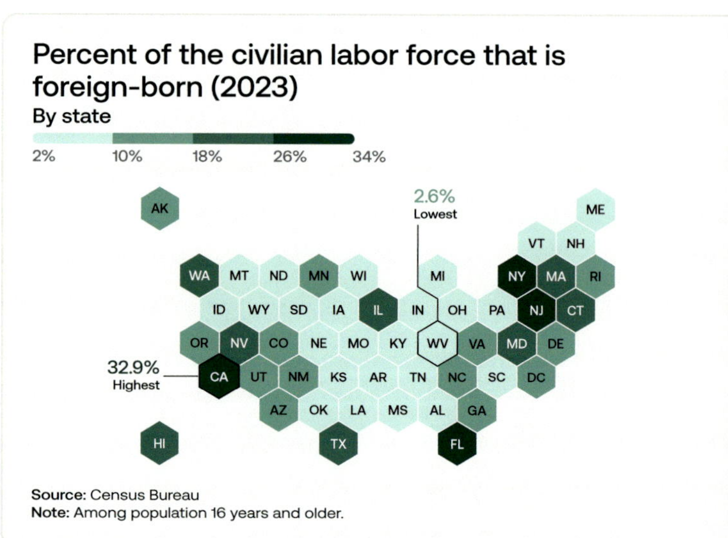

Source: Census Bureau
Note: Among population 16 years and older.

What industries rely the most on foreign-born workers?

Educational and health services employed the most foreign-born workers in 2023 — 5.5 million people, accounting for 14.8% of all workers in the sector. The industries with the biggest shares of foreign-born workers were construction (28.6% of the total), professional and business services (22.9%), and "other services," which spans 11 activities that don't fit in other sectors, including dry cleaning, ministry, grantmaking, and equipment repair (21.9%).[xiii] Foreign-born people were least represented in public administration (10.0%).

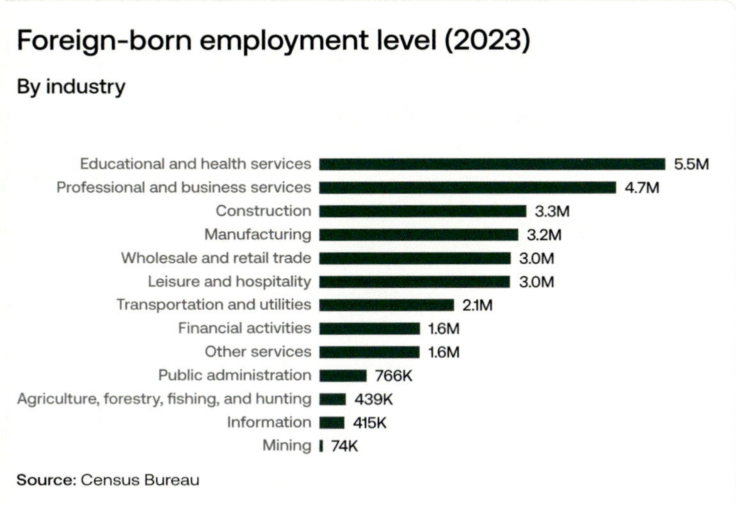

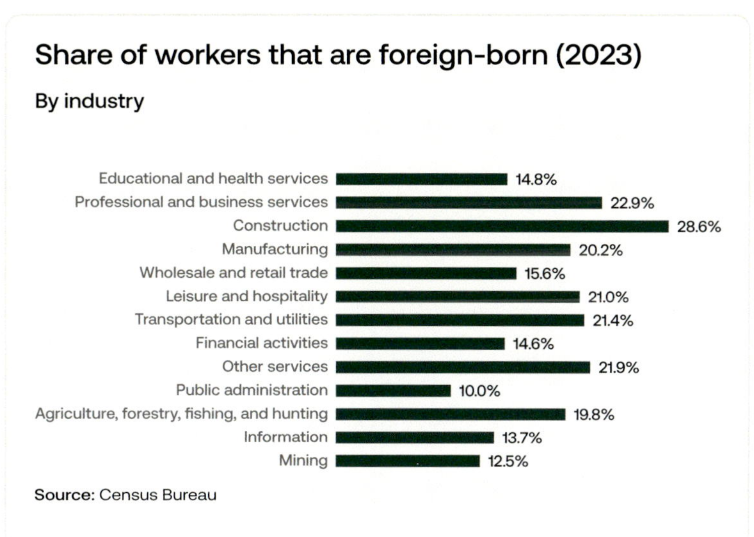

How many work visas does the US give and for what types of occupations?

The 1.1 million work visas awarded in FY 2024 (a 5% drop from FY 2023) were the second most since at least FY 1997. Around 29% of FY 2024 work visas were given to temporary agricultural (H-2A) workers, up by about 5,000 people over FY 2023. H-2B visas, which are for temporary non-agricultural workers, rose 6%, and were the only other major class of work visa that grew in FY 2024. H-1B visas for people in specialty occupations made up about 20% (220,000) of issued work visas, down 17% from a record high in FY 2023.

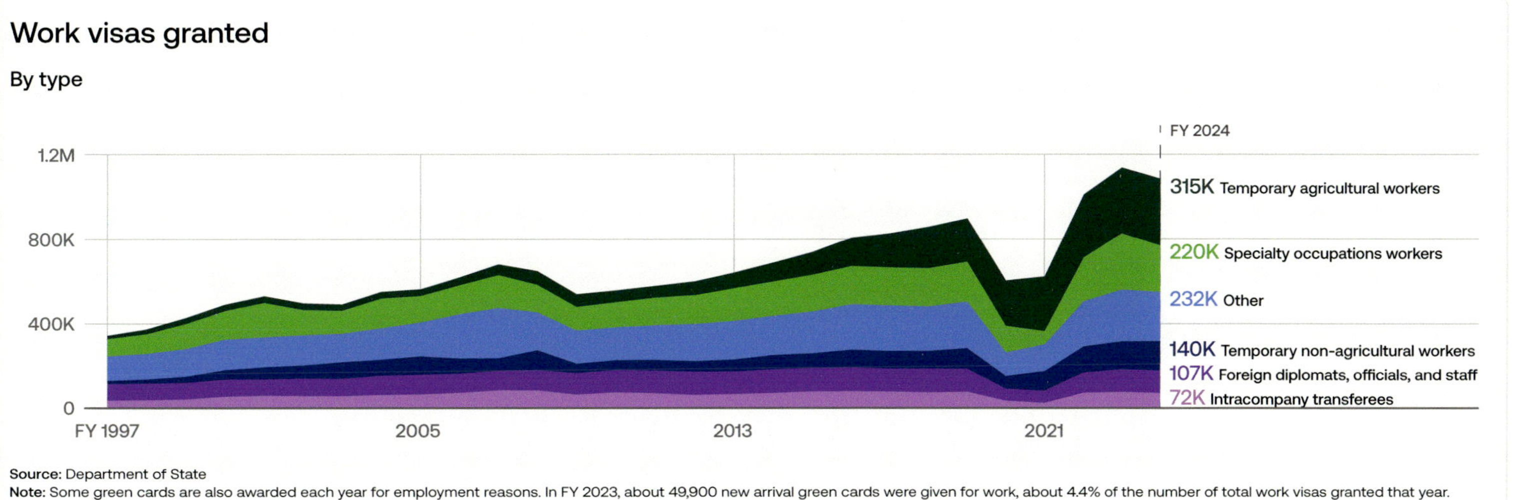

Chapter sources and data timeliness

Publishing agency	Program	Publication name	Release date	Most recent period in the data
Bureau of Consular Affairs (under Department of State)	Nonimmigrant visa statistics	Nonimmigrant worldwide issuance and refusal data by visa category	Not listed	FY 2024
		Nonimmigrant visa issuances by visa class and nationality	Not listed	FY 2024
Bureau of Labor Statistics	Current Population Survey	Employment Situation Summary	Updates monthly for most recently completed month	
Census Bureau	American Community Survey	1-year estimates	Sep. 2024	2023
		Public Use Microdata Sample	Oct. 2024	2023
	Current Population Survey, Annual Social and Economic Supplement	Foreign-born detailed tables	March 2024	2023
Citizenship and Immigration Services (within Department of Homeland Security)	Immigration and citizenship data	All USCIS application and petition form types, quarterly release	June 2025	FY 2025, Q2
Customs and Border Patrol (within Department of Homeland Security)	CBP enforcement statistics	Office of Field Operations inadmissibles	Not listed	July 2025
	Stats and summaries	Nationwide encounters	Not listed	July 2025
Executive Office for Immigration Review (within Department of Justice)	Adjudication statistics	Asylum decisions	July 2025	FY 2025, Q3
		Pending cases, new cases, and total completions	July 2025	FY 2025, Q3
		Immigration judge hiring	July 2025	FY 2025, Q3
Customs and Border Patrol (within Department of Homeland Security)		Annual Report	Dec. 2024	FY 2024
Office of Homeland Security Statistics (within Department of Homeland Security)	Immigration enforcement	Immigration enforcement and legal processes monthly tables	Jan. 2025	Nov. 2024
	Lawful permanent residents (LPRs)	LPR Yearbook tables expanded: Adjustments of status and new arrivals	Aug. 2023	FY 2022
	Refugees and asylees	Annual Flow Report	Oct. 2024	FY 2023
		Asylum workload by top twenty-five nationalities	Nov. 2023	FY 2022
	Illegal aliens	Estimates of the illegal alien population residing in the United States	April 2024	FY 2022

Office of Homeland Security Statistics (within Department of Homeland Security)	Yearbook of Immigration Statistics	Tables 1–12: Lawful permanent residents	Sep. 2024	FY 2023
		Tables 13–15: Refugees	Nov. 2024	FY 2023
		Tables 16–19: Asylees	Oct. 2024	FY 2023
		Tables 33–42: Enforcement actions	Nov. 2023	FY 2022
Refugee Processing Center (within Department of State)	Admissions and arrivals	Cumulative summary of refugee admissions	Jan. 2025	2024

See sources and notes section at the end of this report for detailed citation information.

Data in this chapter comes from nine different agencies, highlighting the diffuse nature of immigration data. The Office of Homeland Security Statistics (OHSS) synthesizes data from Immigration and Customs Enforcement (ICE), Customs and Border Patrol (CBP) — which itself brings together data from the Office of Field Operations (OFO) and Border Patrol (USBP) — the Executive Office for Immigration Review (EOIR), the Department of State, and US Citizenship and Immigration Services (USCIS). OHSS products are dependent on timely and accurate releases from the agencies that generate the source data, and they must reckon with methodological, structural, and semantic differences. In assembling this year's chapter, we noticed some specific challenges and themes:

- Some OHSS products are delayed. The Yearbook of Immigration Statistics for 2023 is partially released, notably lacking the enforcement actions tables. The asylum workload statistics that allow for disaggregated analysis are similarly delayed, as is data sorting new arrival green cards by country of origin and immigration reason. It's unclear whether the delays are happening at OHSS or the reporting agencies.
- ICE has not released data since January 2025 (although its dashboard indicates it should update quarterly), which presumably contributes to the delay in the release of the OHSS Immigration Enforcement and Legal Processes Monthly Tables. These were last released in January 2025, and prior to then had been a consistent monthly release.
- Data sources don't always define or describe populations the same way. Data on where refugees and visa recipients come from provides information by "country of nationality," and data on new arrival green card holders is given by "country of birth." To compile the data, we assume that it is equivalent, even though some people receiving green cards may have been born in one country and be a citizen of another.
- Some immigration processes and outcomes are governed by multiple agencies, like asylum (managed by EOIR and USCIS) or noncitizen removals (conducted by ICE and USBP). Understanding them requires looking at fragmented data published with different structures, documentation, and reporting timelines. OHSS often streamlines it, but waiting for OHSS to collect and clean agency data adds more wait time, bringing the source data further out of date.
- Sources across the immigration landscape vary in terms of how many years of data they present. For a given time series, additional data may exist but be difficult to find or not comparable across time, or not exist at all. In general, explanations that clarify how much historical data is available are not offered.

CHAPTER 06

Population

Population facts

The United States population grew faster in 2024 than during the previous 15 years. Birth rates remain near historic lows and Americans continue to age, while migration accounts for most population growth. This snapshot of who lives in the US today shows how the country's population is changing and offers context for policymakers weighing decisions on spending, immigration, government programs, and more.

Population growth

- In 2024, 340.1 million people lived in the US.
- The population grew by 3.3 million compared to 2023, a growth rate of 1.0%.
- Net migration has recently been driving population growth and was responsible for more than half the growth since 2021. In 2024, it accounted for 84% of new additions to the US population.
- Between 2023 and 2024, the population grew fastest in Florida, Texas, Utah, and Washington, DC.

Deaths and births

- The death rate decreased for the third consecutive year in 2024, dropping to 917.3 deaths per 100,000 people.
- The birth rate decreased in 2023 before bumping up slightly in 2024 — from 1,074 births per 100,000 people to 1,080 — according to preliminary data.
- The 2023 birth rate was the lowest since at least 1980, and the 2024 rate was the second-lowest.

Changing demographics

- The US population is aging. As of 2024, 18.0% of people are aged 65 or older, up from 11.3% in 1980.
- The composition of households continues to shift. The percentage of households led by adults with children decreased in 2024, continuing a decades-long trend. The share of people living alone has increased.
- The population is also becoming more diverse. In 2024, white, non-Hispanic people were 57% of the US population — down from 76% in 1990 and 69% in 2000. Between 2000 and 2022, the size of the multi-racial population grew faster than any other demographic, from 3.5 million people to 8.4 million people, a 145% increase.

What is the US population? Is the population growing?

The US population hit 340.1 million people in 2024. Population growth slowed beginning in 2016 before reaching a low in 2021, when the population grew by 522,000 people, or 0.2%. In 2024, the population grew by 3.3 million people, for a growth rate of 1.0%. Net migration — the difference between the number of people moving into and out of the country — is now the most significant contributor to population growth. It exceeded natural population growth (the effect of births and deaths) over the last four years and was responsible for 84% of the population growth from 2023 to 2024.

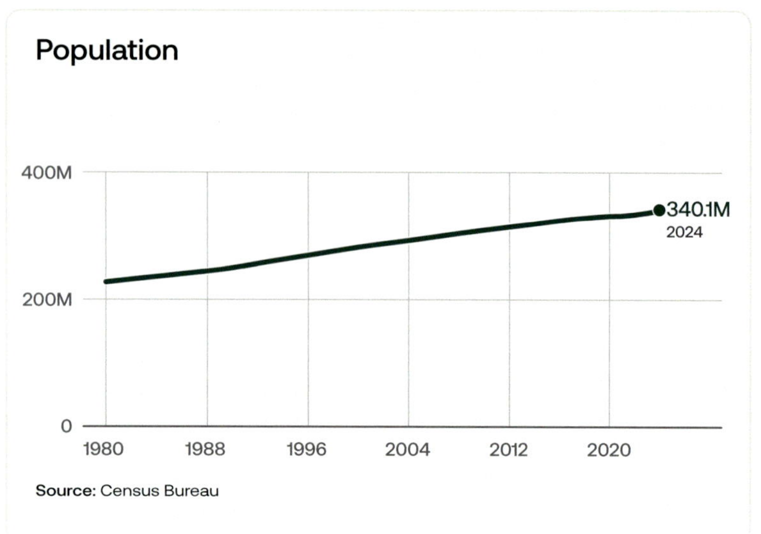

Source: Census Bureau

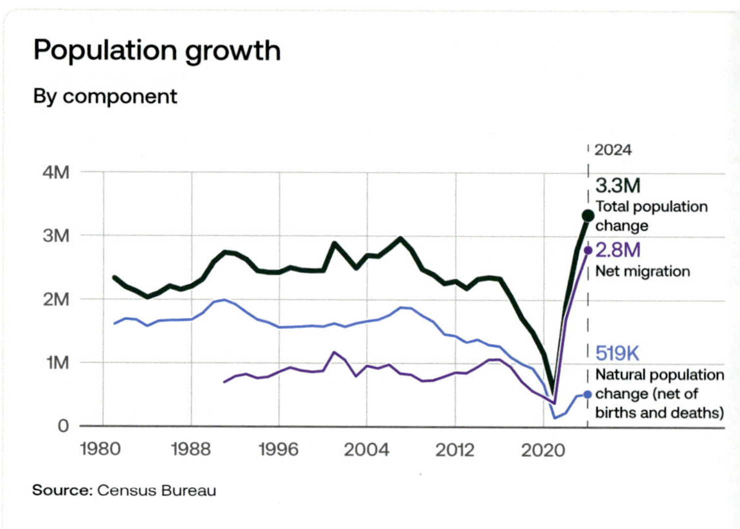

Source: Census Bureau

How have death and birth rates changed over time?

According to preliminary data, the death rate fell for the third consecutive year in 2024, to 917.3 deaths per 100,000 people; it remains above pre-pandemic levels. The birth rate increased to 1,080 per 100,000 people in 2024, slightly higher than 2023's record low of 1,074 births per 100,000 people.

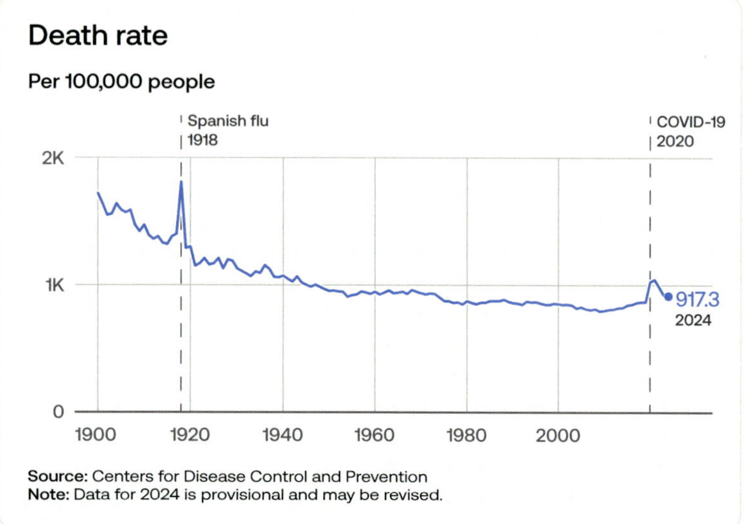

Source: Centers for Disease Control and Prevention
Note: Data for 2024 is provisional and may be revised.

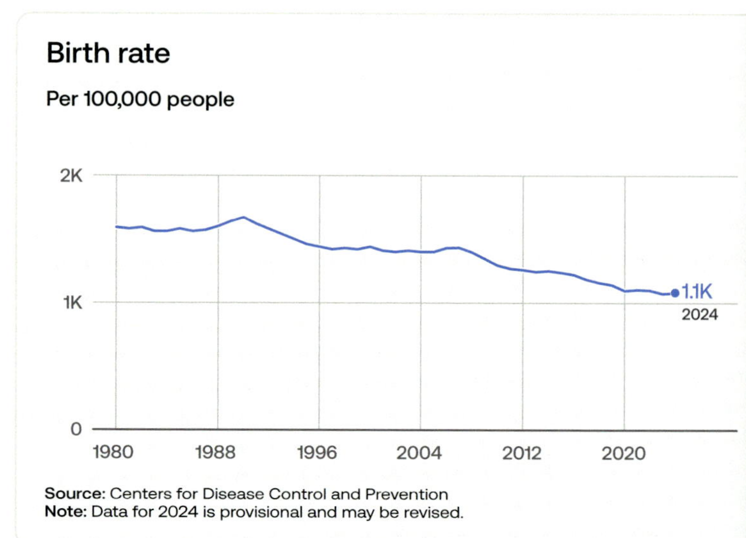

Source: Centers for Disease Control and Prevention
Note: Data for 2024 is provisional and may be revised.

How have state populations changed in the last year?

From 2023 to 2024, the populations of 13 states and Washington, DC, grew by more than 1%. The growth rate was highest in Washington, DC (2.2%), Florida (2.0%), Texas (1.8%), and Utah (1.8%), while the population declined in Mississippi, Vermont, and West Virginia.

Components of population change (2023 vs. 2024)

By state

State	Percent change in population	Natural change (births minus deaths)	Net domestic migration	Net international migration
Alabama	0.8%	-1,732	26,028	15,763
Alaska	0.5%	3,372	-3,774	4,029
Arizona	1.5%	9,660	34,902	64,486
Arkansas	0.6%	-727	13,465	6,152
California	0.6%	110,466	-239,575	361,057
Colorado	1.0%	17,294	5,422	33,227
Connecticut	0.9%	1,813	-6,060	36,214
Delaware	1.5%	-21	8,155	7,283
District of Columbia	2.2%	2,761	-337	12,502
Florida	2.0%	-7,321	64,017	411,322
Georgia	1.1%	28,252	25,321	63,088
Hawaii	0.3%	2,271	-9,321	11,893
Idaho	1.5%	6,195	16,383	7,899
Illinois	0.5%	11,012	-56,235	112,955
Indiana	0.6%	9,159	4,268	30,852
Iowa	0.7%	3,829	-231	19,439
Kansas	0.6%	5,232	-4,701	18,530
Kentucky	0.8%	-892	7,294	31,430
Louisiana	0.2%	3,959	-17,405	23,142
Maine	0.4%	-5,157	5,329	5,196
Maryland	0.7%	11,604	-18,509	53,100
Massachusetts	1.0%	6,718	-27,480	90,217
Michigan	0.6%	-2,855	-7,656	67,608
Minnesota	0.7%	11,780	-1,161	29,540
Mississippi	-0.004%	-1,984	-4,939	6,789
Missouri	0.6%	1,521	12,289	23,569
Montana	0.5%	12	5,410	506
Nebraska	0.9%	6,135	-1,498	12,978
Nevada	1.7%	3,058	16,853	33,005
New Hampshire	0.5%	-2,363	4,889	4,290
New Jersey	1.3%	26,010	-35,554	130,692
New Mexico	0.4%	-1,437	-1,571	12,103
New York	0.7%	43,701	-120,917	207,161
North Carolina	1.5%	12,632	82,288	69,792
North Dakota	1.0%	2,725	-291	5,126
Ohio	0.5%	-425	-2,462	62,378
Oklahoma	0.8%	3,136	14,036	14,358
Oregon	0.4%	-3,731	-1,162	23,590
Pennsylvania	0.5%	-9,311	-11,500	82,101
Rhode Island	0.8%	-362	-305	9,525
South Carolina	1.7%	-517	68,043	23,234
South Dakota	0.7%	2,588	2,132	1,616
Tennessee	1.1%	3,358	48,476	27,648
Texas	1.8%	158,753	85,267	319,569
Utah	1.8%	23,986	3,220	33,133
Vermont	-0.03%	-1,723	-511	2,024
Virginia	0.9%	15,150	5,284	56,155
Washington	1.3%	16,437	2,671	81,581
West Virginia	-0.03%	-7,844	4,520	2,841
Wisconsin	0.5%	2,040	6,332	22,146
Wyoming	0.4%	403	861	1,285

Source: Census Bureau

How has the age of the population and types of households in the US changed?

The proportion of people aged 65 and older in the population is rising while the proportion of people under 18 is falling. The share of the population 65 and older has risen nearly 7 percentage points since 1980, reaching 18.0% in 2024. At the same time, the percentage of children in the population decreased by 6.5 points, to 21.5%. The composition of US households also shifted: Married-parent households fell from 30.9% of households in 1980 to 17.7% in 2024, while the percentage of people living alone increased.

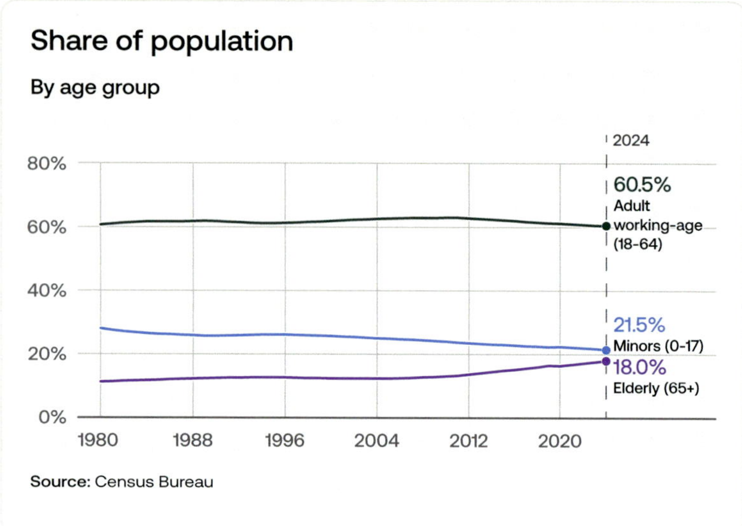

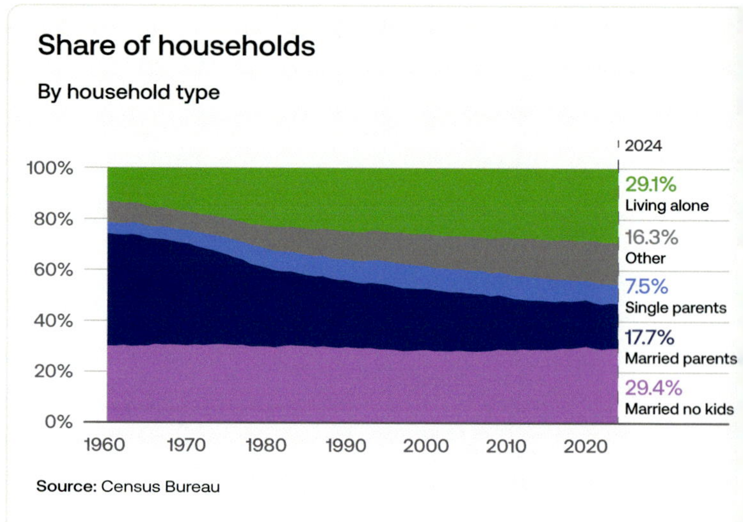

How is the population's racial and ethnic makeup changing?

In 2024, white non-Hispanic people were 57% of the population, down from 76% in 1990 and 69% in 2000. Hispanic people made up 20% of the population and Black people 13%. Between 2000 and 2024, the multiracial population increased faster than any other racial or ethnic group (up 145%), followed by Asian or Pacific Islanders (110%) and Hispanics (91%).

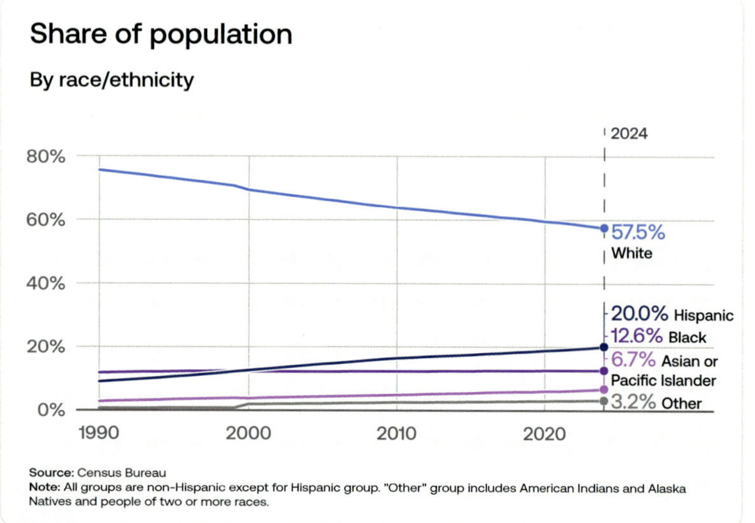

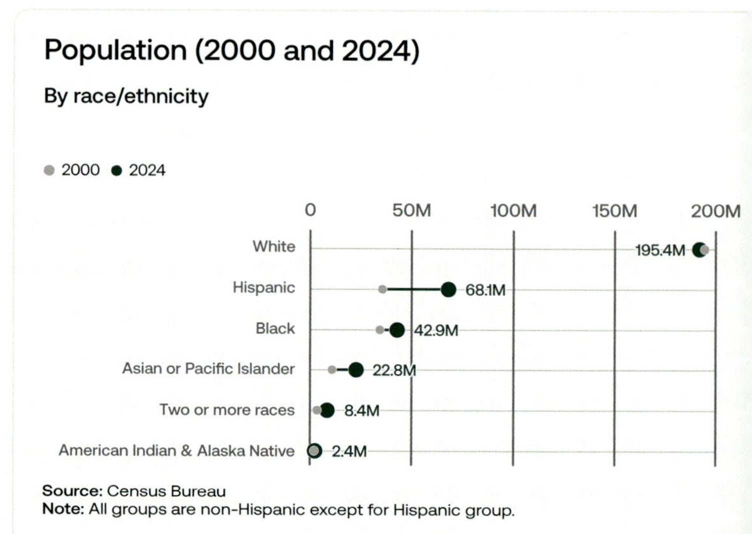

Chapter sources and data timeliness

Publishing agency	Program	Publication name	Release date	Most recent period in the data
Centers for Disease Control and Prevention	CDC Wonder	Multiple causes of death data	Typically released in January or February for two years prior	2023 (final) and 2024 (provisional)
		Natality information		
Census Bureau	Population Estimates Program	National population totals and components of change	Dec. 2024	2024
		National population by characteristics	June 2025	2024
		State population totals and components of change	Dec. 2024	2024
	Current Population Survey, Annual Social Economic Supplement	Historical households tables	Nov. 2024	2024
		Historical families tables	Nov. 2024	2024

See sources and notes section at the end of this report for detailed citation information.

- USAFacts relies on Census population estimates as of July 1 of each year whenever possible. These are known as “intercensal “or “postcensal” estimates and may differ from the decennial counts.
- The Census Bureau releases population estimates by different geographies and demographic characteristics at various points each year. Age and sex data typically come out each April, while race and ethnicity data is released in June.
- At the time of publishing, the CDC’s 2024 death and birth data were provisional and remain subject to revision.

Sources & notes

Endnotes

i. Social Security Administration (SSA) (2025). *Benefits Paid by Type of Beneficiary* (Time series report; Select beneficiary type(s): Retired workers & dependents, Survivors, Disabled workers & dependents; Frequency: Monthly (September of each year)). https://www.ssa.gov/oact/ProgData/icp.html.

ii. Census Bureau (2010 and 2023). *American Community Survey*. (S0101 Age and sex). https://data.census.gov/table/ACSST1Y2010.S0101?q=age.

iii. National Center for Education Statistics (2024). *Digest of Education Statistics* (Table 204.10. Number and percentage of public school students eligible for free or reduced-price lunch, by state). https://nces.ed.gov/programs/digest/d23/tables/dt23_204.10.asp.

iv. Immigrant entries by "nationality" includes new arrival green cards given to people born in the specified country. Green card data from DHS does not include breakouts by nationality. In many countries, birth in the country does not automatically provide nationality, and many people can become nationals of a country without having been born there.

v. Department of Homeland Security (2024). *Annual Flow Report: Refugees.* https://ohss.dhs.gov/topics/immigration/refugees-and-asylees/rfa-annual-flow-report. According to DHS and Title 8 of the US Code, "a refugee is a person who is unable or unwilling to return to their country of nationality (or country of last habitual residence, if stateless) because of persecution or a well-founded fear of persecution on account of race, religion, nationality, membership in a particular social group, or political opinion." Refugees are required to apply for Lawful Permanent Resident ("green card") status one year after being admitted.

vi. National Archive (2024). *Presidential Determination on Refugee Admissions for Fiscal Year 2025.* https://www.federalregister.gov/documents/2024/10/18/2024-24321/presidential-determination-on-refugee-admissions-for-fiscal-year-2025.

vii. The White House (2025). *Realigning the United States Refugee Admissions Program.* https://www.whitehouse.gov/presidential-actions/2025/01/realigning-the-united-states-refugee-admissions-program/.

viii. The released and paroled figure includes people paroled into the country for humanitarian reasons, significant public benefit, or on conditional parole. See endnote ix and its corresponding paragraph for more detail.

ix. Additional parole mechanisms include "advance parole" (for people already in the US with pending adjustments of status to permit travel abroad), "parole in place" (for people already in the US who are close family members of people who are veterans of or in the US military), and "paroled for deferred inspection" (for people presenting to ports of entry who are not preliminarily eligible for admission but will receive a full inspection at a later date). Conditional parole, or temporary release from custody, is a tool used by ICE and USBP to ease capacity constraints at their detention facilities. This is different from the kinds of parole discussed in this section, and is most akin to parole from prison, or supervised, conditional release. For more details, see: https://www.uscis.gov/policy-manual/volume-7-part-b-chapter-2#footnotelink-50.

x. The White House (2025). *Securing Our Borders.* https://www.whitehouse.gov/presidential-actions/2025/01/securing-our-borders/.

xi. US Citizenship and Immigration Services (n.d.). *Obtaining Asylum in the United States*. https://www.uscis.gov/humanitarian/refugees-and-asylum/asylum/obtaining-asylum-in-the-united-states.

xii. Executive Office of Immigration Review (2025). *Make a Difference – Apply for an Immigration Judge Position*. https://www.justice.gov/eoir/Adjudicators.

xiii. US Bureau of Labor Statistics (2024). *Industries at a Glance: Other Services*. https://www.bls.gov/iag/tgs/iag81.htm#:~:text=Establishments%20in%20this%20sector%20are,pet%20care%20services%2C%20photofinishing%20services%2C.

Chart sources and notes

For each **chapter**, all chart names are listed, and additional information is provided for each.

1. Chart sources and notes are structured as follows:
   Chart title: Source(s)
   Note(s):
2. For all population-adjusted data where the source does not provide adjustments, we use intercensal/postcensal estimates from the US Census Bureau, unless otherwise noted. Source details can be found in the citations for the "Population" chart below.
3. Fiscal years (FY) are equivalent to the federal fiscal year, unless otherwise noted. The federal fiscal year begins on October 1 of the previous year and ends on September 30 of the following year. For example, FY 2024 began on October 1, 2023, and ended on September 30, 2024.
4. USAFacts compiles data for government revenue, spending, and debt, as well as on family and individual income and taxes from various government sources, including the Office of Management and Budget, the Census Bureau, the Bureau of Economic Analysis, and the Federal Reserve. The full citations are not included below; to see detailed descriptions and notes about our methodology for compiling this data, please visit: https://usafacts.org/methodology.

Federal government finances

Federal government finances (FY 2024): USAFacts aggregation of data from Office of Management and Budget (OMB), Census Bureau, and Bureau of Economic Analysis (BEA). For more information on our methodology, see: https://usafacts.org/methodology/.

Federal government revenue (FY 1980 vs. FY 2024): Ibid.

Federal government revenue: Ibid.

Federal government spending (FY 1980 vs. FY 2024): Ibid.

Federal government spending: Ibid.

Federal government spending, by type: Ibid.

Components of mandatory spending (FY 2024): Ibid.

Components of discretionary spending (FY 2024): Ibid.

Social Security spending: Ibid.

Social Security as a share of federal spending: Ibid.

Social Security recipients, by type: (1) For Social Security: Social Security Administration (SSA) (2025). *Benefits Paid by Type of Beneficiary* (Time series report; Select beneficiary type(s): Retired workers & dependents and Survivors; Frequency: Monthly (September of each year)). https://www.ssa.gov/oact/ProgData/icp.html; (2) For disability insurance: SSA (2025). *Benefits Paid by Type of Beneficiary* (Time series report; Select beneficiary type(s): All under Disabled workers & dependents; Frequency: Monthly (September of each year)). https://www.ssa.gov/oact/ProgData/icp.html.

Social Security average monthly benefit, by type: Ibid.

Medicare spending: USAFacts aggregation of data from OMB, Census Bureau, and BEA. For more information on our methodology, see: https://usafacts.org/methodology/.

Medicare as a share of federal spending: Ibid.

Medicare enrollment: Centers for Medicare and Medicaid Services (CMS) (2025). *Medicare Trustees Report* (Table V.B3.—Medicare Enrollment). https://www.cms.gov/oact/tr/2025.

Average Medicare cost per beneficiary: CMS (2025). *Medicare Trustees Report* (Table V.D1.—HI and SMI Average Incurred per Beneficiary Costs). https://www.cms.gov/oact/tr/2025.

Federal Medicaid and CHIP spending: USAFacts aggregation of data from OMB, Census Bureau, and BEA. For more information on our methodology, see: https://usafacts.org/methodology/.

Federal Medicaid and CHIP as a share of federal spending: Ibid.

Medicaid and CHIP enrollment: CMS (2024). *Historical National Health Expenditure Data* (NHE Tables, Table 21. Expenditures, Enrollment, and Per Enrollee Estimates of Health Insurance). https://www.cms.gov/data-research/statistics-trends-and-reports/national-health-expenditure-data/historical.

Medicaid and CHIP average spending per enrollee: Ibid.

Net interest payments on the debt as a share of federal spending: USAFacts aggregation of data from OMB, Census Bureau, and BEA. For more information on our methodology, see: https://usafacts.org/methodology/.

Federal government debt: US Department of the Treasury (Multiple issues). *Treasury Bulletin* (Ownership of Federal Securities; TABLE OFS-1—Distribution of Federal Securities by Class of Investors and Type of Issues, TABLE OFS-2—Estimated Ownership of U.S. Treasury Securities). https://fiscal.treasury.gov/reports-statements/treasury-bulletin/current.html.

Federal government debt held by the public as a percent of GDP: Ibid.

Federal government finances: USAFacts aggregation of data from OMB, Census Bureau, and BEA. For more information on our methodology, see: https://usafacts.org/methodology/.

Federal individual income taxes

Total individual income tax collected: Internal Revenue Service (IRS) (2024). *SOI Tax Stats - Individual Statistical Tables by Size of Adjusted Gross Income* (All Returns: Selected Income and Tax Items. Published as: Individual Complete Report (Publication 1304), Table 1.1 [multiple years].xls). https://www.irs.gov/statistics/soi-tax-stats-individual-statistical-tables-by-size-of-adjusted-gross-income.

Number of tax returns filed: Ibid.

Average tax return adjusted gross income: Ibid.

Long-term capital gains as a share of AGI: Ibid.

Share of AGI from long-term capital gains (2022), by AGI: Ibid.

Average effective federal income tax rate, by AGI: IRS (Multiple years). *SOI Tax Stats - Individual Statistical Tables by Size of Adjusted Gross Income* (All Returns: Selected Income and Tax Items. Published as: Individual Complete Report (Publication 1304), Table 1.1 [multiple years].xls). https://www.irs.gov/statistics/soi-tax-stats-individual-statistical-tables-by-size-of-adjusted-gross-income.

Average effective federal income tax rate, by state: IRS (Multiple years). SOI Tax Stats (Table 1. Returns with Positive Gross Income (AGI): Number of Returns, Shares of AGI and Total Income Tax, AGI Floor on Percentiles, and Average Tax Rates (Table 1 [multiple years].csv)). https://www.irs.gov/statistics/soi-tax-stats-adjusted-gross-income-agi-percentile-data-by-state.

Share of federal income taxes collected, by AGI: IRS (2024). *SOI Tax Stats - Individual Statistical Tables by Size of Adjusted Gross Income* (All Returns: Selected Income and Tax Items. Published as: Individual Complete Report (Publication 1304), Table 1.1 [multiple years].xls). https://www.irs.gov/statistics/soi-tax-stats-individual-statistical-tables-by-size-of-adjusted-gross-income.

Share of federal tax returns filed, by AGI: Ibid.

Share of returns claiming itemized deductions, by AGI: (1) IRS (Multiple years). *SOI Tax Stats - Individual Statistical Tables by Size of Adjusted Gross Income* (Individual Income Tax Returns with Itemized Deductions: Sources of Income, Adjustments, Itemized Deductions by Type, Exemptions, and Tax Items. Published as: Individual Complete Report (Publication 1304), Table 2.1 [multiple years].xls). https://www.irs.gov/statistics/soi-tax-stats-individual-statistical-tables-by-size-of-adjusted-gross-income; (2) IRS (Multiple years). *SOI Tax Stats - Individual Statistical Tables by Size of Adjusted Gross Income* (All Returns: Sources of Income, Adjustments Deductions and Exemptions, and Tax Items. Published as: Individual Complete Report (Publication 1304), Table 1.4 [multiple years].xls). https://www.irs.gov/statistics/soi-tax-stats-individual-statistical-tables-by-size-of-adjusted-gross-income.

Number of returns and amount claimed, by itemized deduction (2022): Ibid.

Share of returns claiming itemized deductions, by type of deduction: Ibid.

Share of returns claiming SALT deduction, by AGI: Ibid.

Average SALT deduction, by AGI: IRS (Multiple years). *SOI Tax Stats - Individual Statistical Tables by Size of Adjusted Gross Income* (Individual Income Tax Returns with Itemized Deductions: Sources of Income, Adjustments, Itemized Deductions by Type, Exemptions, and Tax Items. Published as: Individual Complete Report (Publication 1304), Table 2.1 [multiple years].xls). https://www.irs.gov/statistics/soi-tax-stats-individual-statistical-tables-by-size-of-adjusted-gross-income.

Share of returns claiming SALT deduction, by state: IRS (Multiple years). *Historic Table 2* (Historic Table 2 state data tax year [multiple years].csv). https://www.irs.gov/statistics/soi-tax-stats-historic-table-2.

Share of tax returns claiming charitable contributions deduction, by AGI: (1) IRS (Multiple years). *SOI Tax Stats - Individual Statistical Tables by Size of Adjusted Gross Income* (Individual Income Tax Returns with Itemized Deductions: Sources of Income, Adjustments, Itemized Deductions by Type, Exemptions, and Tax Items. Published as: Individual Complete Report (Publication 1304), Table 2.1 [multiple years].xls). https://www.irs.gov/statistics/soi-tax-stats-individual-statistical-tables-by-size-of-adjusted-gross-income; (2) IRS (Multiple years). *SOI Tax Stats - Individual Statistical Tables by Size of Adjusted Gross Income* (All Returns: Sources of Income, Adjustments Deductions and Exemptions, and Tax Items. Published as: Individual Complete Report (Publication 1304), Table 1.4 [multiple years].xls). https://www.irs.gov/statistics/soi-tax-stats-individual-statistical-tables-by-size-of-adjusted-gross-income.

Average charitable deduction, by AGI: IRS (Multiple years). *SOI Tax Stats - Individual Statistical Tables by Size of Adjusted Gross Income* (Individual Income Tax Returns with Itemized Deductions: Sources of Income, Adjustments, Itemized Deductions by Type, Exemptions, and Tax Items. Published as: Individual Complete Report (Publication 1304), Table 2.1 [multiple years].xls). https://www.irs.gov/statistics/soi-tax-stats-individual-statistical-tables-by-size-of-adjusted-gross-income.

Share of returns claiming charitable contributions deduction, by state: IRS (Multiple years). *Historic Table 2* (Historic Table 2 state data tax year [multiple years].csv). https://www.irs.gov/statistics/soi-tax-stats-historic-table-2.

Share of returns claiming home mortgage interest deduction, by AGI: (1) IRS (Multiple years). *SOI Tax Stats - Individual Statistical Tables by Size of Adjusted Gross Income* (Individual Income Tax Returns with Itemized Deductions: Sources of Income, Adjustments, Itemized Deductions by Type, Exemptions, and Tax Items. Published as: Individual Complete Report (Publication 1304), Table 2.1 [multiple years].xls). https://www.irs.gov/statistics/soi-tax-stats-individual-statistical-tables-by-size-of-adjusted-gross-income; (2) IRS (Multiple years). *SOI Tax Stats - Individual Statistical Tables by Size of Adjusted Gross Income* (All Returns: Sources of Income, Adjustments

Deductions and Exemptions, and Tax Items. Published as: Individual Complete Report (Publication 1304), Table 1.4 [multiple years].xls). https://www.irs.gov/statistics/soi-tax-stats-individual-statistical-tables-by-size-of-adjusted-gross-income.

Average home mortgage interest deduction, by AGI: IRS (Multiple years). *SOI Tax Stats - Individual Statistical Tables by Size of Adjusted Gross Income* (Individual Income Tax Returns with Itemized Deductions: Sources of Income, Adjustments, Itemized Deductions by Type, Exemptions, and Tax Items. Published as: Individual Complete Report (Publication 1304), Table 2.1 [multiple years].xls). https://www.irs.gov/statistics/soi-tax-stats-individual-statistical-tables-by-size-of-adjusted-gross-income.

Share of returns claiming home mortgage interest deduction (2022), by state: IRS (Multiple years). *Historic Table 2* (Historic Table 2 state data tax year [multiple years].csv). https://www.irs.gov/statistics/soi-tax-stats-historic-table-2.

Share of tax returns claiming QBI deductions (2022): (1) IRS (Multiple years). *SOI Tax Stats - Individual Statistical Tables by Size of Adjusted Gross Income* (Individual Income Tax Returns with Itemized Deductions: Sources of Income, Adjustments, Itemized Deductions by Type, Exemptions, and Tax Items. Published as: Individual Complete Report (Publication 1304), Table 2.1 [multiple years].xls). https://www.irs.gov/statistics/soi-tax-stats-individual-statistical-tables-by-size-of-adjusted-gross-income; (2) IRS (Multiple years). *SOI Tax Stats - Individual Statistical Tables by Size of Adjusted Gross Income* (All Returns: Sources of Income, Adjustments Deductions and Exemptions, and Tax Items. Published as: Individual Complete Report (Publication 1304), Table 1.4 [multiple years].xls). https://www.irs.gov/statistics/soi-tax-stats-individual-statistical-tables-by-size-of-adjusted-gross-income.

Average QBI deduction (2022), by AGI: IRS (Multiple years). *SOI Tax Stats - Individual Statistical Tables by Size of Adjusted Gross Income* (Individual Income Tax Returns with Itemized Deductions: Sources of Income, Adjustments, Itemized Deductions by Type, Exemptions, and Tax Items. Published as: Individual Complete Report (Publication 1304), Table 2.1 [multiple years].xls). https://www.irs.gov/statistics/soi-tax-stats-individual-statistical-tables-by-size-of-adjusted-gross-income.

Share of returns claiming QBI deduction (2022), by state: IRS (Multiple years). *Historic Table 2* (Historic Table 2 state data tax year [multiple years].csv). https://www.irs.gov/statistics/soi-tax-stats-historic-table-2.

Average QBI deduction, by state (2022): Ibid.

EITC distribution (2022), by AGI: IRS (2024). *SOI Tax Stats - Individual Statistical Tables by Size of Adjusted Gross Income* (Individual Income Tax Returns with Earned Income Credit. Published as: Individual Complete Report (Publication 1304), Table 2.5 [2022].xls). https://www.irs.gov/statistics/soi-tax-stats-individual-statistical-tables-by-size-of-adjusted-gross-income.

EITC credits (2022), by AGI: Ibid.

Distribution of EITC benefits (2022), by number of qualifying children: Ibid.

EITC credits (2022), by number of qualifying children: Ibid.

Child Tax Credit provisions: (1) Adapted from: McDermott, Brendan (2025). *The Child Tax Credit: How it Works and Who Receives It*. CRS Report R41873. https://www.congress.gov/crs-product/R41873; (2) One Big Beautiful Bill Act, HR 1, 119th Congress (2025).

Number of returns claiming the CTC, by refundability: IRS (2024). *SOI Tax Stats - Individual Statistical Tables by Size of Adjusted Gross Income* (All Returns: Selected Income and Tax Items. Published as: Individual Complete Report (Publication 1304), Table 1.1 [multiple years].xls). https://www.irs.gov/statistics/soi-tax-stats-individual-statistical-tables-by-size-of-adjusted-gross-income.

Share of returns claiming the CTC, by AGI: Ibid.

Total value of CTC benefits, by refundability: (1) IRS (2024). *SOI Tax Stats - Individual Statistical Tables by Size of Adjusted Gross Income* (All Returns: Selected Income and Tax Items. Published as: Individual Complete Report (Publication 1304), Table 1.1 [multiple years].xls). https://www.irs.gov/statistics/soi-tax-stats-individual-statistical-tables-by-size-of-adjusted-gross-income; (2) IRS (2024). SOI Tax Stats - Advance Child Tax Credit payments in 2021 (Table 1: Classified by adjusted gross income). https://www.irs.gov/statistics/soi-tax-stats-advance-child-tax-credit-payments-in-2021.

Total value of CTC benefits, by AGI: IRS (2024). *SOI Tax Stats - Individual Statistical Tables by Size of Adjusted Gross Income* (All Returns: Selected Income and Tax Items. Published as: Individual Complete Report (Publication 1304), Table 1.1 [multiple years].xls). https://www.irs.gov/statistics/soi-tax-stats-individual-statistical-tables-by-size-of-adjusted-gross-income.

Average CTC benefit, by AGI: Ibid.

Standard of living

Real gross domestic product, per capita: BEA (2024). *FRED* (Real gross domestic product per capita (A939RX0Q048SBEA)). Federal Reserve Bank of St. Louis. https://fred.stlouisfed.org/series/A939RX0Q048SBEA#0.

Real GDP per capita (2024), by state: (1) BEA (2024). *Real gross domestic product (GDP) by state: Millions of chained 2017 dollars (SAGDP1).* Retrieved from interactive data tables. https://www.bea.gov/itable/regional-gdp-and-personal-income; (2) *Census Bureau (2024).* State population totals and components of change: 2020-2024 (Annual estimates of the resident population for the United States, regions, states, District of Columbia and Puerto Rico: April 1, 2020 to July 1, 2024 (NST-EST2024-POP)). https://www.census.gov/data/tables/time-series/demo/popest/2020s-state-total.html.

Percent change in real GDP per capita (2023 vs. 2024), by state: Ibid.

Average total market income (2000 and 2022): USAFacts calculations using data from the IRS and the Census Bureau. For more information on our methodology, see: https://usafacts.org/methodology/.

Average taxes paid (2000 and 2022): Ibid.

Average transfers received (2000 and 2022): Ibid.

Median annual wages: BLS (2025). Occupational Employment and Wage Statistics (Multiple years, National, XLS Version). https://www.bls.gov/oes/tables.htm.

Median annual wages (2024), by state: Ibid.

Annual percent change in inflation-adjusted median wage: (1) BLS (2025, May 2). *Occupational Employment and Wage Statistics* (Multiple years, National, XLS Version). https://www.bls.gov/oes/tables.htm; (2) US Bureau of Labor Statistics (2025). *CPI for All Urban Consumers (CPI-U)* (All items in US city average, all urban consumers, not seasonally adjusted (CUUR0000SA0)). https://data.bls.gov/timeseries/CUUR0000SA0.

Change in inflation-adjusted median wage (May 2023 to May 2024), by state: (1) BLS (2025, May 2). *Occupational Employment and Wage Statistics* (Multiple years, State, XLS Version). https://www.bls.gov/oes/tables.htm; (2) US Bureau of Labor Statistics (2025). *CPI for All Urban Consumers (CPI-U)* (All items in US city average, all urban consumers, not seasonally adjusted (CUUR0000SA0)). https://data.bls.gov/timeseries/CUUR0000SA0.

Number of people claiming unemployment benefits each week, annual average: US Employment and Training Administration (2025). Continued Claims (Insured Unemployment) [CCNSA], retrieved from FRED, Federal Reserve Bank of St. Louis. https://fred.stlouisfed.org/series/CCNSA.

Share of people claiming unemployment insurance benefits each week, annual average: (1) US Employment and Training Administration (2025). Continued Claims (Insured Unemployment) [CCNSA], retrieved from FRED, Federal Reserve Bank of St. Louis. https://fred.stlouisfed.org/series/CCNSA; (2) Bureau of Labor Statistics (2025). *Labor Force Statistics from the Current Population Survey (CPS) (Civilian noninstitutional population*, 16 years and over [LNU00000000]). https://www.bls.gov/cps/lfcharacteristics.htm.

Poverty rate, by age group: Census Bureau (2024, August 16). *Historical Poverty Tables: People and Families - 1959 to 2020* (Table 3. Poverty Status of People by Age, Race, and Hispanic Origin: 1959 to 2023). https://www.census.gov/data/tables/time-series/demo/income-poverty/historical-poverty-people.html.

Poverty rate (2023), by state: Census Bureau (2023). *Historical Poverty Tables: People and Families - 1959 to 2023* (Table 19. Number of Poor and Poverty Rate by State: 1980 to 2023). https://www.census.gov/data/tables/time-series/demo/income-poverty/historical-poverty-people.html.

Share of households receiving public assistance income: Census Bureau (2024). *American Community Survey (ACS): (Multiple Years) 1-year estimates* (B19057 Public Assistance Income in the Past 12 Months for All Households). https://data.census.gov/table?q=B19057&g=010XX00US,$0400000.

Share of households receiving public assistance income (2023), by state: Ibid.

Share of households receiving Supplemental Security Income: Census Bureau (2024). *ACS: (Multiple Years) 1-year estimates* (B19056 Supplemental Security Income in the Past 12 Months for All Households). https://data.census.gov/table?q=B19056&g=010XX00US,$0400000.

Share of households receiving Supplemental Security Income (2023), by state: Ibid.

Share of households receiving Social Security Income: Census Bureau (2024). *ACS:* (Multiple Years) 1-year estimates (B19055 Social Security Income in the Past 12 Months for All Households). https://data.census.gov/table?q=B19055&g=010XX00US,$0400000.

Share of households receiving Social Security Income (2023), by state: Ibid.

Share of households that are housing burdened: (1) For renters: US Census Bureau (2023). *American Community Survey: (Multiple Years) 1-year estimates* (B25070 Gross Rent as a Percentage of Household Income in the Past 12 Months). https://data.census.gov/table/ACSDT1Y2022.B25070?q=&g=010XX00US,$0400000; (2) For homeowners: US Census Bureau (2023). *American Community Survey: (Multiple years) 1-year estimates* (B25091 Mortgage Status by Selected Monthly Owner Costs as a Percentage of Household Income in the Past 12 Months). https://data.census.gov/table/ACSDT1Y2022.B25091?q=&g=010XX00US,$0400000.

Share of households that are housing burdened, by state (2023): Ibid.

Share of population living in subsidized housing: (1) For 2004-2008: Department of Housing and Urban Development (HUD) (2025). *Picture of Subsidized Households for 2004-2008* (Select Year, US total, Total for all HUD programs, people_total). https://www.huduser.gov/portal/picture/query.html; (2) For 2009-2024: HUD (2025). *Picture of Subsidized Households* (Select Year, US total, Summary of all HUD programs, Number of people: Total). https://www.huduser.gov/portal/datasets/assthsg.html#2009-2017_query; (3) 2004-2010: Census Bureau (2017). *Population Estimates* (2010>2010-eval-estimates>co-est2010-alldata.csv). https://www2.census.gov/programs-surveys/popest/datasets/; (4) 2011-2019: Census Bureau (2021). NST-EST2020-ALLDATA.csv (National Population Totals). https://www.census.gov/programs-surveys/popest/technical-documentation/research/evaluation-estimates/2020-evaluation-estimates/2010s-totals-national.html; (5) 2020-2024: Census Bureau (2024). NST-EST2024-ALLDATA.csv. https://www.census.gov/data/tables/time-series/demo/popest/2020s-national-total.html.

Share of population living in subsidized housing (2024), by state: (1) HUD (2025). *Picture of Subsidized Households* (2024, State, Summary of all HUD programs, Number of people: Total). https://www.huduser.gov/portal/datasets/assthsg.html#2009-2017_query; (2) Census Bureau (2024). *State population totals and components of change: 2020-2024* (Annual estimates of the resident population for the United States, regions, states, District of Columbia and Puerto Rico: April 1, 2020 to July 1, 2024 (NST-EST2024-POP)). https://www.census.gov/data/tables/time-series/demo/popest/2020s-state-total.html.

Subsidized housing units available, per 1,000 people: (1) For 2004-2008: HUD (2025). *Picture of Subsidized Households for 2004-2008* (Select Year, State, Total for all HUD programs, months_waiting). https://www.huduser.gov/portal/picture/query.html; (2) For 2009-2024: HUD (2025). *Picture of Subsidized Households* (Select Year, State, Summary of all HUD programs, Average months on waitlist). https://www.huduser.gov/portal/datasets/assthsg.html#2009-2017_query.

Average months on subsidized housing waitlist: (1) For 2004-2008: HUD (2025). *Picture of Subsidized Households for 2004-2008* (Select Year, US total, Total for all HUD programs, months_waiting). https://www.huduser.gov/portal/picture/query.html; (2) For 2009-2024: HUD (2025). *Picture of Subsidized Households* (Select Year, US total, Summary of all HUD programs, Average months on waitlist). https://www.huduser.gov/portal/datasets/assthsg.html#2009-2017_query.

Share of households that are food insecure: US Department of Agriculture (USDA) Economic Research Service (2023). *Food Security in the US* (Food Security Data file, Food security, all households). https://www.ers.usda.gov/topics/food-nutrition-assistance/food-security-in-the-u-s/interactive-charts-and-highlights/#trends.

Share of households that are food insecure (2021-2023 average), by state: USDA Economic Research Service (2025). *Food Security in the US* (Food Security Data file, Food insecurity by state). https://www.ers.usda.gov/topics/food-nutrition-assistance/food-security-in-the-u-s/interactive-charts-and-highlights/#trends.

Nutrition assistance (SNAP) average monthly recipients: USDA Food and Nutrition Service (2024). *SNAP Data Tables* (National Level Annual Summary: Participation and Costs, 1969-2023). https://www.fns.usda.gov/pd/supplemental-nutrition-assistance-program-snap.

Nutrition assistance (SNAP) average monthly benefit per person: Ibid.

Average monthly WIC recipients: USDA Food and Nutrition Service (2025). *WIC Data Tables* (National Level Annual Summary [FY 1974-2024]). https://www.fns.usda.gov/pd/wic-program.

WIC average monthly food costs per person: Ibid.

Average monthly number of children receiving free or reduced lunch: Ibid.

Share of school lunches served at free or reduced prices: USDA Food and Nutrition Service (2025). *Child Nutrition Tables* (National Level Annual Summary Tables: FY 1969-2024 [National School Lunch - Participation and Meals Served]). https://www.fns.usda.gov/pd/child-nutrition-tables.

Economy

Consumer Price Index, 12-month percent change: BLS (2025). *CPI for All Urban Consumers (CPI-U)* (All items in US city average, all urban consumers, seasonally adjusted (CUSR0000SA0). Retrieved from BLS One-Screen Data Search, All Urban Consumers (Current Series)). https://data.bls.gov/PDQWeb/cu.

Percent change in Consumer Price Index, by select categories, from January 2021: (1) BLS (2025). *CPI for All Urban Consumers (CPI-U)* (CUSR0000SAA, CUSR0000SAE, CUSR0000SAF, CUSR0000SAG, CUSR0000SAH, CUSR0000SAM, CUSR0000SAR, CUSR0000SAT). Retrieved from BLS One-Screen Data Search, All Urban Consumers (Current Series). https://data.bls.gov/PDQWeb/cu.

Components of year-over-year percent change of CPI-U: BLS (2025). Consumer Price Index (Current Release, Table 7. Consumer Price Index for All Urban Consumers (CPI-U): US city average, by expenditure category). https://www.bls.gov/news.release/cpi.t07.htm.

Federal funds rate: Board of Governors of the Federal Reserve System (2025). *FRED* (Federal Funds Effective Rate [FEDFUNDS]). Federal Reserve Bank of St. Louis. https://fred.stlouisfed.org/series/FEDFUNDS.

Personal Consumption Expenditures price index, 12-month percent change: BEA (2024, February). *FRED* (Personal Consumption Expenditures: Chain-type Price Index [PCEPI]). Federal Reserve Bank of St. Louis. https://fred.stlouisfed.org/series/PCEPI.

Yield on 10-year Treasury securities vs. 30-year mortgage rate, monthly average: (1) BEA (2025). *FRED* (Market Yield on US Treasury Securities at 10-Year Constant Maturity, Quoted on an Investment Basis [DGS10]). Federal Reserve Bank of St. Louis. https://fred.stlouisfed.org/series/DGS10; (2) BEA (2025). *FRED* (30-Year Fixed Rate Mortgage Average in the United States [MORTGAGE30US]). Federal Reserve Bank of St. Louis. https://fred.stlouisfed.org/series/MORTGAGE30US.

Annual percent change in real gross domestic product (GDP): BEA (2025). *National Income and Product Accounts* (Table 1.1.1. Percent Change from Preceding Period in Real Gross Domestic Product, Series: Annual). Retrieved from interactive data tables. https://www.bea.gov/itable/national-gdp-and-personal-income.

Percent change in real GDP (2023 vs. 2024): BEA (2025). *State annual gross domestic product (GDP) summary* ([SAGDP1] Real gross domestic product (million of chained 2017 dollars)). Retrieved from interactive data tables. https://www.bea.gov/itable/regional-gdp-and-personal-income.

Net change in employment (jobs): US Bureau of Labor Statistics (2025). *Employment, Hours, and Earnings from the Current Employment Statistics survey (National)* (All employees, thousands, total nonfarm, not seasonally adjusted (CEU0000000001); Data type: "All employees, thousands", Super sector: "Total nonfarm", More formatting options: "12-Month Net Change" view). https://data.bls.gov/PDQWeb/ce.

Percent change in annual average employment (2023 vs 2024), by state: BLS (2025). *State and Metro Area Employment, Hours, & Earnings* (Table 1. Employees on nonfarm payrolls in States and selected areas by major industry). https://www.bls.gov/sae/tables/annual-average/home.htm.

Unemployment rate, annual average: BLS (2025). *Labor Force Statistics from the CPS* ((Unadj) Unemployment Rate (LNU04000000)); Retrieved from BLS One-Screen Data Search, Labor Force Statistics. https://data.bls.gov/PDQWeb/ln.

Unemployment rate (2024 average), by state: BLS (2025). *Unemployment Rates for States*, 2024 Annual Averages. https://www.bls.gov/lau/lastrk24.htm.

Labor force participation rate: BLS (2025). *Labor Force Statistics from the CPS* ((Unadj) Labor Force Participation Rate (LNU01300000)). Retrieved from BLS One-Screen Data Search, Labor Force Statistics. https://data.bls.gov/PDQWeb/ln.

Labor force participation rate (2024 average), by state: BLS (2025). *Economic News Release*. Table 1. Employment status of the civilian noninstitutional population 16 years of age and over by region, division, and state, 2023-24 annual averages. https://www.bls.gov/news.release/srgune.t01.htm.

Job openings rate: BLS (2025). *Job Openings and Labor Turnover Survey* (Table A. Job openings, hires, and total separations by industry, not seasonally adjusted). Retrieved from BLS One-Screen Data Search, Job Openings and Labor Turnover Survey. https://data.bls.gov/PDQWeb/jt.

Job openings rate (2024 annual average), by state: BLS (2025). *Job Openings and Labor Turnover Survey* (Industry: Total nonfarm; Data Elements: Job openings; Rate and/or level: Rate; Seasonal Adjustment: Not seasonally adjusted, select all states). Retrieved from BLS One-Screen Data Search, Job Openings and Labor Turnover Survey. https://data.bls.gov/PDQWeb/jt.

Layoff and discharge rate: BLS (2025). *Job Openings and Labor Turnover Survey* (Table A. Job openings, hires, and total separations by industry, not seasonally adjusted). Retrieved from BLS One-Screen Data Search, Job Openings and Labor Turnover Survey. https://data.bls.gov/PDQWeb/jt.

Layoff and discharge rate (2024 annual average), by state: BLS (2025). *Job Openings and Labor Turnover Survey* (Industry: Total nonfarm; Data Elements: Layoffs and discharges; Rate and/or level: Rate; Seasonal Adjustment: Not seasonally adjusted). Retrieved from BLS One-Screen Data Search, Job Openings and Labor Turnover Survey. https://data.bls.gov/PDQWeb/jt.

Trade balance: BEA (2025). *International Trade in Goods and Services* (Current Release, US Trade in Goods and Services, 1960-present, Table 1. US International Trade in Goods and Services). https://www.bea.gov/data/intl-trade-investment/international-trade-goods-and-services.

Net trade of goods and services: Ibid.

Imports (2024), by goods and services: (1) BEA (2025). *International Transactions, International Services, and International Investment Position Tables* (Table 3.1. US International Trade in Services). Retrieved from interactive data tables. https://www.bea.gov/itable/international-transactions-services-and-investment-position.

Exports (2024), by goods and services: Ibid.

Imports and exports (2024), by area: BEA (2025). *International Transactions, International Services, and International Investment Position Tables* (Table 1.5. US International Trade in Goods and Services by Area and Country, Series: Annual). Retrieved from interactive data tables. https://www.bea.gov/itable/international-transactions-services-and-investment-position.

Total trade value, with top trading partners: BEA (2025). *International Trade in Goods and Services* (Current Release, US Trade in Goods and Services by Selected Countries and Areas, 1999-present, Table 3. US International Trade by Selected Countries and Areas). https://www.bea.gov/data/intl-trade-investment/international-trade-goods-and-services.

Net trade balance with top trading partners: Ibid.

Total and top 5 US imports (2024), by top trading partner: BEA (2025). *International Transactions, International Services, and International Investment Position Tables* (Table 1.5. US International Trade in Goods and Services by Area and Country, Series: Annual). Retrieved from interactive data tables. https://www.bea.gov/itable/international-transactions-services-and-investment-position.

Total and top 5 US exports (2024), by top trading partner: Ibid.

Average effective tariff rate: US International Trade Commission (2025). *US imports for consumption, duties collected, and ratio of duties to value, 1891-2024* (Table 1). https://www.usitc.gov/documents/dataweb/ave_table.pdf.

Customs duties revenue: USAFacts aggregation of data from OMB, Census Bureau, and BEA. For more information on our methodology, see: https://usafacts.org/methodology/.

Customs duties revenue, as a share of federal revenue: Ibid.

Immigration

When describing new authorized immigrant arrivals, terms are defined as follows:

1. New arrival green card data only includes green cards granted to new immigrants to the US. It excludes green cards granted through an adjustment of status to immigrants who are already in the US on a visa.

2. Non-tourist visa data excludes temporary visitors for business or pleasure (including with Border Crossing Cards), transit aliens, and transit crew (airline, cruise ship, etc.).

3. Asylees are excluded. Even though this population becomes "authorized" when they are granted asylum, they may or may not have legal status prior to a grant of asylum. Additionally, they are not new arrivals because they must be in the country to apply for asylum.

New authorized immigrant arrivals, total and by type: (1) Green cards: Office of Homeland Security Statistics (OHSS) under US Department of Homeland Security (DHS) (Multiple Years). *Yearbook of Immigration Statistics* (Lawful Permanent Residents [Year] Data Tables, Table 6. Persons Obtaining Lawful Permanent Resident Status by Type and Major Class of Admission). https://ohss.dhs.gov/topics/immigration/yearbook/2023; (2) Visas: US Department of State (State) (2024). *Nonimmigrant Visa Statistics* (Nonimmigrant Visa Issuances by Visa Class and by Nationality, FY1997-2023 NIV Detail Table). https://travel.state.gov/content/travel/en/legal/visa-law0/visa-statistics/nonimmigrant-visa-statistics.html; (3) Refugees: Refugee Processing Center (RPC) (2024). *Admissions and Arrivals* (Refugee Admissions Report). US Department of State. https://www.wrapsnet.org/admissions-and-arrivals/.

New authorized immigrant arrivals (FY 2023), by region of birth/nationality: (1) Green cards: OHSS under DHS (2023). *Yearbook of Immigration Statistics* (LPR Yearbook Tables 8 to 11 Expanded, Table 10. Persons Obtaining Lawful Permanent Resident Status by Type and Broad Class of Admission and Region and Country of Birth). https://ohss.dhs.gov/topics/immigration/lawful-permanent-residents/lpr-yearbook-tables-8-11-expanded; (2) Visas: State (2023). *Nonimmigrant Visa Statistics* (Nonimmigrant Visa Issuances by Visa Class and by Nationality, FY1997-2023 NIV Detail Table). https://travel.state.gov/content/travel/en/legal/visa-law0/visa-statistics/nonimmigrant-visa-statistics.html; (3) Refugees: OHSS under DHS (2024). *Yearbook of Immigration Statistics* (Refugees [Multiple years] Data Tables, Table 14. Refugee Arrivals by Region and Country of Nationality). https://ohss.dhs.gov/topics/immigration/yearbook/2023.

Note(s): Disaggregated 2023 new arrival green card data from OHSS describing new arrivals by country of origin was not available as of report publication, so this chart uses the 2022 data for 2023. This approach is imperfect: totals change each year (466,000 new arrivals in 2022 vs. 558,000 in 2023), but the reasons for migration and countries of origin appear more stable over time.

New authorized immigrant arrivals (FY 2023), by reason for granted entry: (1) Green cards: OHSS under DHS (2024). *Yearbook of Immigration Statistics* (Lawful Permanent Residents 2023 Data Tables, Table 6. Persons Obtaining Lawful Permanent Resident Status by Type and Major Class of Admission: Fiscal Years 2014 to 2023). https://ohss.dhs.gov/topics/immigration/yearbook/2023/table6; (2) Visas: State (2023). *Nonimmigrant Visa Statistics* (Nonimmigrant Visa Issuances by Visa Class and by Nationality, FY1997-2023 NIV Detail Table). https://travel.state.gov/content/travel/en/legal/visa-law0/visa-statistics/nonimmigrant-visa-statistics.html; (3) Refugees: OHSS under DHS (2024). Yearbook of Immigration Statistics (Refugees [Multiple years] Data Tables, Table 14. Refugee Arrivals by Region and Country of Nationality). https://ohss.dhs.gov/topics/immigration/yearbook/2023.

New authorized immigrant arrivals, by country of birth/nationality: (1) Green cards: OHSS under DHS (Multiple Years). *Yearbook of Immigration Statistics* (LPR Yearbook Tables 8 to 11 Expanded, Table 10. Persons Obtaining Lawful Permanent Resident Status by Type and Broad Class of Admission and Region and Country of Birth). https://ohss.dhs.gov/topics/immigration/lawful-permanent-residents/lpr-yearbook-tables-8-11-expanded; (2) Visas: State (2023). *Nonimmigrant Visa Statistics* (Nonimmigrant Visa Issuances by Visa Class and by Nationality, FY1997-2023 NIV Detail Table). https://travel.state.gov/content/travel/en/legal/visa-law0/visa-statistics/nonimmigrant-visa-statistics.html; (3) Refugees: OHSS under DHS (2024). *Yearbook of Immigration Statistics* (Refugees [Multiple years] Data Tables, Table 14. Refugee Arrivals by Region and Country of Nationality). https://ohss.dhs.gov/topics/immigration/yearbook/2023.
Note(s): Disaggregated 2023 new arrival green card data from OHSS describing new arrivals by country of origin and reason for migration was not available as of report publication, so this chart uses the 2022 data for 2023. This approach is imperfect: totals change each year (466,000 new arrivals in 2022 vs. 558,000 in 2023), but the reasons for migration and countries of origin appear more stable over time.

Reasons for authorized immigration, by reason for entry: Ibid.
Note(s): See notes for chart *New authorized immigrant arrivals (FY 2023), by region of birth/nationality and reason for granted entry.*

Refugee ceiling and admissions: RPC (2024). *Admissions and Arrivals* (Refugee Admissions Report). US Department of State. https://www.wrapsnet.org/admissions-and-arrivals/.

Refugees admitted, by region: OHSS under DHS (2024). *Yearbook of Immigration Statistics* (Refugees [Multiple years] Data Tables, Table 14. Refugee Arrivals by Region and Country of Nationality). https://ohss.dhs.gov/topics/immigration/yearbook/2023.

Annual border enforcement actions, by agency: (1) Border Patrol encounters, 2021–2024: US Customs and Border Protection (CBP) (2025). *Nationwide Encounters* (Nationwide Encounters by Area of Responsibility). https://www.cbp.gov/document/stats/nationwide-encounters; (2) Border Patrol encounters, 1980–2020: CBP (2021). *Nationwide Encounters*. https://www.cbp.gov/sites/default/files/assets/documents/2021-Aug/U.S. Border Patrol Total Apprehensions (FY 1925 - FY 2020) (508).pdf; (3) Office of Field Operations (OFO) inadmissibles, 2017–2024: CBP (2025). *CBP Enforcement Statistics* (Total CBP Enforcement Actions). https://www.cbp.gov/newsroom/stats/cbp-enforcement-statistics; (4) OFO inadmissibles, 2015–2016: CBP (2017). *CBP Enforcement Statistics* FY 2017 (Total CBP Enforcement Actions). https://www.cbp.gov/newsroom/stats/cbp-enforcement-statistics-fy2017.
Note(s): Due to the COVID-19 pandemic, between 2020 and 2023, both OFO and USBP expelled certain people at the border without opportunity to seek asylum under Title 42.

Monthly border enforcement actions, by agency (recent months): CBP (2025). *Nationwide Encounters* (Nationwide Encounters by Area of Responsibility). https://www.cbp.gov/document/stats/nationwide-encounters
Note(s): See notes for chart *Annual border enforcement actions, by agency.*

Outcomes of southwest border encounters (FY 2024): OHSS under DHS (2025). *Immigration Enforcement and Legal Processes Monthly Tables* (CBP SW Border Encounters by Agency; Nationwide CBP Encounters by Type and Region; CBP SW Border Book-Outs by Agency). https://ohss.dhs.gov/topics/immigration/immigration-enforcement/monthly-tables
Note(s): Encounters by OFO are recorded in this chart as inadmissibles and encounters by USBP are apprehensions.

Asylum application cases received, by type: OHSS under DHS (2024). *Annual Flow Report* (Asylees: [2023]; Refugees and Asylees: [Multiple years]). https://ohss.dhs.gov/topics/immigration/refugees-and-asylees/rfa-annual-flow-report.

Note(s): Data is from DHS OHSS, which analyzes data from USCIS (which handles affirmative cases) and EOIR (which handles defensive cases). The EOIR source lists affirmative cases, but this refers only to their origin, i.e., they began as affirmative cases with USCIS which were denied and were subsequently refiled as defensive cases.

Individuals granted affirmative or defensive asylum, by region: OHSS under DHS (Multiple Years). *Yearbook of Immigration Statistics* (Refugees and Asylees [Year] Data Tables: Table 17, Individuals Granted Asylum Affirmatively by Region and County of Nationality; Table 19. Individuals Granted Asylum Defensively by Region and Country of Nationality). https://ohss.dhs.gov/topics/immigration/yearbook/2023.
Note(s): DHS continues to revise estimates for past years with each new Yearbook of Immigration Statistics. Because of the nature of the reporting, total, affirmative, and defensive asylum claims granted statistics are historically revised through 1990. Meanwhile, asylum claims by region are only revised for the ten years before each year's report. Because of this, regional breakdowns may not sum to the total number of asylum claims granted for years more than 10 years in the past.

Decisions for asylum cases, among affirmative and defensive asylum cases closed each year: (1) Defensive case decisions: Executive Office for Immigration Review (EOIR) under DHS (2025). *Workload and Adjudication Statistics* (Asylum Decisions). https://www.justice.gov/eoir/workload-and-adjudication-statistics; (2) Affirmative case decisions, 2014–2022: OHSS under DHS (2023). *Asylum Workload by Top Twenty-Five Nationalities* (Fiscal Years 2014 to 2022). https://ohss.dhs.gov/topics/immigration/refugees-and-asylees/asylum-workload; (3) Affirmative case decisions, 2023: US Customs and Immigration Service (USCIS) under DHS (2023). *All USCIS Application and Petition Form Types, Fiscal Year 2023, Quarter 4* (F-YTD Form I-589). https://www.uscis.gov/tools/reports-and-studies/immigration-and-citizenship-data.
Note(s): (1) OHSS has not released the 2023 Asylum Workload by Top Twenty Nationalities data as of publication of this report; the 2022 release provides the data for affirmative claims for FY 2014 through FY 2022. Since affirmative claims are handled by US Citizenship and Immigration Service (USCIS), the 2023 data comes from that agency. (2) Cases closed equals total case completions less the sum of grants and denials.

New case receipts and total case completions: EOIR under DHS (Multiple Years). *Workload and Adjudication Statistics* (Pending Cases, New Cases, and Total Completions). Retrieved from: (a) For 2015–2024 https://www.justice.gov/eoir/workload-and-adjudication-statistics; (b) For 2008–2014: https://www.justice.gov/d9/pages/attachments/2020/01/31/1_pending_new_receipts_and_total_completions.pdf.
Note(s): Initial case receipts include removal, deportation, exclusion, asylum-only, and withholding-only cases.

Pending immigration cases at the end of the fiscal year, total and per judge: (1) EOIR under DHS (2025). *Workload and Adjudication Statistics* (Pending Cases, New Cases, and Total Completions). https://www.justice.gov/eoir/workload-and-adjudication-statistics; (2) EOIR under DHS (2025). *Workload and Adjudication Statistics* (Immigration Judge Hiring; Pending Cases, New Cases, and Total Completions). https://www.justice.gov/eoir/workload-and-adjudication-statistics.
Note(s): (1) Pending case counts include removal, deportation, exclusion, asylum-only, and withholding-only cases. (2) 2024 count reflects the number of immigration judges on board during the last pay period of FY 2024 and accounts for hiring made in anticipation of attrition during the first quarter of FY 2025.

Administrative arrests by ICE Enforcement and Removal Operations, monthly and annual: OHSS under DHS (2025). *Immigration Enforcement and Legal Processes Monthly Tables* (ERO Administrative Arrests by Selected Citizenship). https://ohss.dhs.gov/topics/immigration/immigration-enforcement/monthly-tables.

Noncitizen removals: (1) For total removals (1892–2022) and criminal removals (1993–2022): OHSS under DHS (2023). *Yearbook of Immigration Statistics* (Immigration Enforcement Actions Data Tables, Table 39). https://ohss.dhs.gov/topics/immigration/yearbook/2022; (2) For total removals (2023–2024): OHSS under DHS (2025). *Immigration Enforcement and Legal Processes Monthly Tables* (DHS Removals by Criminality). https://ohss.dhs.gov/topics/immigration/immigration-enforcement/monthly-tables.
Note(s): (1) Data for 1976 includes the 15 months from July 1, 1975, to September 30, 1976, because the end date of fiscal years was changed from June 30 to September 30. (2) 2023 and 2024 totals come from the OHSS Immigration Enforcement and Legal Processes Monthly Tables rather than the Yearbook of Immigration Statistics enforcement actions section, the 2023 version of which has not been released as of the publication of this report. The Monthly Tables do provide criminal vs. non-criminal removals but appear to count them differently than in the Yearbook, and are not included in these charts.

Noncitizen returns: (1) For 1927–2022: OHSS under DHS (2023). *Yearbook of Immigration Statistics* (Immigration Enforcement Actions Data Tables, Table 39). https://ohss.dhs.gov/topics/immigration/yearbook/2022; (2) For 2023–2024: OHSS under DHS (2025). *Immigration*

Enforcement and Legal Processes Monthly Tables (DHS Enforcement Returns by Selected Citizenship; DHS Administrative Returns by Selected Citizenship). https://ohss.dhs.gov/topics/immigration/immigration-enforcement/monthly-tables.
Note(s): Data for 1976 includes the 15 months from July 1, 1975 to September 30, 1976 because the end date of fiscal years was changed from June 30 to September 30.

Foreign-born population, by naturalization status: (1) For 1970–2000: Gibson, C. and Jung, K. (2006). *Working Paper No. 81, Historical Census Statistics on the Foreign-Born Population of the United States: 1850 to 2000* (Table 12. Citizenship Status of the Foreign-Born Population: 1890 to 1950 and 1970 to 2000). US Census Bureau (Census Bureau), Population Division. https://www.census.gov/content/dam/Census/library/working-papers/2006/demo/POP-twps0081.pdf; (2) For 2005–2009: Data retrieved from ACS table listed above through ACS API at https://www.census.gov/data/developers/data-sets/acs-1year.2005.html; (3) For 2010–2023: Census Bureau (Multiple Years). *ACS 1-Year Estimates Subject Tables* (Table S0501. Selected Characteristics of the Native and Foreign-Born Populations). https://data.census.gov/table?q=S0501.
Note(s): This excludes 2020 data that relies on the ACS because of the pandemic's impact on data collection and quality. For more information, see: https://usafacts.org/articles/what-low-response-rates-mean-for-2020-acs-data/.

Estimated unauthorized immigrant population: OHSS under DHS (Multiple Years). *Estimates of the Illegal Alien Population Residing in the United States*. https://ohss.dhs.gov/topics/immigration/illegal/population-estimates.
Note(s): Estimation methodology changed in 2015, though estimates from 2015-2018 continued to rely on the 2010 Census.

Foreign-born residents, as a share of the population: (1) For 1970–2000: Gibson, C. and Jung, K. (2006). *Working Paper No. 81, Historical Census Statistics on the Foreign-Born Population of the United States: 1850 to 2000* (Table 12. Citizenship Status of the Foreign-Born Population: 1890 to 1950 and 1970 to 2000). Census Bureau, Population Division. https://www.census.gov/content/dam/Census/library/working-papers/2006/demo/POP-twps0081.pdf; (2) For 2005–2009: Data retrieved from ACS table listed above through ACS API at https://www.census.gov/data/developers/data-sets/acs-1year.2005.html; (3) For 2010–2023: Census (Multiple Years). *ACS 1-Year Estimates Subject Tables* (Table S0501. Selected Characteristics of the Native and Foreign-Born Populations). https://data.census.gov/table?q=S0501.
Note(s): See notes for chart *Foreign-born population, by naturalization status*.

Selected characteristics of foreign- and native-born populations (2023), share of population with each characteristic: Census Bureau (2024). *ACS 1-Year Estimates Subject Tables* (Table S0501. Selected Characteristics of the Native and Foreign-Born Populations). https://data.census.gov/table?q=S0501.

Annual average labor force participation rate, by nativity: (1) Foreign-born: BLS (2025). *FRED* (Labor Force Participation Rate - Foreign Born [LNU01373395]). Federal Reserve Bank of St. Louis. https://fred.stlouisfed.org/series/LNU01373395; (2) Native-born: BLS (2025). *FRED* (Labor Force Participation Rate - Native Born [LNU01373413]). Federal Reserve Bank of St. Louis. https://fred.stlouisfed.org/series/LNU01373413.

Annual average unemployment rate, by nativity: (1) Foreign-born: BLS (2025). *FRED* (Unemployment Rate - Foreign Born [LNU04073395]). Federal Reserve Bank of St. Louis. https://fred.stlouisfed.org/series/LNU04073395; (2) Native-born: BLS (2025). *FRED* (Unemployment Rate - Native Born [LNU04073413]). Federal Reserve Bank of St. Louis. https://fred.stlouisfed.org/series/LNU04073413.

Annual average civilian labor force level, total and foreign-born: (1) Foreign-born: BLS (2025). *FRED* (Civilian Labor Force Level - Foreign Born [LNU01073395]). Federal Reserve Bank of St. Louis. https://fred.stlouisfed.org/series/LNU01073395; (2) Native-born: BLS (2025). *FRED* (Civilian Labor Force Level - Native Born [LNU01073413]). Federal Reserve Bank of St. Louis. https://fred.stlouisfed.org/series/LNU01073413.

Percent of the civilian labor force that is foreign-born (2023), by state: Census Bureau (2024). *ACS 1-Year Estimates Public Use Microdata Sample* (MDAT, Custom Query: PUMS person weight [PWGTP]; all states; ESR; NATIVITY). https://data.census.gov/app/mdat/ACSPUMS1Y2023.

Foreign-born employment level (2023), by industry: Census Bureau (2024). *Characteristics of the Foreign-Born Population by Nativity and U.S. Citizenship Status* (Table 1.8. Industry of Employed Civilian Workers 16 Years and Over by Sex, Nativity, and U.S. Citizenship Status: 2023). US Census Bureau, Current Population Survey Detailed Tables. https://www.census.gov/data/tables/2023/demo/foreign-born/cps-2023.html.

Share of workers that are foreign-born (2023), by industry: Ibid.

Work visas granted, by type: (1) For 1997–2023: State (2024). *Nonimmigrant Visa Statistics* (Nonimmigrant Visa Issuances by Visa Class and by Nationality, FY1997-2023 NIV Detail Table). https://travel.state.gov/content/travel/en/legal/visa-law0/visa-statistics/nonimmigrant-visa-statistics.html; (2) For 2024: State (2025). *Nonimmigrant Worldwide Issuance and Refusal Data by Visa Category* (FY 2024 NIV Workload by Visa Category). https://travel.state.gov/content/dam/visas/Statistics/Non-Immigrant-Statistics/NIVWorkload/FY%20 2024NIVWorkloadbyVisaCategory.pdf.
Note(s): "Temporary agricultural workers" is for H-2A visas; "Specialty occupations workers" is for H-1B; "Temporary non-agricultural workers" is for H-2B; "Foreign diplomats, officials, and staff" is for A-1, A-2, or A-3 (A-2 visas were the 4th-largest individual visa category by number of visas granted in 2024); "Intracompany transferees" is for L-1.

Population

Population: (1) Population 1980-1989: Census Bureau (2016). *Population Estimates 1980-1990* (rqi files beginning with e[YY], Month: 7[YY], Geography: 999). https://www2.census.gov/programs-surveys/popest/tables/1980-1990/national/asrh/; (2) Population 1990-1999: Census Bureau (2016). *us-est90int-07-[Year]* (Intercensal Estimates of the United States Resident Population by Age and Sex: Multiple Years, July 1 Total). https://www2.census.gov/programs-surveys/popest/tables/1990-2000/intercensal/national/; (3) Population 2000-2009: Census Bureau (2016, August 24). *us-est00int-01* (Table 1. Intercensal Estimates of the Resident Population by Sex and Age for the United States: April 1, 2000 to July 1, 2010). https://www2.census.gov/programs-surveys/popest/tables/2000-2010/intercensal/national/; (4) Population 2010-2019: Census Bureau (2021). *NST-EST2020* (Annual Estimates of the Resident Population for the United States, Regions, States, the District of Columbia, and Puerto Rico: April 1, 2010 to July 1, 2019; April 1, 2020; and July 1, 2020). https://www2.census.gov/programs-surveys/popest/tables/2010-2020/national/totals/; (5) Population 2020-2023: Census Bureau (2023). *NST-EST2023-POP* (Annual Estimates of the Resident Population for the United States, Regions, States, the District of Columbia, and Puerto Rico: April 1, 2020 to July 1, 2023). https://www2.census.gov/programs-surveys/popest/tables/2020-2023/state/totals/.
Note(s): (1) Population statistics are from intercensal estimates and postcensal estimates produced on July 1 of each year. These may differ from the official decennial counts which are measured as of April 1 in years ending in 0. (2) This population figure excludes territories, such as Puerto Rico.

Population growth, by component: (1) 1981-1990: Census Bureau (2016). *1981 to 1989 Intercensal Estimates of the Resident Population of States, and Year-to-Year Components of Change* (1980-1990>state>8090com.txt.txt). https://www2.census.gov/programs-surveys/popest/tables/; (2) 1991-2000: Census Bureau (2005). *Population Estimates Tables* (1990-2000>estimates-and-change-1990-2000>2000c8_00.txt2010). https://www2.census.gov/programs-surveys/popest/tables/; (3) 2001-2010: Census Bureau (2017). *Population Estimates* (2010>2010-eval-estimates>co-est2010-alldata.csv). https://www2.census.gov/programs-surveys/popest/datasets/; (4) 2011-2020: Census Bureau (2021). *NST-EST2020-ALLDATA.csv* (National Population Totals). https://www.census.gov/programs-surveys/popest/technical-documentation/research/evaluation-estimates/2020-evaluation-estimates/2010s-totals-national.html; (5) 2021-2023: Census Bureau (2023). *NST-EST2023-ALLDATA.csv*. https://www.census.gov/data/tables/time-series/demo/popest/2020s-national-total.html.
Note(s): Population change shows the estimate of change in population as measured on July 1 of each year compared to July 1 of the previous year.

Death rate, per 100,000 people: (1) For 1900-1998: National Center for Health Statistics (NCHS) (2015). *Mortality Data: HIST290A* (Unpublished Tables: HIST290A_0039; _4049; _5059; _6067; _6878; _7998). Centers for Disease Control and Prevention (CDC). https://www.cdc.gov/nchs/nvss/mortality/hist290a.htm; (2) For 1999-2020: CDC (2022). *CDC WONDER Underlying Cause of Death, 1999-2020 Request* (Group Results by: Year). https://wonder.cdc.gov/ucd-icd10.html; (3) For 2021-2023: CDC (2024). *CDC WONDER Provisional Mortality Statistics, 2018 through Last Month Request* (Group Results by: Year). https://wonder.cdc.gov/controller/datarequest/D176.
Note(s): (1) Detailed mortality data between 1900-1932 was only available in certain areas, referred to as "Death Registration Areas". For these years, we report the age-adjusted death rates reported by NCHS, which are calculated using only the death and population counts of the Death Registration Areas in a given year. (2) The 2024 death count is calculated from provisional CDC data that is updated frequently. The death rate calculated here uses provisional numbers current as of 6/6/2025.

Birth rate, per 100,000 people: (1) For 1980-2006: NCHS (2019). *Health, United States - 2019* (Table 1. Crude birth rates, fertility rates, and birth rates, by age, race, and Hispanic origin of mother: United States, selected years 1950–2018). CDC. https://www.cdc.gov/nchs/data/hus/2019/001-508.pdf; (2) For 2007-2022: CDC (2024). *CDC WONDER Natality, 2007-2022 Request* (Group By: Year, Measures selected:

Birth rate). https://wonder.cdc.gov/controller/datarequest/D66; (3) For 2023: CDC (2024). *CDC WONDER Provisional Natality, 2023 Through Last Month* (Group By: Year, Measures selected: Births). https://wonder.cdc.gov/controller/datarequest/D192.
Note(s): (1) Birth rate is calculated as total number of live births per 100,000 people in the population. (2) Birth rate for 2021-2024 calculated by USAFacts using CDC births data and Census population data. Birth rate for all other years reported as calculated by CDC.

Components of population change (2023 vs. 2024), by state: Census Bureau (2023, December 18). *NST-EST2023-ALLDATA.csv*. https://www.census.gov/data/tables/time-series/demo/popest/2020s-national-total.html.

Share of population, by age group: (1) 1980-1989: Census Bureau (2021, October 9). *State Intercensal Tables: 1980-1990* (State Population Estimates and Demographic Components of Change: 1980 to 1990, by Single Year of Age and Sex). https://www.census.gov/data/tables/time-series/demo/popest/1980s-state.html; (2) 1990-1999: CDC (2020). *CDC WONDER: Bridged-Race Population Estimates 1990-2020 Request* (Group by: Age, Yearly July 1st Estimates). https://wonder.cdc.gov/Bridged-Race-v2020.HTML; (3) 2000-2009: Census Bureau (2021, December 17). *Population and Housing Unit Estimates Tables - 2009* (National Intercensal Tables: 2000-2010, Sex and Age, Table 1. Intercensal Estimates of the Resident Population by Sex and Age for the United States: April 1, 2000 to July 1, 2010). https://www.census.gov/programs-surveys/popest/data/tables.2009.List_58029271.html; (4) 2010-2019: Census Bureau (2021, October 8). *State Population by Characteristics: 2010-2020* (Age, Sex, Race, and Hispanic Origin - 6 race groups (5 race alone groups and one multiple race group), Annual State Resident Population Estimates for 6 Race Groups (5 Race Alone Groups and Two or More Races) by Age, Sex, and Hispanic Origin: April 1, 2010 to July 1, 2019; April 1, 2020; and July 1, 2020 (SC-EST2020-ALLDATA6)). https://www.census.gov/programs-surveys/popest/technical-documentation/research/evaluation-estimates/2020-evaluation-estimates/2010s-state-detail.html; (5) 2020-2023: Census Bureau (2024, April 11). *nc-est2023-agesex-res.csv* (Annual Estimates of the Resident Population by Single Year of Age and Sex for the United States: April 1, 2020 to July 1, 2023). https://www.census.gov/data/tables/time-series/demo/popest/2020s-national-detail.html.
Note(s): This population figure excludes territories, such as Puerto Rico.

Share of households, by household type: (1) Census Bureau (2023, November). *Historical Households Tables* (Tables; Table HH-1. Households by Type: 1940 to Present, Table HH-4. Households by Size: 1960 to Present). https://www.census.gov/data/tables/time-series/demo/families/households.html; (2) Census Bureau (2023, November). *Historical Families Tables* (Tables, Table FM-1. Families by Presence of Own Children Under 18: 1950 to Present). https://www.census.gov/data/tables/time-series/demo/families/families.html.
Note(s): Other includes both other family households (such as two single relatives living together), as well as other nonfamily households (such as nonmarried partners living together, or roommates).

Share of population, by race/ethnicity: Census Bureau (2023, June 20). *National Population by Characteristics: {Multiple Years}* (Annual Estimates of the Resident Population by Sex, Race, and Hispanic Origin for the United States: April 1, 2020 to July 1, 2022 (NC-EST{Year}-SR11H)). https://www.census.gov/data/tables/time-series/demo/popest/2020s-national-detail.html.
Note(s): (1) The Census first allowed respondents to select more than one race in the 2000 Census. Comparisons between pre-2000 and post-2000 data should be made with caution. (2) The Census Bureau added the racial category of 'Two or more races' beginning in 2000.

Population (2000 vs. 2024), by race/ethnicity: Census Bureau (2023, June 20). *National Population by Characteristics: {Multiple Years}* (Annual Estimates of the Resident Population by Sex, Race, and Hispanic Origin for the United States: April 1, 2020 to July 1, 2022 (NC-EST{Year}-SR11H)). https://www.census.gov/data/tables/time-series/demo/popest/2020s-national-detail.html.

Photo credits

Front/inside cover: Photo by diy13 on Adobe Stock

Page 21: Photo by Stephen on Adobe Stock

Page 70: Photo by Piotr Mitelski on Adobe Stock

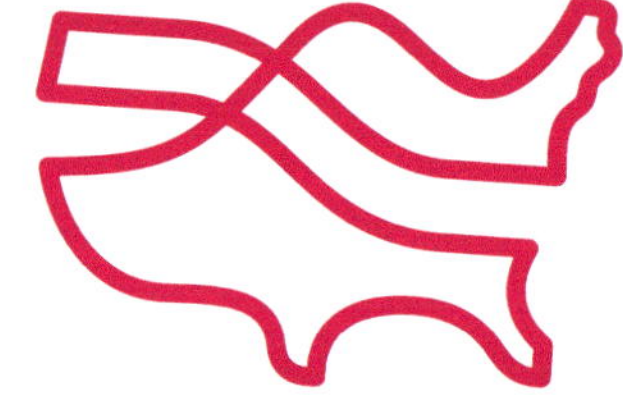

USAFacts

To request printed copies, please contact:

congress@usafacts.org